A Devotional Guide to
BIBLE LANDS

A Devotional Guide to
BIBLE LANDS

Batsell Barrett Baxter
&
Harold Hazelip

BAKER BOOK HOUSE
Grand Rapids, Michigan

Photo Credits

Eugene Henderson and Batsell Barrett Baxter: 23, 59, 67, 75, 81, 129, 145, 211, 217, 225, 233, 239, 253, 259, 275, 281 287; Jack Finegan: 121; Israel Office of Information: 89, 95, 107, 137, 151, 173, 203, 245, 265; Levant Photo Service: 37, 43, 113, 159, 187; Matson Photo Service: 29; Oriental Institute, University of Chicago: 101; Charles F. Pfeiffer: 15, 193; Trans World Airlines: 1; George A. Turner: 51, 165, 179.

Scripture Credit

Scripture quotations are from the Revised Standard Version of the Bible, copyrighted 1946, 1952, © 1971, 1973.

Preface

From June 14 through July 8, 1979, Batsell Barrett and Wanda Baxter, Harold and Helen Hazelip, and Eugene and Colleen Henderson went on a special mission to Bible lands. The visit had been conceived as an effort to bring to life for the Herald of Truth radio audience the sights and sounds of Bible lands today. The visit began in Egypt (three days), continued in Jordan (three days), and concluded in Israel (sixteen days).

Thirty-nine programs, each of thirty minutes length, were planned. They were to be presented on a group of sixty-five NBC stations and nearly three hundred additional independent stations in the United States from September 1, 1979, through May 31, 1980. Actually, forty-three programs were taped. Alternate programs had been prepared in the event that the party might be barred from some areas because of political unrest.

The greatest difficulties turned out to be the summer heat in the Middle East (often rising to above 100° Fahrenheit), along with the general absence of air-conditioned vehicles for travel, and food differences (occasionally resulting in a queasy stomach or worse). Days consumed by travel and time spent in searching for sites suitable for recording combined to present us with a tiring schedule which often required three or four programs to be produced in one day.

The eight-minute sermons, each built on a biblical text which in some way concerned the general area or on an incident which occurred near the place where the recording was being done, had been fully scripted before we left the United States. With the help of copious research cards, the sites were discussed in dialogue fashion. The research was ordinarily reviewed by the speakers separately on the evening preceding the broadcast, and the discussion was rehearsed between them immediately before each recording session. Direction was given to the discussion by the speaker who had charge of the specific program. The sermons are presented in this book in nearly the same form in which they were delivered, while the historical and geographical information about biblical sites was written by the two speakers from the notes used for the discussions.

This series of Herald of Truth programs was not intended to create a reverence for the physical places where biblical events occurred. Actually, the precise locations are usually uncertain after so many centuries have passed. Rather, our intention was to give a real sense of history—of the events having happened—and a renewed awareness of the relevance of biblical events for our lives. Each discussion segment related biblical events which had happened at each location and gave brief descriptions of the places today. Additional historical and archaeological information was incorporated as time permitted or need dictated.

The history of Palestine has been recorded in many places. Glimpses into that history occur in the background information included in this volume. Generally speaking, biblical sites began to be marked, often with shrines, following the acceptance of Christianity by Constantine, the Roman emperor, in the early fourth century. His mother, Helena, sought out the various spots in Palestine and led in their being memorialized. The Muslim conquest of Palestine in the seventh century resulted in the destruction of many of these shrines (usually chapels or church buildings), or their conversion into mosques. The Crusaders (the first Crusade conquered Jerusalem in A.D. 1099) sought to avenge the shame which they thought the Muslim conquest had brought to Christianity. They rebuilt many of the church buildings over the fourth-century remains. Reconquest by Muslims in the twelfth century repeated the process of destruction of churches or conversion into mosques. Most of the present buildings were erected in the late nineteenth and twentieth centuries.

Unless otherwise indicated, all Scripture quotations are from the Revised Standard Version.

We hope that you will be able to share our experiences and will be drawn more deeply into biblical events and the biblical message for your life through this volume. We are especially indebted to the elders of the Fifth and Highland Church of Christ in Abilene, Texas, who made possible the Herald of Truth Bible Lands radio series. Harold Shank provided extremely helpful research materials for the sermons; Eugene Henderson was the recording engineer and producer of the broadcast; and Jim Chester, along with his Harding Academy Chorus, provided special music for these programs. But the finished product is ours and we hope you enjoy it and profit from it.

Batsell Barrett Baxter
Harold Hazelip

Contents

The Forty Sites

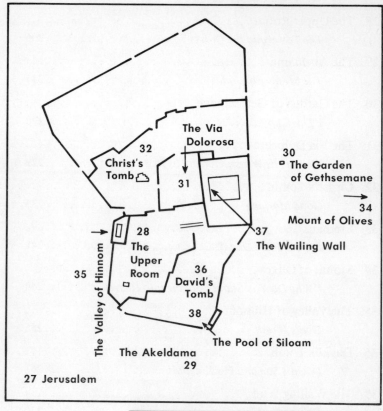

The Via Dolorosa

32 Christ's Tomb

30 ▫ The Garden of Gethsemane

31

→ 34 Mount of Olives

28 The Upper Room

35 The Valley of Hinnom

37 The Wailing Wall

36 David's Tomb

38 The Pool of Siloam

The Akeldama 29

27 Jerusalem

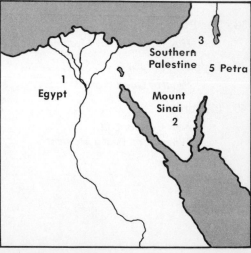

3 Southern Palestine 5 Petra

1 Egypt

Mount Sinai 2

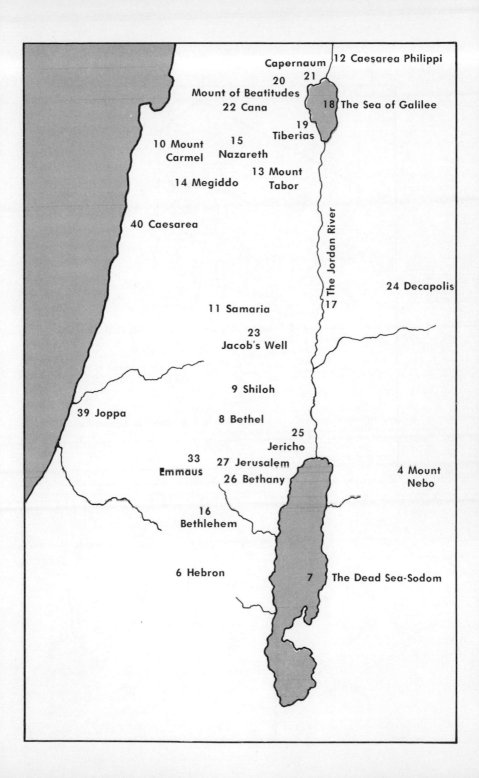

Pyramids and Sphinx

1 Egypt

After an overnight flight from New York, in the early afternoon we found ourselves looking down at the beautiful blue of the Mediterranean Sea. Soon we were flying over the northern edge of the Sahara Desert in North Africa. Later the desolate sand was separated by a green strip running north and south. It was the Nile River basin and we were over Egypt.

After landing at Cairo's modern international airport we found ourselves in the jostling, noisy crowd that always seems to be present at customs. A short time later we were in our room on the eighth floor of the Nile Hilton, looking down from our balcony on the glistening waters of the Nile. We were ready to turn the calendar back and review the biblical story of ancient Egypt and its famous river.

The word *Egypt* appears in the Bible over 600 times, while the word *Egyptian* occurs an additional 124 times, with the Hebrew word for the Nile appearing 52 times. It is quite obvious that Egypt played a very important role in Bible history, most prominently in the period beginning with Joseph and concluding with Moses.

The Nile has played a vital role in the history of Egypt, because life is totally dependent upon the river. Without the waters of the Nile, all of Egypt would be a desert. The Nile is 4,160 miles long and its basin contains over a million square miles. The Nile Valley, where almost the entire population resides, is rarely more than twelve miles wide. In fact, the Nile Valley comprises only 4 percent of Egypt's land, leaving 96 percent as desert. Ninety-nine percent of Egypt's 40,000,000 people live on this 4 percent of the land. The annual rainfall at Alexandria, near the mouth of the Nile, is seven-and-one-half inches, while at Cairo it is only an inch, and upstream at Aswan none at all, except for an extremely rare shower or cloudburst.

History of Ancient Egypt

The history or a united Egypt begins with Menes, the first pharoah of the first dynasty. Menes, according to Manetho (an Egyptian historian of the third century B.C.), united Upper and Lower Egypt and began a series of thirty dynasties covering Egyptian history from 3,000 B.C. to Roman times. The fourth dynasty, which began in 2613 B.C., was known as the pyramid age. The patriarchs of the Bible are thought to have lived during the eleventh and twelfth dynasties. Asiatic invaders called the Hyksos ("rulers of foreign lands") constituted the fifteenth and sixteenth dynasties. The Hyksos were hated by the native Egyptians; it is thought that Joseph probably entered Egypt during the time of the Hyksos when the pharaoh would have been more open to outsiders. The Hyksos ruled from 1720 to 1570 B.C.

With the eighteenth dynasty began the New Kingdom (the Empire), which continued to 1065 B.C. It was during this period that the exodus took place, though no general agreement exists about the date. Both 1290 and 1447 have been suggested. Noteworthy rulers of the eighteenth dynasty include Thutmose III (1504–1450), Amenhotep II (1450–1425), and Tutankhamon (1361–1352). If the theory which posits an early date for the exodus (1447) is correct, Thutmose III was the pharaoh of the oppression and Amenhotep II the pharaoh of the exodus. Noteworthy rulers of the nineteenth dynasty include Seti I (1318–1304) and Ramses II (1304–1237). If the theory which posits a late date for the exodus (1290) is correct, Seti I was the pharaoh of the oppression and Ramses II the pharaoh of the exodus. Because the date of the exodus is unsure, it is not known whether Moses lived before or after King Tut (Tutankhamon). The pyramids were over one thousand years old when Tut and Moses lived in Egypt.

God's People and Egypt

The modern city of Cairo was founded in A.D. 638 by Arab conquerors who exploited the ruins of Memphis for building materials. Ancient Memphis was located on the Nile some ten miles south of modern Cairo. Nine miles to the north of Cairo is the site of ancient On. Potiphera, Joseph's father-in-law, was the priest of On (Gen. 41:45, 50; 46:20). Heliopolis is the modern name for the city called On in the Scriptures. It must have been in this general area along the Nile, bounded by Memphis on the south and On on the north, where Joseph lived and worked. It would also be in this same area where, several centuries later, Jochebed, the mother of Moses, had her son hidden in an ark of bull-rushes along the edge of the Nile River. There the princess found him and began the training of the man who would ultimately lead the Israelites out of bondage.

After 430 years, the Israelites left Egypt, numbering 603,550 men, possibly a total of as many as two million people. God had demonstrated his power through a series of plagues, in which the Nile River figured prominently, as when the river was turned to blood (Exod. 7). The Israelites left behind them the store cities of Pithom and Raamses (Exod. 1:1–14), but they took with them many possessions of the Egyptians. God led them through the Red Sea on dry land, and then destroyed the pursuing Egyptians as the waters came back together (Exod. 14). The story of God's deliverance of his people, in which Moses and Aaron played such prominent roles, is a thrilling part of biblical history.

The Pyramids

There are approximately a hundred pyramids in various groups along an eighty-mile stretch of the Nile River just west of modern Cairo. Most of them were built in the period from 2700 to 2400 B.C. The Great Pyramid of Cheops is so accurately laid out that modern compasses can be checked against it. The margin of error in the squaring of the sides is nowhere more than .09 percent. The Great Pyramid measures nearly 800 feet along each base line and was originally over 450 feet high. The three major pyramids are the Great Pyramid of Cheops, the pyramid of Chephren, and the pyramid of Mykerinus.

When they were built, each pyramid was encased in a sheath of shining white limestone which reflected the sun like a mirror. The stones were put together so tightly and with such accuracy that a piece of paper could hardly pass between the joints. The Sphinx stands below and east of the three major pyramids. The oldest of the pyramids, known as the Step Pyramid, is approximately ten miles south of the three major ones. It is thought that more than twenty years were required to build the largest of them. Herodotus, the Greek historian, visited the pyramids at Gizeh approximately twenty-five hundred years ago and reported that a roofed stone causeway ran from the Nile to the pyramid complexes. He thought the causeway must have taken as long to build as the pyramids themselves.

King Tut

King Tut is best known for his tomb. On the morning of November 4, 1922, Howard Carter, who had spent eighteen years hunting for the boy-king's tomb, found it. Digging in the Valley of the Kings near the tomb of Ramses VI, the archaeologist uncovered a series of sixteen steps leading down to a door marked with a seal reading: "Tutankhamun." A tunnel, thirty feet in length, leading to the tomb was filled with dirt, rocks, and rubble. After various problems the four-room tomb was opened. It contained over 5,000 objects, some 1,703 in the burial chamber itself.

In the rooms were found a fleet of model ships, several full-sized chariots, gold-covered couches, thrones, jewelry cases, gameboards, statues of the Egyptian gods, and the mummy of King Tut himself. The royal mummy was found inside three shrines completely covered with gold. The sarcophagus was fashioned from granite. The lid alone weighed 3,000 pounds. Inside the stone sarcophagus was a body-shaped coffin made of wood and covered with gold. A second body-shaped casket was inside; made of pure gold, it weighed 2,450 pounds (worth about sixteen million dollars in 1979). The king had 143 pieces of precious jewelry on his body. King Tut was a boy-king who ruled for only nine years. Though in wealth and power he was not among the more significant of the pharaohs, it took ten years to remove the treasures from his tomb. Today, except for a brief trip for a few of these objects to America and a few other nations, most of the treasures of King Tut's tomb are to be found in the Museum of Egyptian Antiquities in Cairo.

The modern city of Alexandria was founded by Alexander the Great on the Mediterranean some fourteen miles west of the branch of the Nile known as the Canopic. There Greek-speaking Jewish scholars produced the Septuagint, the Greek translation of the Old Testament. The Rosetta Stone, which proved to be a remarkable means of deciphering Egyptian hieroglyphics, was discovered by a soldier of Napoleon's army on the Rosetta branch of the Nile.

A visit to Egypt takes one back to the very roots of Bible history. To stand beside the same river where Moses was found as a baby, and to visit the pyramids which looked down upon Abraham, Joseph, Moses, and perhaps even Jesus, make the expense and the effort of visiting Egypt eminently worthwhile.

"Let My People Go"

Batsell Barrett Baxter

I have often wished there were some way by which we could visualize the events connected with the deliverance of the ancient Israelites from Egyptian bondage. Our visit to Egypt makes it a bit easier for us to recapture the significance of some of those momentous events some fifteen hundred years before Christ. As it is told in the Book of Exodus, the Israelites had been in bondage to the Egyptians for a number of generations when God responded to their pleas for deliverance by raising up a deliverer. He carefully guided the training of Moses and then sent him, together with Aaron his spokesman, to break the yoke of slavery that bound the Hebrews.

Confrontations with Pharaoh

There were a number of dramatic confrontations between Moses and Pharaoh. In Exodus 5:1, we read, "Afterward Moses and Aaron went to Pharaoh and said, 'Thus says the Lord, the God of Israel, "Let my people go, that they may hold a feast to me in the wilderness."'" Pharoah was little impressed by this rather grandiloquent request from a man who was "slow of speech and of tongue," representing a people who had no weapons of war by which to implement a revolt. There follow in the succeeding pages of the Book of Exodus six other occasions, interspersed with the various plagues and the hardening of Pharaoh's heart, on which Moses used the same key expression, "The Lord, the God of the Hebrews, sent me to you, saying, 'Let my people go, that they may serve me in the wilderness...'" (Exod. 7:16; cf. 8:1, 20; 9:1, 13; 10:3). Although these people were in abject slavery their complete bondage to their Egyptian masters was broken by God's power. It is thrilling to read how they ultimately walked out of Egypt free men, carrying the spoils of Egypt with them as they went.

Why This Ancient Story?

But why should I remind you of this ancient story? Simply because I believe there is a very meaningful parallel between the bondage of God's people then and the different kind of bondage of God's people today. We of the twentieth century are not subject to a dictatorial ruler like Pharaoh, but we are subject to an even more devastating kind of slavery, planned and perpetrated by the archenemy of mankind and the archrival of God, Satan. He seeks to bring God's children into bondage on a far more widespread and more destructive scale than Pharaoh could ever have done. We remember the words of the apostle Peter, "Be sober, be watchful. Your adversary the devil prowls around like a roaring lion, seeking someone to devour" (I Peter 5:8).

We Are Often in Bondage

Ours is a day in which Satan has reached out with his octupuslike tentacles to many of our young people throughout the land and has planted doubts and questions in their minds. Ours is a day in which atheism and agnosticism are making inroads among the intellectuals in the colleges and universities. By destroying religious faith, by raising questions, by upsetting the old ethical and moral standards, and by creating a state of uncertainty and confusion the devil is bringing millions of people into a far more serious kind of bondage than the Israelites in Egypt ever knew. Life without God and without faith has little purpose. If there is no God and if there is no life hereafter, then what difference does it all make? How much better it was for the apostle Paul who could say, "I know whom I have believed, and I am sure that he is able to guard until that Day what has been entrusted to me" (II Tim. 1:12).

Another of the major efforts to bring man into bondage is in the realm of sensualism. Millions of people are addicted to sex. The books they read, the magazines they buy, the movies they see, the television they watch, and the general pattern of their lives are all dominated by sex. They are slaves to sex, missing, through their misuse of this one faculty, many of the fine, wholesome things in life. There are many others who are slaves to alcohol and other drugs. Their lives and the lives of their loved ones are cursed by their bondage to these unfortunate habits.

In the midst of all of this we are reminded of the words of the apostle Paul, "Do not be deceived; God is not mocked, for whatever a man sows, that he will also reap. For he who sows to his own flesh will from the flesh reap corruption; but he who sows to the Spirit will from the Spirit reap eternal life" (Gal. 6:7, 8).

Loving the World

Yet another avenue through which Satan brings men into bondage in our day is that of materialism. This is an age in which there are more creature comforts and a higher level of luxurious living than ever before known in the history of the world. As a consequence we who live in this materially blessed society find ourselves dominated by things. We need to heed the warning of the apostle John who wrote, "Do not love the world or the things in the world. If any one loves the world, love for the Father is not in him" (I John 2:15).

We also remember Christ's own words, "Do not lay up for yourselves treasures on earth, where moth and rust consume and where thieves break in and steal, but lay up for yourselves treasures in heaven, where neither moth nor rust consumes and where thieves do not break in and steal. For where your treasure is, there will your heart be also. . . . But seek first his kingdom and his righteousness, and all these things shall be yours as well" (Matt. 6:19–21, 33).

Release for the Captives

When we look deeply into what Christianity is all about, we find that essentially it is God's effort to free man from the bondage of sin. There is a significant paragraph in the Gospel of Luke, "And he came to Nazareth, where he had been brought up; and he went to the synagogue, as his custom was, on the sabbath day. And he stood up to read; and there was given to him the book of the prophet Isaiah. He opened the book and found the place where it was written, 'The Spirit of the Lord is upon me, because he has anointed me to preach good news to the poor. He has sent me to proclaim release to the captives and recovering of sight to the blind, to set at liberty those who are oppressed, to proclaim the acceptable year of the Lord' " (Luke 4:16–19). Jesus came to preach liberty to those who are in bondage to sin.

In Galatians 5:1, we find an excellent summary statement of all that we have been trying to say, "For freedom Christ has set us free; stand fast therefore, and do not submit again to a yoke of slavery." We were in bondage to sin; then Christ came to free us from that bondage. Everyone who has believed in Christ as the Son of God, has made known his faith before his fellow men, has turned away from the world's sins, and has been baptized into Christ has been made free. The blood of Christ washed him clean as he responded to the grace of God.

Satan still tries to bring us into bondage in all the many ways of which we have spoken and many others as well. Ours is a continuing battle to remain free from the sins that would enslave us. May we work constantly and may we diligently pray that God will continue to "deliver us from bondage."

Moses' Choice

Harold Hazelip

Napoleon described Moses as the greatest military genius the world has known. Herman Wouk, in his bestselling *This Is My God,* wrote of Moses, "His were the hands that broke the gods of Egypt, Mesopotamia, Greece, and Rome. . . . He disappeared into the darkness on a mountain and came back with a law. First Israel, then half the world accepted the law as the word of God."

The writer of Hebrews says, "By faith Moses, when he was grown up, refused to be called the son of Pharaoh's daughter, choosing rather to share ill-treatment with the people of God than to enjoy the fleeting pleasures of sin" (Heb. 11:24, 25).

What was Moses like? How was he able to accomplish so much? Why did he choose to identify himself with a group of "strangers and exiles" rather than cling to his opportunities as an Egyptian prince?

Moses' Faith in God

Moses' belief in God was central to his whole life. He was born in Egypt when Israel was enslaved there as a people. Although every male child was supposed to be killed, Moses' mother kept him alive. When he was three months old, she placed him in a basket and set it afloat on the Nile River. Pharaoh's daughter found him and adopted him. She gave him his name *Moses*, which means "one who is drawn out," since she drew him out of the river.

Pharaoh's daughter employed Moses' mother to nurse him. Moses' family must have taught him about the true God. Though he was reared in Pharaoh's palace, and received the finest Egyptian education, he continued to believe in the God who was working through Abraham's descendants to accomplish his goals. The early training by his parents shaped the decision which he later made.

But how was God going to work out his purpose for Israel? One day Moses went out to see his brethren. As a prince, he was far removed from their world of suffering. But the slaves' hunger and suffering touched him. When he saw an Egyptian overseer torturing a slave, he killed the Egyptian.

The next day Moses saw two Hebrews quarreling. When one began to strike the other, Moses intervened. The offender responded: "Who made you a prince and a judge over us? Do you mean to kill me as you killed the Egyptian?" (Exod. 2:14). It was evident that the Hebrews were not going to accept Moses and quick deliverance at this time. Realizing that his slaying of the Egyptian overseer was known, Moses fled from Pharaoh and became a shepherd in the Midian desert.

It was not easy for a young man accustomed to a princely life and the friendship of powerful people to become a fugitive overnight. He had to break with his friends and habits and adapt himself to the life of a refugee. He became a stranger to the Egyptian people, to the Jewish people, and perhaps to himself. He must have seemed an ingrate to the king. He had been rescued from the Nile, had received an excellent education, and now turned against the people who had helped him.

Forty years later, after God spoke to him out of the burning bush, Moses returned to deliver Israel. The slaves often seemed no more ready to leave Egypt than the Pharaoh was ready to let them leave. By sending a series of ten plagues, God delivered Israel. The exodus continued to be marked by miracles—water from rocks, manna from heaven, and quail to eat. There were many disappointments and setbacks for Moses, but the faith his parents had given him in early life supported Moses to the end.

The plagues and the other miracles seemed spectacular. But God's work had been very slow. It had stretched over forty years since Moses first tried to deliver Israel, and there would be another forty years in reaching the Promised Land. When frustrations and difficulties come, we must remember that God often works slowly, but he is with us in our daily struggles.

Honesty About Himself

Moses' faith in God was crucial. But he was also honest about himself. His long years of loneliness as a shepherd had made him aware of his own limitations. When God told him at the burning bush that he was to return to Egypt and deliver Israel, Moses was very open about his limitations: "Who am I that I should go to Pharaoh?... They will not believe me.... I am not eloquent.... O, my Lord, send, I pray, some other person" (Exod. 3:11; 4:1, 10, 13).

Moses was also a man of intense feelings, feelings which he did not hide. He would get angry with the people over their pettiness. Even his prayers are classic in their honesty with God (Exod. 32:11–13). Moses was a man with deep faith in God and complete honesty about himself.

Love for His People

A third factor which made Moses a great leader was his attitude toward the people he was to help. He was a Hebrew by birth, adopted as an Egyptian prince. He could have forgotten his background and have contented himself with his privileges. He must have loved Pharaoh's daughter;

she saved his life. When did he begin to have contact with his slave brothers? When did he become aware of his real origin?

We are told only that he voluntarily made their burden his burden. We all face a choice: we can work to make the world a better place, or we can work to get a better place for ourselves in the world.

Moses made his choice. He gave up the "here and now" securities for a security he could not see as yet. His decision involved patience. When people have been enslaved for centuries, it may take some time before they will be able to act maturely on their own. The Book of Exodus makes it clear that Israel was ill-prepared for the trials in the wilderness. There were mistakes and failures, but giving the people freedom was the only way for them to learn how to act maturely.

Before Moses said anything to Pharaoh, he gathered the elders of the people of Israel and spoke to them about God's promises (Exod. 4:29). He would later endure their rebellions, but love them to the end. When God was on the verge of destroying Israel because the people had made a golden calf while Moses was on the mount receiving the Ten Commandments, Moses interceded for the people with his very life (Exod. 32:30–32).

Our Treasures

Moses is not just a character in ancient history. He is an example for us in many ways. We will not have the courage to give up our own "treasures of Egypt" unless we recognize that there is something more lasting than these temporary values. How do we muster the courage to make such a choice—to give up relying on bank accounts, social position, and all our other "securities"? Moses made his choice and he endured "as seeing him who is invisible" (Heb. 11:27).

People who commit themselves to God's way know that there is life beyond life. When Henry VIII threatened to tie a couple of his opponents in a sack and cast them into the Thames if they did not renounce their faith, they responded, "The road to heaven lies as near by water as by land; and therefore, it is indifferent to us which way we go hither."

And so with Moses. He followed his choice to the end. Nobody was present at his death; nobody knows his resting place. The people of the mountains situate it in the valley, the people of the valley situate it in the mountains. It has become neither temple nor shrine. And, in a way, he still lives. The law God gave through him became the schoolmaster to bring people to Christ. And his example still speaks to all of us as we make life's fundamental choices.

Have you made your choice? Becoming a Christian involves a life-and-death commitment. Spiritually, you begin by dying to sin and being buried with Christ in baptism. For the rest of your life you can look back to that choice as the starting post for every action.

The Providence of God

Batsell Barrett Baxter

The story of Joseph, which unfolded in ancient Egypt, is an undying narrative. It is of deep interest to all: to children, who find in it a simple but powerful story, and also to mature Bible students, who find in it an evidence of one of the most meaningful principles taught in the Bible, the providence of God. The story occupies more space in the Old Testament than any other personal narrative, with the exception of the story of Abraham. One might well ask, "Why is this story given so much space?" Let's look at the story to see.

Although the birth of Joseph is mentioned in an earlier chapter, along with a few facts concerning his position in the family, the story of Joseph begins in earnest in Genesis 37. The story of Joseph really begins with the words, "Joseph, being seventeen years old, was shepherding the flock with his brothers;. . . and Joseph brought an ill report of them to their father. Now Israel [or Jacob] loved Joseph more than any other of his children, because he was the son of his old age; and he made him a long robe with sleeves [often called the coat of many colors]. But when his brothers saw that their father loved him more than all his brothers, they hated him, and could not speak peaceably to him" (Gen. 37:2–4).

Survival in a Strange Land

As you probably remember the story, the older brothers discussed what they might do to get rid of this younger brother who not only had brought an ill report of their behavior to their father, but also had dreamed a dream in which they bowed down to him. After much discussion, they sold Joseph to a caravan of Ishmaelite traders on their way to Egypt. In Egypt Joseph was bought by Potiphar, an officer of Pharaoh, the captain of his guard. After serving as houseboy and ultimately overseer of Potiphar's house, Joseph was unjustly accused and thrown into prison. There he languished for some years, until God enabled him to reveal a dream to the Pharaoh who was on the throne, which brought him freedom and also a position of power, as governor of Egypt.

In the severe famine which followed, Joseph's brethren came down from Canaan to buy grain in order to sustain their own lives and the lives of their loved ones back in Canaan, including their aged father Jacob. Many years had passed since they sold Joseph into Egypt, so they did not recognize him when they came before him to ask for grain. He was now a man of about forty instead of a lad of seventeen; he was now Pharaoh's chief advisor. Undoubtedly his appearance was very different from what it had been at seventeen and undoubtedly he was dressed in a way they never expected to see him. In any case, there is the dramatic moment in the story when he recognizes them, a group dressed much as he had seen them last. The outcome of the story is that he treats them far better than they deserve, gives them grain, and sends additional grain back for their families and for his father Jacob. Ultimately, he sends wagons into Canaan to move his father and the entire patriarchal family down into Egypt, where they are located in a choice section of the country, the land of Goshen.

What Purpose Has This Story?

Is there any design in this story beyond that of entertainment, beyond that of interest for the reader? It is an exciting story. It does have its dramatic moments. It is thrilling to see the mistreated seventeen-year-old boy eventually occupy a position of triumph over his evil brethren. It is also a thrilling success story, just the kind that has been so popular in novels and movies. But, is there any deeper meaning? The answer, of course, is that there are deeper meanings. The stories of the Bible are never for mere entertainment, but have higher and more significant meanings.

To find the deeper meaning in the story of Joseph we begin by reading Genesis 15:13-14, "Then the Lord said to Abram, 'Know of a surety that your descendants will be sojourners in a land that is not theirs, and will be slaves there, and they will be oppressed for four hundred years; but I will bring judgment on the nation which they serve, and afterward they shall come out with great possessions.' " In this passage God made a promise to Abraham that his descendants would be taken into another land, made slaves, and ultimately brought forth again to freedom.

After this promise was given, Abraham completed his life, Isaac lived a long and significant life, and Jacob lived more than a hundred years of his life; yet nothing had happened to move the people into another land. Not until the caravan of wagons traveled from Egypt into Canaan to move Jacob and his whole household into Egypt did God's plan appear to unfold. About two hundred years had passed, yet God had not forgotten. In the most natural ways, the events in the life of Joseph were simply bringing about a plan of God.

God's Plan Fulfilled

God brings about his purposes indirectly and unobtrusively. Almost every event in the story took place without any direct or overt intervention from God. Each of the steps in this story stands like a link in a long chain by which God, having determined that the Hebrews should dwell in Egypt for four hundred years, after predicting it about two hundred years before, draws them down where he wants them to be.

The story of Joseph is a beautiful example of God's providence. By God's providence we mean simply the way that God works in the affairs of men to bring about his ultimate purposes. It was Benjamin Franklin, one of our founding fathers in America, a member of the Constitutional Convention, who said, as he addressed General George Washington, who was presiding, "I have lived, sir, a long time, and the longer I live the more convincing proof I see of this truth—that God governs in the affairs of men. And if a sparrow cannot fall without his notice, is it possible that an empire can rise without his aid?" We, too, believe that God shapes the destinies of men, as we yield our lives in submission to his will. At times he overrules, at times he directs without our knowledge, but always his ultimate plan is fulfilled. If we fail him, then he looks to someone else to carry out his purposes. If we cooperate with his plan, then our lives move to ever higher levels of significance, as did the life of Joseph.

In the New Testament, there is a very impressive comment in the conversion narrative of Saul of Tarsus, in which the Lord says of this brilliant young Jewish lawyer:". . . he is a chosen instrument of mine to carry my name before the Gentiles and kings and the sons of Israel; for I will show him how much he must suffer for the sake of my name" (Acts 9:15, 16). The rest of that story is that Saul of Tarsus yielded his life to God's plan and ultimately did carry the message of Christ to Gentiles, to kings, and to his fellow Jews. In addition, throughout his life he suffered greatly for his Lord's sake. In a beautiful and impressive way Saul, who became the apostle Paul, fulfilled God's plan for his life.

Yielding Our Lives

I would close this meditation by asking if you have yielded your life to the plan of God which he would like for you to follow. Have you believed in the Lord Jesus Christ as the divine Son of God? Have you openly confessed that faith before your fellows? Have you turned from Satan and his kingdom to follow Christ and be part of his kingdom? Have you been buried with your Lord in baptism, as was done by each of those who became a Christian in apostolic times? We would ask those of you who long ago began the Christian walk, "Have you continued to let the Lord guide your life? Have you yielded your will to God's plan for your life?"

All of us have a remarkable capacity to be the captains of our souls, the privilege of determining which way our lives shall go. How tragic it is when we go in a direction different from the direction the Lord would have us go. How wonderful it is when, like Paul of whom we have just spoken, and like Joseph who lived in this land so long ago, we let our lives fit into God's plan and help to fulfill his will. There is no greater purpose in life than to play a role, large or small, in the plan of God. That is your privilege and mine.

Mount Moses, Sinai

2 Mount Sinai

One may reach Mount Sinai by private plane or he may drive. Political control of the Sinai Peninsula reverts from Israel to Egypt as a result of the 1979 peace agreements.

The Sinai Peninsula is a triangle of land with the "base" of the triangle at the top. It stretches some 150 miles from the Gulf of Suez on the west to the Gulf of Aqaba on the east. The triangle also stretches about 260 miles from the Mediterranean Sea on the north to the northern end of the main body of the Red Sea on the south.

The terrain of the area ranges from shifting sand dunes to bare rock and hard-baked soil to naked, craggy mountains. A few palm groves and oases dot the area. The night air is cool but the day may bring temperatures to 120° Fahrenheit.

The books of Exodus and Numbers mention five wilderness areas: the wilderness of Shur in the northwest, east of Goshen; the wilderness of Etham between the Bitter Lakes and Marah; the wilderness of Sin near Elim in the western Sinai; the wilderness of Paran near the Gulf of Aqaba; and the wilderness of Zin near Kadesh-barnea, along what would later be the border of Judah.

The Sinai Peninsula has been a highway for travelers that include Abraham and Sarah; young Joseph, who had been sold by his brothers; and Mary, Joseph, and Jesus during Jesus' early childhood. Moses and the Israelites wandered for forty years in the area. Camel caravans laden with rich goods going from one part of the Fertile Crescent to another knew the area. The Sinai has a population of 35,000 today.

The word *Sinai* appears thirty-seven times in Scripture, *Horeb* seventeen times. No geographical distinction between these terms is noted in the Bible. Elijah went to Horeb in his flight from Ahab and Jezebel (I Kings 19:4–8). It was an eleven-day journey from Kadesh-barnea at the southern edge of Palestine to Horeb (Deut. 1:2).

Israel's Route

The exodus did not take Israel along any of the well-traveled roads. This makes it difficult for modern geographers to trace their route with certainty. The Israelites began at Rameses (Num. 33:5), the capital city which Raamses II built. They left Egypt "by the way of the wilderness toward the Red Sea" (Exod. 13:18), but the exact place of the crossing is not known. Instead of taking one of the direct roads eastward, the Israelites traveled through the desert, making stops at Marah where bitter waters were made sweet (Exod. 15:23–26) and at the oasis of Elim (Exod. 15:27) with its twelve springs and seventy palm trees.

They also stopped at Dophkah, which has been identified with the copper and turquoise mining area operated by the pharaohs. Their last stop before Mount Sinai was at Rephidim, where Moses struck the rock, bringing forth water (Exod. 17:1–7), and Israel fought the Amalekites under Joshua's leadership (Exod. 17:8–16).

Israel at Sinai

The Israelites reached Mount Sinai in the third month after their departure from Egypt and camped at its foot where they could view the summit (Exod.

19:1, 16–20). God revealed himself to Moses, who then called on the people to make a covenant with God (Exod. 19:1–8). When Israel agreed to keep God's words, they were given three days to prepare themselves before the beginning of the events which brought the Ten Commandments and the accompanying laws. The people later heard the law read (Exod. 24:3, 7) and watched as Moses built an altar and sacrificed to the Lord (Exod. 24:4–6). A group composed of Moses, Aaron, Nadab, Abihu, and seventy of the elders of Israel are described as going up and seeing the God of Israel standing on a pavement of sapphire (Exod. 24:9–11). Moses took Joshua into the mountain and stayed forty days; here he was shown the pattern of the tabernacle (Exod. 24:12—31:18).

When Moses returned from the mountain, the people had grown weary with his long absence and had fashioned a golden calf (Exod. 32:1–6). Moses had to persuade God not to slay them (Exod. 32:7–14). Moses destroyed the golden calf and broke the tablets of the law (Exod. 32:15–24). Moses stood at the gate of the camp and asked, "Who is on the Lord's side? Come to me." The Levites responded and were ordered to put to death the idolaters (Exod. 32:25–29). The camp of Israel was hit with a plague (Exod. 32:30–35).

After telling Israel to prepare to leave Sinai and go to the Promised Land and after instructing Moses to set up the tent of meeting, God gave Moses a second set of the stone tablets and revealed several other commands and warnings (Exod. 33–34). After other instructions (Leviticus), the people prepared for the march (Num. 1–10). A census was taken, leaders were appointed in each tribe, the Levites were organized, camp regulations were spelled out, including details about the order of marching; and the people left Sinai (Num. 10:11–13).

In the area around the traditional site of the giving of the law, three mountains tower over the plain: Mount Catherine rises 8,536 feet above sea level on the southwest; Mount Moses 7,363 feet; and Ras es-Safsaf 6,540 feet on the northwest. Several traditional sites have been chosen through the centuries, but none is certain. At 6,900 feet on Jebel Musa (Mount Moses) is the Chapel of Elijah (I Kings 19:8ff.). Also on the side of this mount is the spring which is said to be the place where Moses tended Jethro's flock (Exod. 2:15ff.).

On the northwest slope of Mount Moses, Constantine's mother, Helena, built a small church in the fourth century. The Monastery of St. Catherine, covering about the size of a city block and resembling a fortress, was built on the site of Helena's church and can be traced back to the emperor Justinian in A.D. 527. The monastery library is said by some to be the oldest library in the world. It includes an invaluable list of ancient manuscripts in Greek, Syriac, Georgian, Slavic, and Arabic. The Codex Sinaiticus, a third-century Greek translation of the Bible, was found here and transferred by Konstantin von Tischendorf to the private libraries of the czars in the middle of the nineteenth century. It was later sold to the British Museum.

The monastery was founded to mark the spot where Moses saw the burning bush (Exod. 3). It encloses the Church of St. Catherine, the Chapel of the Burning Bush, and many recent buildings, including a mosque. A government-operated museum is housed a couple of miles to the west of the monastery.

After the encampment at Sinai, Moses and the Israelites moved northeastward and traveled through the wilderness of Paran. It was to this area that Hagar and Ishmael had fled (Gen. 21:21) and from the same region that the spies were sent out (Num. 10:12; 12–16). On the northern border of the wilderness of Paran is the city of Kadesh-barnea. The Israelites' exact itinerary is traced in Numbers 10–12 and 33:16f. Among the stops mentioned are Taberah, where those who murmured against the Lord were consumed by fire (Num. 11:1–3, location unknown), and Kibroth-hattaavah, where those who overate the quail died. At Hazeroth, Miriam and Aaron criticized Moses for his marriage to an Ethiopian woman.

The Sinai is still a bleak, forbidding area, but travel there today is easier than ever before.

Moses and the Ten Commandments

Harold Hazelip

American historian Andrew Hacker has concluded that we are no longer a nation of people but a collection of two hundred million egos, each pursuing its own narrow purposes. We have begun to handle moral choices in the same way we shop for food brands—according to personal taste, social position, and economic ability. Values which are centuries old are being wiped out. We search for direction, for a foundation upon which persons can mature and society can be stable.

In Walker Percy's novel *Lancelot,* Lancelot Lawar broods over his wife's unfaithfulness. He decides "that perhaps there are no evil acts, no good acts either, only acts of sickness on the one hand, and acts flowing from unrecognized self-interest on the other." His wife's sexual betrayal becomes a "philosophical mystery." He finally realizes that he is morally confused and no longer certain of what is good or evil. Lamenting the loss of the old values, he finally rages, "I will not have my son or daughter grow up in such a world."

Our spiritual wells seem to be running low. Tested values that once seemed right are being abandoned. Technology has produced unbelievable progress, but the result is "future shock"—an inability to adjust to massive change. Our future shock is made worse by the absence of any certain foundation for moral behavior.

The Problem of Permissiveness

We call the problems we see in today's moral structures "relativity" and "permissiveness." Everything is relative, we are told; there is no objective standard of behavior. The outcome, when everything is relative, is permissiveness. In the business world the result of permissiveness is that otherwise law-abiding citizens commit white-collar crimes of embezzlement and pilferage. The prevalent philosophy of personal advantage at any cost rips relationships apart.

The problems of permissiveness are nowhere more evident than in sexual behavior. The "playboy" notion of total sexual freedom, shunning the restraints of the "old morality," has resulted in today's "sexual wilderness." There are astonishing statistics of broken marriages, premarital sexual adventures, skyrocketing venereal disease, unprecedented extramarital activity, and staggering aberrant sexual manifestations. Are we really ready for Hemingway's philosophy, "What is moral is what you feel good after, and what is immoral is what you feel bad after"?

Of course, there are new solutions. Solutions which offer a god but deny the devil. These gods do not demand much; they never punish, but do offer some form of reward. Like permissive parents, they give us easy recipes. Twenty minutes of meditation, or of mindlessly chanting some word, or of simply standing on one's head—and everything is made whole again. We are at peace with the world, with our fellows, and with ourselves—very cheaply.

A Word from God

What we need is a word from God. An anchor. G. K. Chesterton once observed, "Morality, like art, consists of drawing a line somewhere." Arthur Sueltz uses his golf game to illustrate this point. When he started golfing, he played with some generous fellows. If he bungled on the first tee, they would say, "Art, we won't count it. We'll call it a 'mulligan.' Hit it again." This resulted in a mutual grace when they went to the green. Imagine that a man's ball lay fifteen feet from the cup. He might say to his friend, "I'll give you yours if you'll give me mine." "Deal."

Do we think we're playing this type of golf in our moral decisions? Do we decide by mutual consent which strokes will count and which won't? But there is a pesky question: where does par come in? Who speaks for par? Does mutual consent in sexual wrong make the act right? Or are we accountable to someone higher than "mutual consent"?

The Bible has an answer. The apostle Paul reflected on the commandments God gave Moses: "Owe no one anything, except to love one another; for he who loves his neighbor has fulfilled the law. The commandments, 'You shall not commit adultery, You shall not kill, You shall not steal, You shall not covet,' and any other commandment, are summed up in this sentence, 'You shall love your neighbor as yourself.' Love does no wrong to a neighbor; therefore love is the fulfilling of the law" (Rom. 13:8–10).

Paul does not mention every one of the Ten Commandments. The fourth commandment ("Remember the sabbath day, to keep it holy,") was never repeated for Christians. The day of worship in Christianity is the day of our Lord's resurrection—the first day of the week. All of the other commandments are repeated and given new emphasis in the New Testament as the basis for morality.

Harry Emerson Fosdick was a well-known theologically liberal minister in New York City during the last generation. After his retirement he made a rather strong statement affirming the need for the Ten Commandments over against the collapse of moral standards in our era. He said, "In my callow youth I reached the conclusion that we had so far spiritually progressed that we could center all attention on Paul's positive ethic, 'Love is the fulfilling of the law,' and that we need no longer stress the negative, 'Thou shalt not.' I take it back. I know human life better. I wish those Ten Commandments could be blazoned in every marketplace, in every schoolhouse, in every church. Thou shalt not kill. Thou shalt not commit adultery. Thou shalt not steal. Thou shalt not bear false witness. Thou shalt not covet."

God Commands—God Cares

No society can survive without restraints and guidelines. God commands because he cares. We keep the commandments because they are God's guidelines. The Ten Commandments never liberated anyone from sin. They are restraints. They have kept people from falling apart personally. The cross offers the healing and forgiveness we need for our failures.

God's Word includes both demands and promises. Either apart from the other distorts his Word. If we know only God's demands, and do not know his grace, we are driven to despair or we may become legalists. On the other hand, if we know only God's grace and promises, and do not know his commandments, we will become pampered children instead of responsible servants.

We need to reclaim the moral foundation of the Ten Commandments and then learn how Jesus handled it. He went beyond the outward action to the state of the heart (Matt. 5:17–48). He made promises but he also made demands. He offers us forgiveness while requiring holy behavior.

So you have failed. Don't despair. "All have sinned and fall short of the glory of God" (Rom. 3:23). But don't take your failures lightly either. Turn to God for forgiveness and strength to follow his will.

You may begin the Christian life through faith in Christ as God's Son. He requires a new mind—a second thought—a turning from the old life to the new in repentance. Baptism becomes the line of demarcation between the world and the church as the Red Sea was the line of separation between Israel and Egypt. Those who are enslaved can be free. And you can be— through God's grace.

Abraham's Well, Beersheba

3 Southern Palestine

The southern area of Palestine is known as the Negeb or, in modern Israeli spelling, Negev. The Hebrew word apparently means "dry country," though sometimes the word is used simply to refer to an area in the south. It occurs some ninety-seven times in the Old Testament. Actually, the Negeb is shaped like an upside-down triangle, with the east-west baseline connecting Gaza on the Mediterranean coast with the southernmost point of the Dead Sea. The eastern side would then run directly south to Ezion-geber (the modern Elat) at the northern tip of the Gulf of Aqaba. The third line of the triangle would run northwest from Ezion-geber back to Gaza. The Negeb

23

has some barren rocky mountains stretching toward the Dead Sea, mountains which reach an elevation of 3,300 feet above sea level at their highest point. To the north and west of these mountains, between Beer-sheba and Kadesh-barnea, there is an area of broad cultivatable wadis which are moistened by heavy dew from the sea and by occasional storms. The southernmost part of the area is incredibly barren and has sand dunes as well as great gorges and tremendous cliffs in the mountain ranges.

Beer-sheba is fifty-four miles south of Jerusalem and some forty-seven miles west of the Dead Sea. The name, meaning "well of seven" or "well of swearing," apparently refers to the covenant between Abraham and Abimelich made there (Gen. 21:31, 32). It is less than fifty miles north of Kadesh-barnea and must have been one of the first areas visited by the twelve spies.

Biblical History

When Abram obeyed God's call to leave Ur of the Chaldees, he first stopped near Bethel, where he built an altar. He then moved on toward the Negeb (Gen. 12:4–9). After dividing the land with Lot, he lived at Hebron by the oaks of Mamre (Gen. 13:18). After the destruction of Sodom and Gomorrah he moved southward "toward the territory of the Negeb, and dwelt between Kadesh and Shur; and he sojourned in Gerar" (Gen. 20:1). Gerar is thought to have been some fifteen miles northwest of Beer-sheba. It was here that Abraham told Abimelech, king of Gerar, that Sarah was his sister (Gen. 20:1–7), and from this area that Ishmael and his mother were expelled (Gen. 21:8–14) and sent away into the "wilderness of Beer-sheba." It was also here that Abraham and Abimelech disagreed over water wells and ultimately made a covenant at Beer-sheba (Gen. 21:31, 32). It was also from here that Abraham journeyed to Mount Moriah (widely assumed to be part of what is now Jerusalem) to offer Isaac as God requested (Gen. 22:1–18).

Isaac was living at Beer-lahai-roi in the Negeb when he first met Rebekah, who was brought to him by his father Abraham's servant to become his wife (Gen. 24:62–67). It was at Beer-lahai-roi that Jacob and Esau were born and that Esau sold his birthright to Jacob (Gen. 25:19–34). Later, at Beer-sheba Rebekah and Jacob deceived Isaac and Esau in the matter of the stolen blessing (Gen. 27), and Jacob was sent to Paddan-aram (Gen. 28:1–10). Apparently, when Jacob returned from Paddan-aram, he did not live in the Negeb, but near Shechem (north of Jerusalem). It was at Beer-sheba, however, that God spoke to Jacob in a vision promising that a great nation would grow out of the relatively few then going into Egypt (Gen. 46:1–7). From there Jacob and his household journeyed into Egypt where they prospered. Their descendants, however, were subjected to slavery.

After the long sojourn in Egypt, the Israelites were eventually freed by God's power from their Egyptian masters. Slightly more than a year after the exodus from Egypt, Moses led the people on an eleven-day journey from Mount Horeb to Kadesh-barnea (Deut. 1:2, 19), where they prepared to enter the Promised Land. It was here that the twelve spies were chosen and sent out. Upon their return, the faithless Israelites were turned back to wander in the Sinai Peninsula for a period of forty years (Num. 13–14). It was also at Kadesh-barnea that a number of other events took place: the giving of additional laws and regulations (Num. 15); the rebellion and death of Korah, Dathan, and Abiram (Num. 16); the budding of Aaron's rod (Num. 17); the giving of the laws of the priests and the Levites (Num. 18); the death of Miriam (Num. 20:1); and the bringing of water from the rock at Meribah (apparently another name for Kadesh), an act in which Moses sinned (Num. 20:2–13).

The prophet Samuel stationed his sons in Beer-sheba to act as judges (I Sam. 8:2). It was during the period of the judges that Beer-sheba was reckoned as the southernmost part of Israelite territory, giving birth to the phrase "from Dan to Beer-sheba" (Judg. 20:1; I Sam. 3:20), which denoted the land in its entire extent from north to south (Dan was located on the slopes of Mount Hermon in the north). During the period of the kings, especially during the reign of Solomon, the land from Dan to Beer-sheba had peace (I Kings 4:25). During this period Solomon also built a fleet of ships at Ezion-geber (modern Elat) on the shore of the Gulf of Aqaba.

Beer-sheba today prominently displays a well which has been excavated to a depth of some sixty-five feet by archaeologists. It is called Abraham's well, though this designation is by no means certain. Today, Beer-sheba is largely a Jewish city. The ancient city is thought to have been some four miles east of the modern city of Beer-sheba, where excavations have found evidence of a massive wall, thirteen feet thick, which existed as far back as the tenth century B.C. No remains dating back to Abraham have been found at the site, since the patriarch lived in tents and seems to have moved a great deal. Apparently the city was founded in the period of the judges.

In the story of Elijah there is the account of the prophet's fleeing from Ahab and Jezebel and stopping at Beer-sheba, where he left his servant. He went on another day's journey into the wilderness and wished for his own death before sleeping under a broom tree. It was there that God came to him through an angel and sustained his life, after which he continued his journey southward to Mount Horeb, or Mount Sinai (I Kings 19:1–8).

From the above it is obvious that the Negeb played an important role in the history of God's people. Those who have been reared in well-watered, fertile areas of the earth find it difficult to understand how the Israelites could have lived for so long in such a barren, desolate area. The spies in their report used the expression, "The land. . . is a land that devours its inhabitants'' (Num. 13:32), a most appropriate description of the entire area of the Negeb. Life must have been difficult for the patriarchs, their families, and their flocks.

"Without Faith It Is Impossible"
Batsell Barrett Baxter

The theme for this message comes from the great eleventh chapter of the Book of Hebrews. You may remember that that chapter is sometimes called "The Hall of Faith" because it tells of a number of the great heroes and heroines of the Bible whose lives were characterized by triumphant faith. Among the many mentioned are Abraham, Isaac, Jacob, Moses, David, Samuel, and others of the prophets. Early in this great chapter we read. "And without faith it is impossible to please him. For whoever would draw near to God must believe that he exists and that he rewards those who seek him" (Heb. 11:6). I have chosen especially that first line, "Without faith it is impossible," because I feel that this phrase captures the essence of the chapter. Of all the great host of people who lived successful lives and whose stories are told in the Bible, the one thing that they had in common was a great faith or trust in God.

The Exodus

The theme of faith has a special appropriateness in relation to the southern portion of the land of Israel. Here there occurred a great demonstration of the power of faith. God had delivered the Israelites from Egyptian bondage with a marvelous display of his divine power. You recall the plagues and the destruction of Pharaoh's army in the Red Sea. Then, three months later the Israelites came to the wilderness of Sinai (Exod. 19:1) and there they were given the law of Moses. Eleven months later they left Sinai (Num. 10:11, 12), moving north to Kadesh-barnea, intent on entering the Promised Land of Canaan. There were some 603,550 grown men, twenty years of age and up, men who were able to go to war. This suggests that the total population of Israel at that time was possibly two million people. Moses and Aaron were their leaders.

Spying Out the Land

In Numbers 13:2 we find God's directions to his people, "Send men to spy out the land of Canaan, which I give to the people of Israel; from each tribe of their fathers shall you send a man, every one a leader among them."

There are two Hebrew verbs that are used in this account to describe the activity of the spies. One means "to explore, to seek the qualities of the land." The other means "to reconnoiter and find weak points for the purpose of attack." The twelve men were to explore the land and to find the best way to enter and subdue it. All of these men were leaders, but only Joshua and Caleb, the men who are described as having great faith in God, are ever mentioned again.

In Numbers 13:17–20 we find the specific instructions to the twelve: "Go up into the Negeb yonder, and go up into the hill country, and see what the land is, and whether the people who dwell in it are strong or weak, whether they are few or many, and whether the land that they dwell in is good or bad, and whether the cities that they dwell in are camps or strongholds, and whether the land is rich or poor, and whether there is wood in it or not. Be of good courage, and bring some of the fruit of the land."

Our text continues: "So they went up and spied out the land from the wilderness of Zin to Rehob, near the entrance of Hamath. They went up into the Negeb, and came to Hebron; and Ahiman, Sheshai, and Talmai, the descendants of Anak, were there." The children of Anak were a tribe of "long-necked" men, who appeared as giants to the smaller people who lived near Hebron. Hebron was famous for many things, but especially as the site where Abraham buried his wife Sarah.

The twelve spies returned and made their report to the people, who were approximately fifty miles south of Beer-sheba. We read, beginning in verse 27, "We came to the land to which you sent us; it flows with milk and honey, and this is its fruit. Yet the people who dwell in the land are strong, and the cities are fortified and very large; and besides, we saw the descendants of Anak there."

Continuing to read, "But Caleb quieted the people before Moses, and said, 'Let us go up at once, and occupy it; for we are well able to overcome it.' Then the men who had gone up with him said, 'We are not able to go up against the people; for they are stronger than we.' So they brought to the people of Israel an evil report of the land which they had spied out."

Same Facts—Different Faith

All twelve of the men sent to spy out the land came back with the same facts. The land was "flowing with milk and honey," a phrase denoting fertility and abundant natural resources. However, ten of the twelve men brought back a negative report—a report of fear and cowardice. Only Joshua and Caleb had unlimited faith in God and trusted confidently that he would help them in overcoming the people of the land. The facts which were observed were the same; the conclusions drawn were vastly different.

The ten wavering spys easily influenced the people to have similar doubts.

What tremendous responsibility leaders have! Movements can so easily be stopped by a few doubting words. Joshua and Caleb tried to persuade the people to trust God, saying, "The land, which we passed through to spy it out, is an exceedingly good land. If the Lord delights in us, he will bring us into this land and give it to us, a land which flows with milk and honey. Only, do not rebel against the Lord; and do not fear the people of the land, for they are bread for us; their protection is removed from them, and the Lord is with us; do not fear them.' But all the congregation said to stone them with stones" (Num. 14:7–10a).

At this point God appeared and spoke to the people, for the text continues: "Then the glory of the Lord appeared at the tent of meeting to all the people of Israel. And the Lord said to Moses, 'How long will this people despise me? And how long will they not believe in me, in spite of all the signs which I have wrought among them?' " (Num. 14:10b, 11).

As one continues to read in this fourteenth chapter of Numbers, he finds that God caused the faithless Israelites to wander forty years in the wilderness, a year for each day that the spies had searched out the land, before allowing their descendants to enter and to conquer the land of Canaan. With the exception of Joshua and Caleb all those who were twenty years old and older died in the wilderness, unworthy to enter the Promised Land, which God eventually gave to their children.

The Life of Trust

The story is simple, the lesson profound. This is essentially a lesson to teach that we must stand with the Lord no matter what. We must stand with him even though the majority go another way. Following the crowd is so appealing. Yet, the fact that the majority believe something, or do something, never does make it right. Only God determines what is right and what is wrong. Only God's inspired Word, the Bible, can be trusted as an ever-faithful guide. If our lives are built upon trust in him, he will give us the victory. If we go our own way, defeat and destruction lie ahead. When we look at the long sweep of history, it is very clear that those who stand on the Lord's side triumph and those who go their own way go down to defeat.

Mount Nebo, with Springs of Moses in the Foreground

4　Mount Nebo

If one wishes to go to the top of Mount Nebo, the place where Moses had his view of the Promised Land, died, and was buried by God in an unmarked grave, one must go to the modern country of Jordan. Jordan is a relatively small country with a population of about three million. The capital city Amman is built on the site of the ancient city of Philadelphia, one of the ten cities of the Decapolis of Jesus' day. The present city is built on a series of low-lying hills, but as one begins the hour-long drive toward the southwest to Mount Nebo, he soon finds himself on the relatively level Plains of Moab. The road approaches from the eastern side of the mountain and almost before one knows it, he finds himself at the top of Mount Nebo, looking down on the Dead Sea and the southern end of the Jordan Valley.

Three peaks are identified today as the area of Nebo. Jebel en-Neba (Arabic for Mount Nebo), the highest of the three, is thought to be the place where Moses' life ended. The name *Nebo* is usually connected with the concept of height, suggesting "high mountain." Since the name *Pisgah* is associated with Nebo in Deuteronomy 34:1, some have suggested that both are names for the same peak. Other opinions are that Pisgah may be a peak near Mount Nebo or that Nebo might be a part of a larger area known as Pisgah. Biblical references to the two include Numbers 21:20; 23:14; 33:47, 48; Deuteronomy 3:17, 27; 4:49; 32;49; 34:1; and Joshua 12:3; 13:20.

Mount Nebo is almost opposite the northern end of the Dead Sea, rising some 4,000 feet above the water's surface. This means that it is actually some 2,700 feet above the sea level, since the Dead Sea is approximately 1,300 feet below sea level. The peak is about twelve miles east of the place where the Jordan River flows into the Dead Sea.

Moses' View

As indicated by Deuteronomy 34:1–3, the view from the mountain is magnificent. On a clear day Mount Hermon, with its snow cap, is visible in the north. Tabor, Ebal, Gerizim, and other heights of Samaria and Judea are also visible. The ridge on which Bethlehem and Hebron are located can be seen to the southwest. On a clear day the modern-day towers on the Mount of Olives, just east of Jerusalem, and the city of Jericho can be seen. Most of the Jordan River cannot be seen, being hidden in a deep gorge. The Dead Sea is clearly visible since it lies immediately below. The area of En-gedi, on the western shore of the sea, can also be seen. It is quite possible that when God gave Moses his look into the Promised Land his view was miraculously enhanced, for Deuternomy 34:2 indicates that Moses could see "all the land of Judah as far as the Western Sea." This is generally taken to be a reference to the Mediterranean Sea, which cannot be seen by the naked eye from Mount Nebo.

The Austrian explorer Alois Musil left this interesting comment concerning the westward view from Moab: "No wonder that at this glorious view the poor Bedouin may feel an irresistible longing to journey westward across the valley into that paradisical land, where there is water-a-plenty, where the rich verdure never seems to disappear, and where he believes he will find everything his heart desires." The same yearning must have been present among the Israelites after their long sojourn in the desolate wastes of the Sinai Peninsula.

Balak and Balaam

Moses' journey to the top of Mount Nebo to view the Promised Land, which he was not permitted to enter because of his sin (Deut. 32:49ff.), is not the only important event connected with this particular mountain in biblical history. This was also the site where Balak, king of Moab, summoned the prophet Balaam to curse the Israelites. In fact, Balak took Balaam "to the field of Zophim, to the top of Pisgah" (Num. 23:14), which, depending upon the relationship of Pisgah and Nebo, may be the same peak on which Moses died. Balak built altars on the top of the mountain where Balaam could get a good view of the encampment of the Israelites and then offered him rich rewards if he would curse the people. Only blessings for Israel came forth from Balaam's mouth, however.

As one stands on Mount Nebo it is extremely difficult to comprehend even a small fraction of the significant events which happened on the mountain and in the valley below. The events of our modern world, about which people get so excited today, lose a great deal of their significance when viewed from Mount Nebo and in the light of the history of the peoples and kingdoms whose affairs have unfolded there.

An old, yet relatively modern, church building stands on the brow of the hill. It is the latest in a long line of buildings which have been erected here, some of which date back at least as far as the fourth century A.D. Unfortunately, these "modern" buildings tend to distract our minds from the significance of the mountain and the momentous events which have happened upon it.

In a familiar poem, Mrs. C. F. Alexander has captured much of the significance of Mount Nebo for the modern religious traveler:

> By Nebo's lonely mountain,
> On this side Jordan's wave,
> In a vale in the land of Moab
> There lies a lonely grave.
>
> And no man knows that sepulchre,
> And no man saw it e'er;
> For the angels of God upturned the sod,
> And laid the dead man there.
>
> O lonely grave in Moab's land;
> O dark Beth-peor hill;
> Speak to these curious hearts of ours,
> And teach them to be still.

God hath His mysteries of grace,
Ways that we cannot tell;
He hides them deep, like the hidden sleep
Of him he loved so well.

Learning to Live with Disappointment

Batsell Barrett Baxter

We do not often encounter Mount Nebo in the Bible, yet it is a very famous mountain. It was here at the very end of his life that God took Moses and allowed him to view the Promised Land, which he was not permitted to enter. It was on Mount Nebo that Moses died, alone, except for God who buried him in an unmarked grave. There is a sad but significant story behind the unusual events that took place on this mountain.

The events which culminated here on Mount Nebo with the death and burial of Moses—outside the Promised Land—began with an incident much earlier at Meribah in the wilderness of Zin, during the early months of the exodus from Egypt. There was no water and the people were murmuring against Moses and Aaron.

The story is found in Numbers 20:7-12: "And the Lord said to Moses, 'Take the rod, and assemble the congregation, you and Aaron your brother, and tell the rock before their eyes to yield its water; so you shall bring water out of the rock for them; so you shall give drink to the congregation and their cattle.' And Moses took the rod from before the Lord, as he commanded him. And Moses and Aaron gathered the assembly together before the rock, and he said to them, 'Hear now, you rebels; shall we bring forth water for you out of this rock?' And Moses lifted up his hand and struck the rock with his rod twice; and water came forth abundantly, and the congregation drank, and their cattle. And the Lord said to Moses and Aaron, 'Because you did not believe in me, to sanctify me in the eyes of the people of Israel, therefore you shall not bring this assembly into the land which I have given them.' ''

Moses' Disappointment

Evidently, because Moses and Aaron arrogated to themselves the power that brought forth water out of the rock and did not honor God, their fate was that they would not enter the Promised Land. Moses' deep disappointment at this closing of the gate of the land of Canaan to him is shown in a prayer which he makes at a later time. "O Lord God, thou hast only begun to show thy servant thy greatness and thy mighty hand; for what god is there in heaven or on earth who can do such works and mighty acts as thine? Let me go over, I pray, and see the good land beyond the Jordan, that goodly hill country, and Lebanon'' (Deut. 3:24, 25). After years of anticipation, years of toil and effort to lead God's people to the land of promise, it was a great disappointment to Moses not to get to enter himself.

As the time for the people to enter the Promised Land came closer, Moses readied them for what lay ahead. In Deuteronomy 4:20–23, he admonished them, ''But the Lord has taken you, and brought you forth out of the iron furnace, out of Egypt, to be a people of his own possession, as at this day. . . . Take heed to yourselves, lest you forget the covenant of the Lord your God, which he made with you. . . .''

I would also like to turn to the description of the events at the close of Moses' life—events which happened right here on Mount Nebo: ''And Moses went up from the plains of Moab to Mount Nebo, to the top of Pisgah, which is opposite Jericho. And the Lord showed him all the land. . . . And the Lord said to him, 'This is the land of which I swore to Abraham, to Isaac, and to Jacob, ''I will give it to your descendants.'' I have let you see it with your eyes, but you shall not go over there.' So Moses the servant of the Lord died there in the land of Moab, according to the word of the Lord, and he buried him in the valley in the land of Moab opposite Beth-peor; but no man knows the place of his burial to this day. Moses was a hundred and twenty years old when he died; his eye was not dim, nor his natural force abated'' (Deut. 34:1, 4–7).

With great confidence and courage Moses led God's people out of Egyptian bondage. With great faith and trust he led the Israelites through the wilderness. With great leadership ability he taught them God's law—known through the centuries as the law of Moses. But, because of his sin he could not lead them into the Promised Land. That was left to his successor Joshua. What disappointment he must have felt!

Disappointment Is Universal

Moses has not been alone in feeling great disappointment. In fact, all of us in the course of our lives will be disappointed many times. The disappointments range all the way from the fading of childhood dreams to the deep lifelong disappointments that come with failure to achieve life's major goals. As a child I dreamed of being an outstanding sports hero and in my fantasy played many a baseball game in Yankee Stadium. As time went on, however, I realized that I would never be a Babe Ruth, or a Lou Gehrig. Those dreams evaporated with the passing of the years.

Thousands of little boys across our land today dream such dreams. Perhaps even more serious are the ambitions of the thousands of high school and college athletes who have achieved certain levels of excellence in their chosen sports, but who are destined to be disappointed as they eventually learn that they are not qualified for stardom among the professionals.

Similarly, many enter marriage with high hopes and great expectations, only to discover later on that their marriages are unfulfilling, or perhaps even worse. What seemed to attractive and so promising has faded with the passing years. The sudden death of a marriage partner can make an enormous difference in the lifestyle and the enjoyment of life. All of these are very real disappointments that come to people all the time.

Children likewise may be disappointing to parents. We parents often have such great dreams for our children and live to see many of those dreams unfulfilled.

Then, too, disappointments come in the realm of our material possessions. So often these possessions for which we labor and toil fail to live up to expectations.

There are also the disappointments connected with aging. As the years pass, our physical bodies inevitably decline in their capabilities. Impaired hearing, defective eyesight, or inability to walk normally brings disappointment. Forgetfulness becomes a problem. Physical weakness and inability to get our work done bring disappointment and regret.

Life's Spiritual Dimensions

My point in all of this is not to play upon the disappointments of life, which are all too real on their own, but to emphasize that these disappointments need not be overwhelming. There is a spiritual dimension to life which will never let us down. If our primary goals are in this life, centered in the things of this world, the here and now, we will inevitably be disappointed. Yet, it is possible for our deepest goals to be anchored in the spiritual values which do not decline as the years pass.

It is this spiritual dimension of life that makes possible the facing of the day-to-day disappointments that must inevitably come. The promises of God give us strength to bear our disappointments. It is God who gives us hope for the future. In the words of Paul, "I know whom I have believed, and I am sure that he is able to guard until that Day what has been entrusted to me" (II Tim. 1:12).

In order to have this security that makes all the difference in terms of our peace of mind here in this life, we must be children of God, members of his family. We become part of God's family by our own deliberate choice. As we believe in Christ as God's Son, confess our faith in him before our fellow men, turn away from the world and its sinfulness, and then are baptized into the name of Christ, God adds us to his family and we become children of

God. Without this relationship with God, life inevitably becomes a disappointment and ultimately a tragedy.

In the long ago Moses faced a great disappointment, but he went right on doing his duty—preparing the people to enter the Promised Land which he himself would not be permitted to enter. When we are disappointed, let's keep right on doing whatever needs to be done. Let's learn to live with the inevitable day-to-day disappointments of life. As children of God, we have the inner spiritual resources to enable us to come through our disappointments triumphantly.

The Treasury, a Royal Tomb at Petra

5 Petra

Petra is aptly named—"the city of Rock." It lies south of the Dead Sea, approximately three hours' drive from Amman, and was the home of the ancient Nabataeans. Little is known of the early history of the Nabataeans, but they may be the people referred to by Obadiah in his condemnation of the Edomites (Obad. 5ff.). These people apparently grew rich by plundering passing caravans.

The road to Petra winds down the hill from the little village of Wadi Musa. One enters Petra either by foot or on horseback. A narrow ravine leads into the ruins, making it possible for a handul of men to defend the city against a large attacking force. At some points the road is twenty feet wide; at others, the rock almost touches overhead.

The basin of the city itself is an open space about a mile long and two-thirds of a mile wide. The site was occupied from about the fifth century B.C. to the fifth century A.D., and was at its heyday during the first centuries B.C. and A.D. From this capital city, the Nabataeans extended their empire as far north as Damascus in the first century B.C. under King Aretas III.

Temples and Tombs

The remains of temples, palaces, baths, and private houses present a brilliantly colored display of ancient sculpture. Great tombs line either side of the gorge leading into the basin. The softness of the sandstone prevented any finely detailed work, but the sculptors devised a style which allowed the tombs to fit perfectly into the giant cliffs.

From the open basin of the townsite, valleys go off in various directions, and days could be spent exploring these ravines. They too are lined with houses and tombs, with occasional flights of steps winding their way up the sides of the mountains. Worshipers apparently climbed these steps to their high places of sacrifice.

The great number of the tombs, their huge size, and variety of form stagger the imagination. Several of the tombs are occupied by Arab families today. These people sell souvenirs to tourists and tend their flocks of goats.

Prosperity and Decline

In 312 B.C., Petra was captured by Antigonus I, and with it a great treasure. The city was probably a storage place for plunder at that time. The Nabataeans apparently found that it was profitable to charge a toll to caravans in exchange for safe conduct through their land. Contact with the outside world introduced the Nabataeans to Greek culture, which influenced the architecture of Petra.

One of the problems the Nabataeans faced was an insufficient water supply from the two springs in the city. A channel was cut in the rock from the springs at Wadi Musa to the heart of the city, which brought a continuous supply of fresh water. To avoid loss of this in time of siege, vast cisterns were cut in the rock and lined with plaster. Channels were cut in the hillsides and rainwater was conducted to the cisterns.

Stories of the wealth of Petra caused the Roman Empire to attempt to capture the city. The first two or three attempts failed, although the Nabataeans as a nation were made to pay tribute. But in A.D. 106, Petra was overcome and became a Roman province. The emperor Trajan built a road which passed through Petra, connecting Syria with the Red Sea. Petra prospered under Roman rule and some of the best monuments date from this period.

However, the prosperity was short-lived. A decline set in by the third century A.D., principally because an easier caravan route caused the abandonment of the route through Petra. The city was occupied, but by declining numbers. Christianity apparently came to Petra in the fourth or fifth century A.D., as evidenced by crosses carved on tombs. By the time of the Arab conquest in the seventh century, nothing remained of Petra but an empty shell. The Crusaders erected a fortress behind the temple, but Petra remained unpopulated.

The very memory of the city seems to have been lost for centuries. Johann Burckhardt, a Swiss explorer, rediscovered the city in 1812. Its giant mausoleums seem strange to a modern civilization, but Petra has a breathtakingly unique beauty which justifies the long, hot drive to the site.

"God Is Our Refuge"

Harold Hazelip

Twin brothers were born to the Old Testament couple, Isaac and Rebekah. Esau, the older brother, became the forefather of the Edomites, and Jacob of the Israelites. These two nations became locked in an endless cycle of hate and retaliation. Of all the enemies living around ancient Israel and harassing her, Edom was perhaps the most despised.

Esau's descendants settled in a land south of the Dead Sea about a hundred miles long and fifty miles wide. It included some well-watered plains. The Edomites were shrewd traders. They made raids on neighboring peoples and then retreated to impregnable strongholds for security.

Our False Security

One of those strongholds was Petra. It was entered by a narrow gorge, over a mile long, between massive cliffs over 700 feet high. The gorge led into a hollow basin over a mile long and two-thirds of a mile broad. There were rock-hewn dwellings, tombs, and temples. Located on an important caravan route, Petra was once a great trading center. But it is desolate today.

The strongest sort of human refuge is insufficient when real trouble comes. When everything on which man has built crumbles—even the solid ground itself—where do we go for refuge?

Psalm 46 was written in a time of trouble for Israel. Fear stalked the land. People were depressed. Many students think the psalm was inspired by the deliverance of Jerusalem from Sennacherib in 701 B.C. Three times in the psalm of eleven verses occurs the refrain: "God is our refuge."

This refrain has made Psalm 46 perhaps the second most popular in the collection of 150 psalms in the Old Testament—second only to Psalm 23. In times of discouragement, Luther would say to Melanchthon, "Come, Philip, let us sing the forty-sixth psalm." They sang it in the hymn, "A Mighty Fortress Is Our God."

There are great lines in the psalm: "God is our refuge and strength, a very present help in trouble." "There is a river whose streams make glad the city of God, the holy habitation of the Most High. God is in the midst of her, she shall not be moved; God will help her right early." "Be still, and know that I am God. I am exalted among the nations, I am exalted in the earth!"

But the key refrain is, "The Lord of hosts is with us; the God of Jacob is our refuge." Here are two titles for God: the Lord of hosts and the God of Jacob.

Lord of Hosts

What does Psalm 46 mean by the phrase "Lord of hosts"? God is Lord of all nature and ruler of all men. He will protect us in the midst of the universe and in the midst of hostile peoples. "Therefore we will not fear though the earth should change, though the mountains shake in the heart of the sea; though its waters roar and foam, though the mountains tremble with its tumult" (vv. 2, 3).

Man is so small in the presence of nature's forces. If you and I had been crouched in that little capsule revolving around the moon, what would have passed through our minds? Through the window one sees the little globe called earth against the background of the stars. From this distance nothing less than a continent can be detected by the eye. The greatest cities are invisible. Human beings are like grains of sand scattered on the surface of the globe.

This view would surely give us a new perspective on man and his achievements. But there is another thought. Through all those billions of miles, on all those planets now coming within view, there seems to be no other creature capable of this kind of exploration. There is something special about this tiny creature called man.

But we are so small. The Milky Way, one of the hundreds of galaxies, has one hundred billion suns or stars. Our sun is 1.3 million times the volume of the earth. If you dropped an earth into the sun every second, it would take over fifteen days to fill the sun. Alpha Hercules is the largest known star.

You could put 512 million suns in Alpha Hercules. And yet it appears as only a tiny dot of light through our largest telescopes.

As vast as the universe is, it has a Master. "The heavens are telling the glory of God; and the firmament proclaims his handiwork" (Ps. 19:1). Jeremiah said, "Ah Lord God! It is thou who hast made the heavens and the earth by thy great power and by thy outstretched arm! Nothing is too hard for thee" (Jer. 32:17).

God of Jacob

The psalmist is sure that though the earth collapse, "the Lord of hosts is with us." His second affirmation is, "the God of Jacob is our refuge." The God who rules the spacious firmament on high also cares about the lives of people. Someone has suggested that we paraphrase this line, "the God of *even* Jacob is our refuge." Jacob's name means "supplanter." He deceived his father and obtained the birthright which belonged to his older brother Esau. There came a night at the brook Jabbok when he wrestled with an angel until daybreak. His name was changed to Israel—"he who strives with God" (Gen. 32:28). God cared for even Jacob.

Whenever we decide that people do not matter to God, we look at Jesus and repent. Nothing was more characteristic of the life of Jesus than concern for individual human beings: the Twelve, Mary and Martha, the woman by Jacob's well, Nicodemus, the widow of Nain, blind Bartimaeus, Zacchaeus, the woman caught in adultery, the thief on the cross, the little children who came to him. Jesus was talking about sparrows when he said, "And not one of them is forgotten before God." He added, "Why, even the hairs of your head are all numbered. Fear not; you are of more value than many sparrows" (Luke 12:6, 7).

You and I are not expendable. We matter to God.

God Cares for You

So you are facing trouble. And you wonder whether to believe that you really do matter to God. Like Jacob, we are very imperfect people. But the central thread of Scripture is, "For God so loved the world that he gave his only Son, that whoever believes in him should not perish but have eternal life" (John 3:16). "God was in Christ reconciling the world to himself, not counting their trespasses against them" (II Cor. 5:19).

"The Lord of hosts is with us; the God of Jacob is our refuge." This is the God we trust, come what may. He commands the powers of the universe, yet pursues the hearts of men. As Paul put it, "The love of Christ leaves us no choice" (II Cor. 5:14, NEB).

Paul looked back on his conversion to Christ and said, "I have been crucified with Christ; it is no longer I who live, but Christ who lives in me; and the life I now live in the flesh I live by faith in the Son of God, who loved me and gave himself for me" (Gal. 2:20). You and I must be crucified with him too. When we die to sin in repentance and are buried with him in baptism, he begins to live in us. And through him, God becomes "our refuge and strength, a very present help in trouble. Therefore we will not fear. . . ." No earthly stronghold can give that security. This is the view of faith.

Hebron in the Hill Country of Judah

6 Hebron

The city of Hebron is located nineteen miles southwest of Jerusalem and about thirteen miles southwest of Bethlehem. It is 3,040 feet above sea level, which makes it the highest city in Israel. Hebron is identified with the Arab city of el-Khalil, which means "the friend of God." This may have some connection with the references in Isaiah 41:8 and James 2:23. Hebron was also known as Kiriath-arba, which means "city of four." According to Jewish tradition, it was so named because four patriarchs—Adam, Abraham, Isaac, and Jacob—were buried there. It is also known as Mamre, after the name of one of the three men who joined with Abram when he went

43

to rescue Lot from Chedorlaomer (Gen. 14:13ff.). The other men who assisted Abram were Aner and Eshcol. According to Numbers 13, the twelve spies brought back a huge cluster of grapes from the Valley of Eshcol. A large number of springs and wells in the area make it possible for apple, plum, fig, pomegranate, apricot, and nut trees to grow. Vegetables, grapes, and melons are also produced in the area's rich soil.

Hebron is mentioned only in the Old Testament, where it occurs some sixty-one times. Kiriath-arba is mentioned six times in the Old Testament, while the oaks or plain of Mamre is mentioned another ten times. Abram moved from the Negeb to Bethel, where strife arose between his herdsmen and those of Lot. Lot moved to Sodom, and Abram moved to Hebron. It was here that his name was changed to Abraham (Gen. 17:5). While sitting at the door of his tent at the oaks of Mamre, Abraham entertained heavenly visitors whose promise of a son caused Sarah to laugh (Gen. 18:1–15). They also warned Abraham of the coming destruction of Sodom and Gomorrah (Gen. 18:16–21). After the angels left, Abraham interceded to God for Sodom (Gen. 18:22–33). Afterward Abraham returned to the territory of the Negeb (Gen. 20:1).

Early History

While Abraham was grazing his flocks at Beer-sheba, Sarah died in Hebron and Abraham came to mourn her passing (Gen. 23:1, 2). Needing to secure an appropriate burial place for Sarah, he entered into negotiations with Ephron the Hittite to purchase the field in which was located the cave of Mach-pelah. He bought it for four hundred shekels of silver, and there buried Sarah. Later, he was also buried in the cave (Gen. 25:7–11). In the course of time Isaac and Rebekah, Jacob and Leah, and others were buried there.

Entrance to the cave of Mach-pelah has been a point of contention for centuries. A decree by the Mamelukes in 1266 forbade Jews from entering the cave. The closest the Jews could get was the seventh step of the staircase leading up to the mosque known as the Haram el-Khalil, which means "sacred precinct of the friend of the merciful one, God." The law was rescinded in 1967. Since that time the mosque has been opened to Jews and the general public. Inside the Mohammedan mosque today, surprisingly, there is a Jewish synagogue; and within close proximity of each other Muslims, Jews, and Christians come to pay their tribute to the patriarchs and their wives. The name *Mach-pelah* occurs six times in the Scriptures.

Sometime in his old age, Isaac moved to Hebron and was buried there (Gen. 35:27–29). The Bible does not specify the exact time when Jacob moved to Hebron. Apparently, Joseph had his dreams of superiority there, encountering his brothers' hatred. It was from Hebron that he was sent to visit with his brothers in Shechem (Gen. 37:1–14). It was to Hebron that they brought their evil report concerning Joseph's death and presented to their father Jacob the blood-stained coat of Joseph (Gen. 37:15–35). Later, when Jacob and his family were in Egypt he charged his sons shortly before his death to bury him with his fathers in the cave of Mach-pelah; and this they ultimately did (Gen. 50:12–14).

Under Joshua the Israelites began to conquer the land. When Hebron had been conquered, Caleb approached Joshua at Gilgal and rehearsed to him the role he had played when, as a forty-year-old man, he was one of the twelve spies whom Moses had sent into the land. Now, at age eighty-five, Caleb reminded Joshua of Moses' promise to him and asked that he be given Hebron. Joshua granted his wish (Josh. 14:13). Hebron was also one of the six cities of refuge (Josh. 20:7) as well as a city of the Levites (Josh. 21:11–13).

David's First Capital

Hebron also played an important role in the life of King David. After the death of Saul, David asked the Lord to which of the cities of Judah he should go. God instructed him to go to Hebron; the men of Judah anointed him king there (II Sam. 2:1–4). Hebron was the capital of David's kingdom for seven-and-one-half years, during which time six of his sons were born, including Absalom and Adonijah (II Sam. 3:2–5). During this time Ish-bosheth ruled the other tribes. The captain of his army, Abner, defected and came to David, but he was treacherously killed by Joab at the gate of the city. David put on clothes of mourning and walked behind the coffin as it moved through the streets of Hebron to the cemetery. When Ish-bosheth was assassinated by two of his own captains, David had them killed because of their treachery. After Ish-bosheth's death, David moved his capital from Hebron to Jerusalem (II Sam. 5:1–13). Later, Hebron became the head-quarters for Absalom's revolt against his father, David (II Sam. 15:7–10).

Archaeological discovery indicates that Hebron was occupied as early as 3300 B.C. In the Amarna Letters "a field of Abram" is listed among the cities conquered by one of the pharaohs. According to Josephus, Judas Maccabaeus captured, burned, and destroyed the city. Crusaders occupied the area, but in A.D. 1187 it was returned to the Muslims, under whose control it has remained until recent years. Few cities have had so influential a role in biblical history as Hebron.

Modern tourists are reminded constantly of the story of the cluster of grapes brought back from Hebron (or the Valley of Eshcol) because a cluster of grapes is the official emblem of the Israeli Department of Tourism, appearing on hundreds of vehicles, on numerous signs, and in much printed material. While visitors are not allowed to go into the depths of the cave of Mach-pelah, it is a moving experience to stand only a few feet above the place where Abraham, Isaac, Jacob, and their wives were buried.

Living—When a Loved One Has Died

Batsell Barrett Baxter

Abraham purchased a field in Hebron and there buried his wife Sarah. Later he himself was buried there, and still later Isaac and Rebekah, Jacob and Leah, were also buried there. The location was the cave of Mach-pelah; note the way in which the story is told in the twenty-third chapter of the Book of Genesis: "Sarah lived a hundred and twenty-seven years; these were the years of the life of Sarah. And Sarah died at Kiriath-arba (that is, Hebron) in the land of Canaan; and Abraham went in to mourn for Sarah and to weep for her. And Abraham rose up from before his dead, and said to the Hittites, 'I am a stranger and a sojourner among you; give me property among you for a burying place, that I may bury my dead out of my sight.' The Hittites answered Abraham, 'Hear us, my lord; you are a mighty prince among us. Bury your dead in the choicest of our sepulchres; none of us will withhold from you his sepulchre, or hinder you from burying your dead'" (Gen. 23:1-6).

There then follows a very interesting account of the negotiations in which Abraham offers to buy the field that he desires. Eventually, after offering to give the field, Ephron the Hittite names his price and Abraham counts out four hundred shekels of silver, thus purchasing the field. At that point the text continues: "After this, Abraham buried Sarah his wife in the cave of the field of Mach-pelah east of Mamre (that is, Hebron) in the land of Canaan. The field and the cave that is in it were made over to Abraham as a possession for a burying place by the Hittites" (Gen. 23:19, 20).

Aching Grief

Abraham's grief is a familiar story. There were many before him, no doubt, who had felt the aching grief that comes with the loss of a loved one. There have been multiplied millions since who have known the agony of the separation which death brings. Parents have known it when their children have been taken from them. Husbands and wives have known it when their companions died. Children have known it when parents have slipped away. For all its frequency, death never ceases to leave behind an emptiness and a pain which burden the lives of the loved ones who remain. How deeply meaningful it is to stand here today in Hebron, just a few yards from the ancient cave where Abraham laid his beloved Sarah to rest. Yet, our thoughts move out from this ancient site to all the thousands and millions across the world who have needed to go on living when a loved one has died.

C. S. Lewis opens his book, *A Grief Observed,* with the words, "No one ever told me that grief is so like fear. I am not afraid, but the sensation is like being afraid." He is speaking of that uneasiness and disquiet that fill the heart of the loved ones left behind. Such sensations can be paralyzing at worst, weakening at best.

The Road of Gratitude

Another who experienced the loss of a loved one and wrote very meaningfully about it was John Claypool, in his fine book *Tracks of a Fellow Struggler.* This book is the record of the author's struggle with his daughter's losing battle with leukemia. The battle lasted eighteen months. Four weeks after the death of his twelve-year-old daughter, he included in one of his sermons, "Though I cannot give the final word on the subject, I have made a few discoveries that may be worthwhile. To be specific, now that I have looked down three alternative roads that seemed to lead out of this darkness, I must report that two of them appear to be dead-ends, while the third holds real promise."

The first of those alternative roads was "unquestioning resignation; assuming nature is ruled by determinism." The second road, also rejected, was "intellectual understanding; a tidy answer to why." Turning from both of these Claypool found meaning in the third alternative, "the road of gratitude." He says: "Only when life is seen as a gift and received with the open hands of gratitude is it the joy that God meant for it to be. And these were the truths God was seeking to emphasize as he waited so long to send Isaac and then asked for him back. Did Abraham realize that all was gift, and not something to be earned or to be possessed, but received, participated in, held freely in gratefulness? This is the most helpful perspective I have found in the last weeks and of all the roads to travel, it offers the best promise of being a way out."

An eminent English woman lived in preoccupied contentment on her baronial estate until the day her little daughter, running to the balcony to welcome her mother home from a concert, fell over the railing and crumpled lifeless at her feet. It was after that tragic day that the mother found the nearby path to the village orphanage she had never seen before. New insights into the meaning of life can come out of the alchemy of suffering. Pain can soften hardness; aching grief can lift one to nobler enterprises.

The Promises of God

Much more can be said and has been said by those who have faced the death of loved ones. The greatest help of all, however, I have saved until last. I speak of the everlasting promises of God. Listen to Jesus as he says to his disciples and through them to all of us, "Let not your hearts be troubled; believe in God, believe also in me. In my Father's house are many rooms; if it were not so, would I have told you that I go to prepare a place for you? And when I go and prepare a place for you, I will come again and will take you to myself, that where I am you may be also" (John 14:1–3). For the Christian, death is simply a transition to a more wonderful world to come, a place where Christ has gone on ahead to prepare for us.

In I Corinthians 15:20 Jesus is described as the first fruits of them that are asleep. The meaning is simple. Christ was raised from the dead never to die again, and his resurrection is God's promise to all of us that we also will be raised. In Revelation 1:18 Jesus says to John, "I died, and behold I am alive for evermore." Earlier Jesus had said, "Because I live, you will live also" (John 14:19).

The apostle Paul wrote to the Thessalonians who were grieving over their departed loved ones, "But we would not have you ignorant, brethren, concerning those who are asleep, that you may not grieve as others do who have no hope. For since we believe that Jesus died and rose again, even so, through Jesus, God will bring with him those who have fallen asleep. For this we declare to you by the word of the Lord, that we who are alive, who are left until the coming of the Lord, shall not precede those who have fallen asleep. For the Lord himself will descend from heaven with a cry of command, with the archangel's call, and with the sound of the trumpet of God. And the dead in Christ will rise first; then we who are alive, who are left, shall be caught up together with them in the clouds to meet the Lord in the air; and so we shall always be with the Lord. Therefore comfort one another with these words" (I Thess. 4:13–18).

Take the time to read the entire fifteenth chapter of I Corinthians, which deals with the resurrection and even talks about the kind of bodies we will have in that wonderful spiritual world. Also read the twenty-first chapter of Revelation for a most meaningful description of heaven. It is still beyond our total grasp, but God opens the door and lets us look inside. Thus he makes it easier for us to say good-bye to our loved ones.

Comfort in Christ

Finally, I would like to point out that it is in Christ that we have this comfort. Those who have never come to Christ do not have these promises.

It is for that reason that I urge you to believe in Christ as divine, then to bring your own stubborn will under control by letting Christ become the Lord of your life. Confess his name before your fellow men. Then, heed the Lord's admonition as found in the words Ananias spoke to Saul, a deeply penitent believer: "Rise and be baptized, and wash away your sins, calling on his name" (Acts 22:16). The Lord will be with you not only in death and bereavement, but in all the other crises of life. He will share the great and happy moments and help in times of sorrow and bewilderment.

The church, made up of God's children, can be such a great help to us in time of grief and uncertainty. The community of faithful Christians stands ready continually to touch our innermost needs with their collective support and the offer of renewed life through the strength of our Lord Jesus Christ.

Standing here on Abraham's ground in ancient Hebron, I am thankful that we have in Jesus Christ blessings which Abraham never knew. How blessed we are! How blessed we are in life and in death!

Storm over the Dead Sea, Qumran Cliffs to the Right

7 The Dead Sea–Sodom

The Dead Sea is called by several different names in the Old Testament. It is called the Salt Sea (Num. 34:3, 12; Deut. 3:17; Josh. 12:3), the Sea of the Arabah (in some of the same passages), and the Eastern Sea (Ezek. 47:18; Joel 2:20; Zech. 14:8). In extrabiblical literature it is also known as the Sea of Sodom, the Sea of Asphalt, and the Sea of Lot. The name *Dead Sea* seems to have been introduced into Greek and Latin usage in the second century A.D. The New Testament makes no reference to the sea.

The Geography

The Great Rift is a deep valley stretching from northern Syria through the Valley of Lebanon to the upper Nile Valley and on into southern Africa. The Jordan Valley, the Dead Sea, the Arabah, the Gulf of Aqaba, and the Red Sea occur along the Great Rift. The trough begins at an altitude of 300 feet above sea level in the north and descends to 1,292 feet below sea level at the Dead Sea, the world's lowest point. From the southern end of the Dead Sea the valley floor rises again to a point 750 feet above sea level, a point known as the Arabah, and then slopes down again to the Gulf of Aqaba.

The Dead Sea is fifty-three miles long, nearly eleven miles wide at the widest point, and only two miles wide at the Lisan or "Tongue," which divides the sea into the 294-square-mile northern section, which reaches a depth of 1,300 feet, and the 99-square-mile shallow southern basin, which reaches depths of from three to thirty feet. The hills which form the walls of the valley are steep and barren on both sides of the Dead Sea. The mountains on the east rise some 3,000 feet above the water level and are often precipitous. The site of the Machaerus prison, where Herod held John the Baptist and beheaded him, is on the northeast shore of the sea. The hills on the west rise 2,500 feet above the shoreline. Not a single stream enters from the Judean wilderness though two springs feed the sea from the west. One spring is near the Qumran site at the northwest corner of the sea and the other is at En-gedi, where David fled from Saul and found refuge in a cave. The Song of Songs 1:14 speaks of the pleasant vineyards at En-gedi.

Masada, the mountain-top fortress of King Herod where later more than nine hundred zealots committed suicide in A.D. 73 rather than fall into the hands of the Romans, is located on the western shore some 2,000 feet above the water level. The southern part of the sea is very shallow and may once have been a plain on which cities existed. Historians mention the presence of bituminous materials in and about the sea, and chunks still rise to the surface in the southern part today, especially during an earthquake. Southwest of the sea is a five-mile salt ridge covered with clay and limestone. The entire mass is known as Jebel Usdum, the Mount of Sodom.

With barely four inches of rain in a year, the Dead Sea gets its water from the Arnon, Udhemi, Zerqa, Zered, and Jordan Rivers. The Jordan adds the most with some six to seven million tons of water daily; but with the hot and arid climate, often rising to 124° Fahrenheit, evaporation keeps pace with the intake. Since there is no outlet the sea is 25 percent solids (some estimates run as high as 33 percent), at least five times the concentration of the ocean, making it the world's densest large body of water. The principal minerals include magnesium, sodium, calcium, potassium, and magnesium bromide. Since the specific gravity of the water exceeds that of the human body, swimming is a bit like floating a cork. The water is bitter, distasteful, and oily to the touch. It is extremely painful to the eyes, making swimming less than an enjoyable experience. Swimming in the sea requires a bath of fresh water immediately afterwards. All forms of marine life find it impossible to live in the sea, even salt-water varieties.

Mineral extraction is being carried on commercially in the shallow southern end of the sea. This practice dates back to Roman and Arab times. It is estimated today that the sea contains twenty-two billion tons of magnesium chloride, eleven billion tons of common table salt, six billion tons of calcium chloride, two billion tons of potassium chloride, 989 million tons of magnesium bromide, and 200 million tons of gypsum.

The Biblical Story

Sodom, located at the southern end of the Dead Sea, came into the biblical story when Abraham and Lot, while living and grazing their flocks near Bethel, decided that they must separate. Conflicts arose between their herdsmen and Abraham did not want the conflict to continue. He urged Lot to choose where he would like to live, and Lot "lifted up his eyes, and saw that the Jordan valley was well watered everywhere like the garden of the Lord, like the land of Egypt, in the direction of Zoar." And Lot "dwelt among the cities of the valley and moved his tent as far as Sodom" (Gen. 13:2-13).

While Lot was living in Sodom four eastern kings made war on the five kings in the valley and carried away many of the people, including Lot. Hearing that his relative was among those captured, Abraham took 318 men and pursued the retreating army as far as Dan. He attacked by night and rescued Lot's family and possessions (Gen. 14:1-16). When he returned he met Melchizedek, king of Salem and priest of God. Abraham gave to Melchizedek a tenth of the plunder which he had recovered and returned the rest to the king of Sodom, taking only what he and his men had eaten on the way (Gen. 14:17-24).

While Abraham lived at the oaks of Mamre three angels came to his tent, in the form of men. The Lord used them to tell Abraham, "Because the outcry against Sodom and Gomorrah is great and their sin is very grave, I will go down to see whether they have done altogether according to the outcry which has come to me; and if not, I will know" (Gen. 18:20, 21). The men of Sodom were guilty of homosexuality, giving rise to the words *sodomy* and *sodomite* in our language today.

Because of his love for Lot, Abraham pleaded with the Lord not to destroy the city, but since not even ten righteous people could be found in the city God did determine to destroy it. While sitting at the gate of Sodom, Lot was warned by two of the angels of its impending doom and urged to take his family and leave. After some hesitation Lot's family fled to the city of Zoar. "Then the Lord rained on Sodom and Gomorrah brimstone and fire from the Lord out of heaven; and he overthrew those cities, and all the valley, and all the inhabitants of the cities, and what grew on the ground" (Gen. 19:24, 25). Lot's wife looked back as she fled and became a pillar of salt. Abraham watched Sodom and Gomorrah go up like the smoke of a furnace, viewing from a distance at his dwelling place near Hebron.

Symbolic Meaning

Sodom and Gomorrah are mentioned numerous times in the Scriptures. Moses, for example, compared the overthrow of the land whose people disobey God to the overthrow of those two ancient cities. He pointed out that the whole land would become "brimstone and salt, and a burnt-out waste, unsown, and growing nothing, where no grass can sprout" (Deut. 29:23). The prophets compared the overthrow of various countries to the overthrow of Sodom and Gomorrah (Isa. 13:19; Jer. 49:18; Lam. 4:6; Amos 4:11). Jesus mentioned Sodom when the Twelve were sent out on their mission and given instructions on preaching (Matt. 10:1–15); in his sermon against Capernaum, Bethsaida, and Chorazin (Matt. 11:20–24); and in describing his second coming (Luke 17:22–38).

Several sites have been proposed as the location of ancient Sodom and Gomorrah. William Albright and others have suggested that the cities may be under what is now the southern part of the Dead Sea. More recent suggestions connect the cities with several sites east of the southern section of the Dead Sea. Excavations in this area indicate that fire played a major role in the destruction of the cities. Of these excavations, Harry Thomas Frank wrote in the *Biblical Archaelogist* (Dec., 1978): "Moreover, they have suggested that many. . . cities in the south met a sudden and violent end." At Bab edh 'Drah, which lies slightly east of the tongue of the Dead Sea and is 540 feet above the level of the sea, another archaeologist notes there is "evidence of severe burning on many of the stones." In this city, which may date back to the thirty-second century B.C., archaeologists uncovered a structure believed similar to the gate at which Lot was sitting when the angels appeared to him. Seeds collected from the debris in this region indicate that it was once a very prosperous area producing wheat, barley, dates, wild plums, peaches, grapes, figs, pistachio nuts, almonds, olives, pine nuts, lentils, chick peas, pumpkins and watermelon. Flax and castor-oil plants were also raised.

A visit to this arid and desolate crevice in the earth's surface, coupled with the awesome biblical story of God's destruction of ancient Sodom and

Gomorrah, leaves one deeply moved. The record of God's righteous indignation against the wickedness of these ancient people still stands in stark relief. One cannot but draw a parallel between the ancient sins and the sins of the modern world and wonder about God's feelings toward the people who inhabit some of the great cities of our own day.

Sodom and Gomorrah: Can It Happen Now?

Batsell Barrett Baxter

In the nineteenth chapter of the Book of Genesis is the sad story of Sodom and Gomorrah. The moral degeneration of these ancient cities is very obvious in the story told in this chapter. Two angels in the form of men came to visit Lot, nephew of Abraham, who lived in Sodom. The men of Sodom threatened great harm to Lot and his family if he did not allow them the opportunity to "know" his visitors. Only God's protective intervention saved Lot and his guests from the homosexual advances of the men of the city.

God had earlier decided to destroy Sodom and Gomorrah because "their sin [was] very grave" (Gen. 18:20). Now, after the threats made upon Lot, God said to Lot (through the angels), "Arise, take your wife and your two daughters who are here, lest you be consumed in the punishment of the city" (Gen. 19:15). When Lot and his family were safely out of the city, we read, "Then the Lord rained on Sodom and Gomorrah brimstone and fire from the Lord out of heaven; and he overthrew those cities" (Gen. 19:24, 25). From a distance Abraham "looked down toward Sodom and Gomorrah and toward all the land of the valley, and beheld, and lo, the smoke of the land went up like the smoke of a furnace" (Gen. 19:28).

Sodomy

The story is very simple. God was displeased by the homosexual immorality of these ancient cities, which has added the word *sodomy* to our language. He destroyed them totally. It is a moving experience to stand in the valley and look toward the site where those ancient cities once stood. One wonders, will the same kind of sin and the other immoralities that are so prominent in our own land lead to the downfall of our nation? Can it happen in America today?

Let's take a look at our modern American culture. John Updike's book *Couples* vividly describes an average, though fictitious, town where ordinary people are caught up in a "playboy" mentality, with recreational sex as the favorite indoor sport. There are alcohol-saturated parties by night and elaborate weekend rendezvous. Anything goes—wife-swapping, sex orgies, and the like. Ours is the age of the so-called *new morality,* which is really not new at all, as a casual reading of the Scriptures will show. Anything is considered right which does not injure the other person, whatever that means.

Harvard sociologist, Pitirim Sorokin, has painted a grim picture of what is happening to the moral fiber of our nation. As high standards give way to permissiveness, the very structure of our society is threatened. William S. Banowsky commented further, "It is significant that Sorokin is a native of Russia and has first-hand knowledge of that culture's free love experiment, which followed the Bolshevik Revolution. The consequences of free love and easy divorce were so devastating that the Russians now enforce a strict sexual code. They have learned that a society's spinal cord is weakened when the integrity of the marriage tie is jeopardized. While we ridicule Puritanism, the Russians practice it."

Like Second-century Rome

Will Durant, one of the most eminent of the world's historians, summarized our century's moral and ethical decline. To Durant contemporary America greatly resembles the Roman Empire. "We," he says, "have reached our zenith, and are beginning to crumble and share with Second Century Rome, great wealth, great freedom, loss of religious faith, and have over-extended ourselves in the world with wide avenues of commitment." Durant then adds that our moral code has withered. The family structure has broken down with the result that individuals are growing more and more violent. We also remember the words of Winston Churchill, "Man has improved himself every way except morally." It is true that we have made great advances in the technological realm. There is no doubt that we have the highest standard of living ever known to man, but, as Thomas Hilton asks, "Have we gained the whole world and lost our own souls?"

The idea so widely heard in modern society, that what consenting adults do in private is solely their own business, is false. What people do in private will inevitably affect their attitudes and behavior in public and will inevitably affect the lives of others. This shibboleth, now so widely accepted, has already laid the foundation for our nation's decline and fall.

What's to Be Done?

The new system of moral and ethical permissiveness confronts the Christian with a serious dilemma. One approach would be for Christians to withdraw from society and form separate communities governed by Christian standards. This approach, however, has been tried in other generations and has never worked. More important, it is not God's way to handle the problem. The Christian way is to remain in the world and to be actively involved with the world, as a leavening and redeeming force. The apostle Paul commented on this very point, ''Look carefully then how you walk, not as unwise men but as wise, making the most of the time, because the days are evil'' (Eph. 5:15, 16). Our role is not to depart from the world but to remain in the world and to have an influence for good.

The influence of majority opinion on behavior was discussed by George Forrell and William Lazareth in their book *Crisis and Marriage* (1978): ''Does it really matter what the Bible says about sexual issues? Can the Bible speak to us when what is 'normal' in sexual attitudes and behavior seems to be determined by updated Kinsey reports and the media? Has the Bible been shown to be historically conditioned and thus irrelevant to us?'' The answer, of course, as God speaks in the Bible is that the *norm* is not what is ''normal.'' What was ''normal'' in the lives of the people in Jerusalem seven hundred years before Christ was what God guided the prophet Isaiah to preach against. What was ''normal'' in Christ's day was exactly what he taught against. What was ''normal'' in first-century Corinth was what the apostle Paul wrote against. Just so, today, Christians must speak out against what is ''normal'' sexual behavior and attitudes in movies, books, discotheques, bedrooms, and bars. What is right is not what is ''normal,'' but what is clearly taught in God's inspired Scriptures.

The unanimous witness of the New Testament is that a Christian is called to a new standard. It isn't that Christians are antisexual, nor that they are antimarriage. When they learn of Christ and accept the Christian way they are introduced into a new world of values. ''For this is the will of God, your sanctification: that you abstain from immorality; that each one of you know how to take a wife for himself in holiness and honor, not in the passion of lust like heathen who do not know God'' (I Thess. 4:3-5). And, ''Do you not know that the unrighteous will not inherit the kingdom of God? Do not be deceived; neither the immoral, nor idolaters, nor adulterers, nor homosexuals, nor thieves, nor the greedy, nor drunkards, nor revilers, nor robbers will inherit the kingdom of God. And such were some of you'' (I Cor. 6:9-11). The old permissiveness belongs to the past. Christians take on a new kind of life, one that is contrary to the accepted values of the day.

Not Conformed to This World

As we look back, it appears that in Bible times faith often had to exist in a world that was as permissive as our own. Indeed, the basic law of the Old

Testament, the Ten Commandments, pictured the man-woman relationship as very different from that which prevailed among the people who surrounded Israel. The Old Testament Scriptures present God's ideal against tendencies in the other direction: toward infidelity, prostitution, homosexuality, and the like. God's people were instructed to live by a standard which seemed odd when compared to the permissive standards of the day. In our day, too, God's people must often be different from those about them. The apostle Paul spoke of Christians as new creatures, and this different kind of life as "a more excellent way." It is to that more excellent way that I would encourage you to come. You will always be glad you did.

Ruins at Bethel

8   Bethel

In 1838 Edward Robinson identified Beitin of modern Israel as the biblical Bethel, on the basis of the geographical references in the Bible and in Eusebius. Nearly a hundred and fifty years later this identification is still generally accepted by archaeologists and Bible scholars.

Bethel means "house of God." *El* was one of the several terms for God. The Hebrew name *Bethel* had its roots in Jacob's vision of the ladder which went up into heaven, with angels ascending and descending upon it. The city was once called Luz, meaning "place of refuge." The name *Bethel* has been preserved in the modern Arabic *Beitin* by the normal shift of consonants.

Bethel is ten-and-one-half miles north of Jerusalem and is located between the site of ancient Ai on the east and Mizpah on the west. Gibeah, one-time capital of Saul, is located on a hill across the valley to the southwest; and Ramah, the home of Samuel, is on a hill still further south. Both are visible from the road which runs from Bethel to Jerusalem. Shiloh and Shechem are on the same road north of Bethel. The city was located at the junction of the tribes of Benjamin and Ephraim. It lay on an important east-west route going from the Mediterranean to Jericho and to the area beyond the Jordan. Bethel is mentioned more times in the Old Testament than any other city except Jerusalem. Strangely, it is not mentioned in the New Testament.

Biblical History

The biblical history of this site began when Abraham moved from Ur of the Chaldees and Haran to Canaan, with Sarah, his wife, and Lot, his nephew. He built an altar at Shechem and then pitched his tent on the mountain east of Bethel. Sometime later he moved on south to the Negeb (Gen. 12:4–9). After dwelling in the Negeb, Abraham moved, along with Lot and his herdsmen, back to Bethel, to the same spot where he had lived before; he built another altar where he called on the name of the Lord. The land, however, was not large enough to support the flocks of both Lot and Abraham, so the two separated, with Lot moving to Sodom and Abraham to Hebron (Gen. 13).

Later, Jacob fled from his brother Esau in Beer-sheba, after gaining the birthright through his deception of his father Isaac. Upon reaching Bethel he camped for the night, using one of the stones for a pillow. While he slept, he dreamed that there was a ladder reaching from earth to heaven with angels going up and down and God standing at the top. The Lord promised to bless Jacob and to give him many descendants. When he awoke he said, "How awesome is this place! This is none other than the house of God, and this is the gate of heaven" (Gen. 28:17). Jacob then took his stone pillow and set it up for a pillar, pouring oil over it. He called the place Bethel (House of God), though it had previously been known as Luz.

Hosea alluded to this event when he wrote, "[Jacob] met God at Bethel and there God spoke with him" (Hos. 12:4). When Jacob prepared to leave Laban's house in Paddan-aram several years later, God appeared to him and said, "I am the God of Bethel, where you anointed a pillar and made a vow to me. Now arise, go forth from this land, and return to the land of your birth" (Gen. 31:13).

After living at Shechem for a time, Jacob was called by God to move to Bethel. Before going, he ordered all his household to turn in their idols and purify themselves. Jacob hid the gods under a tree at Shechem. When he arrived at Bethel, Jacob built an altar and God renewed his promise that he would bless Jacob and make him a mighty nation. It was at Bethel that Deborah, Rebekah's nurse, died (Gen. 35:8).

After Egyptian Bondage

At a much later time, after the Israelites had escaped Egyptian bondage and wandered in the wilderness for forty years, they began the conquest of Canaan. After winning the city of Jericho, Joshua sent a small force to take Ai, but his army met defeat (Josh. 7:1–5). Joshua took care of the internal problem, growing out of the disobedience of Achan, before sending a contingent of soldiers to lie in ambush between Ai and Bethel. He approached the city with the main body of troops and then retreated as the men of Ai pursued. Joshua gave the sign and the men in hiding entered the city and set it on fire. The battle was soon won (Josh. 8:1–29).

Later the house of Joseph went up against Bethel by first sending spies. The spies saw a man coming out of the city, and they persuaded him to reveal the entrance to the city in exchange for his life. They took the city and spared the man's life (Judg. 1:22–26).

A number of other biblical events are connected with Bethel and the region around it. Deborah, Israel's only woman judge, judged Israel between Ramah and Bethel under the palm of Deborah in the hill country of Ephraim. It was here that she told Barak to assemble the men at Mount Tabor to fight Sisera (Judg. 4:4–10). Samuel also passed through Bethel, Gilgal, and Mizpah on his yearly circuit to judge the people, but he always came back to his home in Ramah (I Sam. 7:15–17).

Just before his translation, Elijah tried to persuade Elisha to stay while he went on, but the younger prophet insisted on following Elijah from Gilgal to Bethel (where the sons of the prophets asked Elisha if he knew that Elijah was about to be taken away) and on to Jericho (II Kings 2:1–4). After Elijah was taken, Elisha left Jericho for Bethel; and on the way, young boys from Bethel jeered at the prophet, saying, "Go up, you baldhead!" He cursed the boys and two bears came out against them (II Kings 2:23, 24).

King Saul gathered two thousand men in the hill country of Bethel to fight against the Philistines (I Sam. 13:2). Later, David rewarded the city of Bethel after some of his successful military operations by sending its people some of the spoil of war (I Sam. 30:26, 27). When Jeroboam (931–910 B.C.) became king of Israel he said to his people, "You have gone up to Jerusalem long enough. Behold your gods, O Israel, who brought you up out of the land of Egypt." With this statement, he set up two golden calves, one at Dan, the other at Bethel. The king proclaimed a feast day and burned incense on an altar in Bethel to the golden calf there, but God sent a young prophet to condemn the idolatry and in the course of his prophecy Jeroboam's hand was miraculously withered (I Kings 12:25—13:10). The young prophet himself later fell into trouble and was killed by a lion for disregarding God's directions not to eat or drink while in Bethel and to return by a different route (I Kings 13:11–34). Still later, after Israel had been taken into captivity, Ezra 2:28 reports that 223 men of Bethel and Ai returned under Zerubbabel. Bethel was one of the villages settled by the returnees.

Amos from Tekoa near Bethlehem in the southern kingdom did his prophetic work at Bethel during the reign of Jeroboam II (790–749 B.C.). Therefore, we have an entire book of the Old Testament written in connection with Bethel. In it Amos acted as God's spokesman: "Hear, and testify against the house of Jacob . . . that on the day I punish Israel for his transgressions, I will punish the altars of Bethel, and the horns of the altar shall be cut off and fall to the ground" (Amos 3:13, 14).

Archaeological excavations at Bethel in 1934, 1954, and 1960 have revealed that the area around the springs was originally a camping ground for shepherds. It became a village in about 3200 B.C. A sanctuary was located on the northwest corner of the mound. Dark stains from blood and traces of numerous bonfires were found. Animal bones and artifacts such as cooking pots and flint knives suggest that Bethel was an open-air sanctuary before the village grew up.

To stand on the site of ancient Bethel, surrounded by some of the stones of the ancient buildings, on a mound that has been only partially excavated, amid the sounds of goats and goatherds, is a moving experience. To go back and read again the story of Jacob's vision and from this site to preach a lesson for present-day America, by means of modern recording techniques, is an experience long to be remembered. History becomes so very real when one stands on the hill at Bethel and thinks back to the events that happened around it through three millenniums of time.

Climbing Jacob's Ladder

Batsell Barrett Baxter

One day when Isaac was a very old man he was sitting in his tent, thinking. He was virtually blind, and his other physical faculties had also begun to fade. He knew that the end of life was not far away. There was something yet to be done before the end came. The loose ends of life needed to be tied up. One very important thing remained to be done: the calling of his elder son and the giving to him of the special patriarchal blessing. This blessing was not some vague expression of goodwill, such as we sometimes convey when we say, "God bless you." It was a very important official act. The pronouncing of the patriarchal blessing carried with it authority, prestige, prosperity, and special powers of a lifelong, far-reaching nature. Once the blessing had been pronounced, it could not be taken back or changed.

Jacob's Deception

The twenty-seventh chapter of the Book of Genesis tells how Isaac's intended blessing for his elder son Esau was stolen by his younger son Jacob through trickery. Esau had been sent into the fields to seek game and to prepare a special meal for his father. While he was gone, Jacob came to his father's tent and said, "My father." Isaac replied, "Here I am; who are you, my son?" Jacob lied to his nearly blind father, "I am Esau your first-born. I have done as you told me; now sit up and eat of my game, that you may bless me" (Gen. 27:18, 19). Isaac at first did not believe his son could have so quickly found game for the meal. So he asked his son to come near that he might feel him and thus make sure of his identity. Jacob's deception was well planned; his father ultimately thought him to be Esau and pronounced upon him the blessing.

Later in the day Esau returned from his hunting trip and began to prepare the special meal for his father, only to learn that his younger brother had stolen away the birthright and blessing. Later in the same chapter we read, "Now Esau hated Jacob because of the blessing with which his father had blessed him, and Esau said to himself, 'The days of mourning for my father are approaching; then I will kill my brother Jacob'" (Gen. 27:41). When Esau's angry threat against Jacob was told to their mother Rebekah, she called Jacob to her and said, "Behold, your brother Esau comforts himself by planning to kill you. Now therefore, my son, obey my voice; arise, flee to Laban my brother in Haran, and stay with him a while, until your brother's fury turns away; until your brother's anger turns away, and he forgets what you have done to him" (Gen. 27:42–45).

God Reaches Down

It was as Jacob fled from his own home to protect himself against his brother's wrath that a momentous thing happened. The text reads, "And he came to a certain place, and stayed there that night, because the sun had set. Taking one of the stones of the place, he put it under his head and lay down in that place to sleep. And he dreamed that there was a ladder set up on the earth, and the top of it reached to heaven; and behold, the angels of God were ascending and descending on it! And behold, the Lord stood above it and said, 'I am the Lord, the God of Abraham your father and the God of Isaac; the land on which you lie I will give to you and to your descendants; and your descendants shall be like the dust of the earth, and you shall spread abroad to the west and to the east and to the north and to the south; and by you and your descendants shall all the families of the earth bless themselves. Behold, I am with you and will keep you wherever you go, and will bring you back to this land; for I will not leave you until I have done that of which I have spoken to you'" (Gen. 28:11–15).

Early in the morning as he awakened, Jacob took the stone which he had put under his head and set it up for a pillar, pouring oil on the top of it. He called the name of that place Bethel, which means "House of God." Jacob was so deeply moved that he made a vow, saying, "If God will be with me, and will keep me in this way that I go, and will give me bread to eat and clothing to wear . . . then the Lord shall be my God, and . . . of all that thou givest me I will give the tenth to thee" (Gen. 28:20–22). Jacob fulfilled his promise that the Lord would be his God and regularly tithed. As his life moved through the years, he became the leader of the nation Israel and one of the pillars in the history of the Old Testament.

Why Jacob?

We cannot but wonder why it was that God blessed Jacob. Was he not a deceiver and a liar in the incident of stealing his brother's blessing? Even his name means "supplanter," or, in our own vernacular, "trickster." It is obvious that Jacob was not worthy of any blessing from God. Yet, it may be in the very fact that he was weak and unworthy we find the reason why God blessed him. God saw in this self-centered deceiver possibilities of greatness. It may be that God chose him just because he was so unworthy, in order to say to all of us down through the centuries that God's love is not based upon our own merits, but upon his divine nature. If each of us had to be worthy of the blessings that we receive at God's hands, we would never receive any blessings at all. God loves us and blesses us, in spite of our unworthiness.

Jacob's magnificent dream left him a changed man. He had discovered the presence of God. Indeed, so impressed was Jacob that he named the place Bethel—the "House of God." Before this experience Jacob had apparently lived by his wits. Our impression from the story of the birthright and the blessing is that Jacob had lived for himself—so much so that he was fleeing from the one he had deceived. But now God's mercy had changed him. Jacob's life now belonged to God. This is reflected in his words, ". . . and of all that thou givest me I will give the tenth to thee."

The same thing is true of us. God comes to us though we have done nothing to deserve it. He gives us a new outlook that changes the way we perceive our homes and jobs and families. His mercy can change us. It may even lead us to cease living for ourselves and to begin living for the God who created us.

God Reaches Down to All of Us

This story is a little bit of a preview of what God did for the whole human race in the sending of Christ into the world as our Savior and Lord. God, through Christ, reaches down to all of us and lifts us up from the selfish, unworthy things in our lives, cleanses us from the past, and sets us on a new course in life. What a thrilling thing it is to be able to begin life over again. When we come to Jesus we have the promise that his blood will cleanse us from all our past sins (I John 1:7). As we believe in him as the divine Son of God, as we genuinely regret our past sins and turn away from them, and as we confess the name of Jesus and are baptized, he cleanses us and starts us on the road to heaven. Like Jacob in the long ago, we are unworthy of God's love and blessings. Yet, that is why Christ came into the world. He loves us and he does for us what we could never have done for ourselves.

Jacob's life matured and developed until he was a great man, a leader of God's people, so very different from the boy he had been. As we live with Christ we are transformed into his likeness. The old ways of thinking, the old patterns of speech, the old attitudes and goals are put behind us, and in their place God gives us new attitudes and habits and goals for which to live. God has been in the business of making men over since time began and he yearns to help each of us if only we will allow him to do so.

What about you? Is there a bit of Jacob in you? Are you willing to let Christ open the gates of heaven for you? The God of Jacob is our God, too.

Tomb at Shiloh

9 Shiloh

Shiloh is an abandoned site today, but a new Israeli village is springing up alongside its ruins. Shiloh was a city in Ephraim some twenty miles north of Jerusalem, twelve miles south of Shechem, and ten miles northeast of Bethel. It is identified with Tell Seilun, about three miles east of the main road. Eusebius and Jerome (fourth century) made this identification, as did Edward Robinson in 1838.

According to recent excavations, Shiloh flourished in the Middle Bronze II period (ca. 1800–1550 B.C.) when the twelve-acre mound was surrounded by a substantial wall. It was destroyed at the end of that period, perhaps by an Egyptian army, but was occupied on a lesser scale from about 1400 B.C. until its sudden destruction about 600 B.C. The site remained unoccupied until the late Greek or early Roman days, but a prosperous city was built here during the Roman and Byzantine days. After the Muslim conquest, the site lost its importance and gradually became uninhabited.

Shiloh was well suited as a quiet place of worship. Hills surround it on all sides except the southwest, offering abundant pasture lands. A water supply was close at hand. Built on a low mound, Shiloh was not easily defended. The fact that it was located off the main roads detracted from its economic importance.

In the blessing of Jacob, the phrase "until Shiloh come" has occasioned much discussion (Gen. 49:10). Although the passage is not cited in the New Testament as a messianic passage, nor is Shiloh used elsewhere in the Bible as a personal name, Christian interpreters since the sixteenth century have understood Shiloh as the Messiah.

Joshua moved his headquarters from Gilgal to Shiloh. Since seven tribes had not yet received their inheritance, he called the whole congregation together at Shiloh. The tabernacle was set up there. The land lay subdued before the people (Josh. 18:1). Joshua asked for three men from each tribe to go out and look at the land, "writing a description of it with a view to their inheritances" (Josh. 18:4). The description was written, lots were cast, and the land was divided (Josh. 18:8–10). The inheritances of Benjamin, Simeon, Zebulun, Issachar, Asher, Naphtali, and Dan were allotted at Shiloh (Josh. 18:11—19:51). Here the six cities of refuge (Josh. 30) and the Levitical cities (Josh. 21) were named.

Eli and Samuel

In the period of the judges, Elkanah of Ramathaim-zophim in the hill country of Ephraim, and his wives, Hannah and Peninnah, went up annually to sacrifice and worship at Shiloh. The priests at Shiloh were Eli's sons, Hophni and Phinehas. When Elkanah sacrificed, he would give Hannah only one portion while giving Peninnah several, since Hannah had provided him with no children. Peninnah used the occasion to taunt Hannah.

Finally, on one occasion, Hannah refused to eat and began to cry, prompting her husband to calm her. After she had eaten and drunk, Hannah approached Eli, who was "sitting beside the doorpost of the temple of the Lord." Distressed and weeping she prayed, "O Lord of hosts, if thou wilt indeed look on the affliction of thy maidservant, and remember me, and not forget thy maidservant, but wilt give to thy maidservant a son, then I will give him to the Lord all the days of his life, and no razor shall touch his head" (I Sam. 1:11).

Eli thought she was drunk but Hannah convinced him otherwise. Eli blessed the woman and asked the Lord to grant her request. After worshiping the next morning, Elkanah and his family went back to their house in Ramah (I Sam. 1:19). "Hannah conceived and bore a son, and she called his name Samuel, for she said, 'I have asked him of the Lord' " (I Sam. 1:20).

Hannah did not go with Elkanah to the next yearly sacrifice, but waited until Samuel was weaned. Then she gave Samuel to Eli and sang a song of praise (I Sam. 1:21—2:10).

Samuel grew up ministering to the Lord in the presence of Eli the priest. Eli's sons were worthless men who had intercourse with women at the entrance to the tabernacle. When asked by their father why they did such things, they refused to listen to him. Samuel, however, grew in stature and in reputation with man and God (I Sam. 2:22-26). He wore a linen ephod; his mother would make a new robe each year and take it to him when she came up to Shiloh for the sacrifice. Later Hannah was to bear three sons and two daughters.

Young Samuel was lying down in the temple when the Lord called his name twice. Thinking it was the nearly blind Eli, who had gone to bed, Samuel ran to him but was told that he had not called. When this happened a second time and a third, Eli told Samuel what to say. When the fourth call from God came, Samuel listened as God pronounced judgment on Eli's house. The boy waited until morning before telling the old priest what had happened.

Later when Israel went out against the Philistines, they took the ark into battle with them. They were defeated and the ark of God was captured (I Sam. 4:2-11). Eli's two sons were killed. When news reached Shiloh, Eli, the ninety-eight-year-old father, fell over backwards, broke his neck, and died. He had judged Israel for forty years (I Sam. 4:12-18). The wife of Phinehas heard the news, causing her to give birth to a child whom she named Ichabod (I Sam. 4:19-22). Samuel apparently left Shiloh at this point and moved about the country.

God Forsakes Shiloh

Psalm 78:60 reads, "He forsook his dwelling at Shiloh, the tent where he dwelt among men." The background to this verse is found in I Samuel 4. The wife of Phinehas realized that the glory of the Lord had departed (Ichabod means "the glory has departed"). The capture of the ark, the symbol of God's glory, represented the Lord's departure.

When Abijah, the son of Jeroboam I fell sick, the king told his wife to disguise herself and go to Shiloh to seek information about the illness from the prophet there. She took ten loaves, some cakes, and a jar of honey and went to the house of Ahijah, the prophet of Shiloh. The old prophet was blind, but God told him that the woman who was approaching was the king's wife. Ahijah greeted her when she entered his house and told her the word of the Lord. God was displeased with the way Jeroboam was making images and ignoring the commandments. The prophecy continued: God would cut off Jeroboam and his son would die when his mother entered the city. She returned and the boy died (I Kings 14:1–18).

The prophet Jeremiah mentions Shiloh several times. He warns that the temple in Jerusalem will suffer the same fate as Shiloh (recall I Samuel 4): "Therefore I will do to the house which is called by my name, and in which you trust, and to the place where I gave to you and to your fathers, as I did to Shiloh" (Jer. 7:14; cf. 26:6, 9; 41:5).

A Home Without Restraints

Harold Hazelip

American parents worry about how to rear their children. They feel uncertain about the proper balance between permissiveness and firmness. They fear they are neglecting their children. Yet they may resent the demands their children make. They wonder whether they are doing a good job as parents, yet are unable to define just what a good job is. In droves, they seek expert advice.

This concern with rearing children is neither new nor uniquely American. Within forty years after the first settlers came to Plymouth Colony, they were afraid their children had lost the religious conviction of the founding generation. But our fears have grown more intense. The feeling of not being in control as parents, the lack of guidelines for raising children, the widespread sense of personal guilt—these are the problems of today's parents.

Parental Neglect

We are not the first parents to neglect our responsibilities. The Old Testament book, I Samuel, tells the story of Eli, a high priest at the tabernacle at Shiloh before the temple was built. Eli was a good man. As a child Samuel the prophet served under him.

But something was missing in Eli's home. His two sons served as priests, though they lacked their father's character. They "were worthless men; they had no regard for the Lord" (I Sam 2:12). They "treated the offering of the Lord with contempt" (v. 17). We are even told that "they lay with the women who served at the entrance to the tent of meeting" (v. 22). Eli was very old. He reasoned with them, "Why do you do such things?" (v. 23). Although he was a good and pure man, Eli was weak and indecisive as a father. The Bible says that "he did not restrain" his sons from doing evil (I Sam. 3:13).

Two things seem to be missing in Eli's sons: discipline to restrain their desires, and a viable faith to provide a sense of right and wrong.

Love Your Child

There are five basic suggestions which can be made to help parents in rearing their children. First, genuinely love your child as he or she is. Children become secure and stable, not through access to material things, but through real love in the home. The Old Testament includes some classic pictures of parental love. Imagine what Abraham must have felt on the long walk to the land of Moriah to sacrifice Isaac. In instructing Abraham God had told him: "Take your son, your only son Isaac, whom you love..." (Gen. 22:2).

And what father cannot sympathize with the weeping David? He has just heard that his son Absalom has been killed. Stunned and grieving, he gropes his way to a private place where he can mourn unashamedly: "O my son Absalom, my son, my son Absalom! Would I had died instead of you, O Absalom, my son, my son!" (II Sam. 18:33).

Even though we love them, children will misbehave. And a surprising number of texts in the Bible deal with discipline. From the Bible's point of view, true parental love includes willingness to train and discipline children. There are stern proverbs: "Folly is bound up in the heart of a child, but the rod of discipline drives it far from him" (Prov. 22:15); "He who spares the rod hates his son, but he who loves him is diligent to discipline him" (13:24). From these proverbs came the old saying, "Spare the rod and spoil the child."

This is not, of course, a license for child abuse. Statistics indicate that two thousand to five thousand children are killed yearly in America and perhaps as many as one million are subjected to some form of emotional, physical, or sexual abuse. The Bible, on the other hand, presents a profound understanding of what proper discipline is. Paul's words sum it up: "Fathers, do not provoke your children to anger, but bring them up in the discipline and instruction of the Lord" (Eph 6:4). There is a training, a teaching which comes from God. "Discipline and instruction of the Lord" should not be taken as synonymous with punishment. "Responsibility" captures the idea better. We are to teach our children that they are responsible to God, not only in the religious sphere, but in every area of their lives.

Encourage Your Child

The second suggestion is that you encourage your child. Paul emphasized this: "Fathers, do not provoke your children, lest they become discouraged" (Col. 3:21). Harshness by the parent can destroy the relationship between parent and child as surely as can disobedience by the child. A half million youngsters run away from American homes each year.

This is not to suggest that parents should be afraid to say no, for fear of injuring the child's personality. A home that makes no demands, sets no firm rules or limits, is a breeding ground for trouble. Children should be reared in a positive atmosphere. If they constantly hear the words, "Stop," "Don't," it will be difficult for them to develop stable internal controls and to grow into maturity. We may overreact when a small child enjoys playing with clothespins and breaks them or loses them. Or when an older child makes ruts by riding his bike or playing ball on the grass. But eventually we realize we can buy new clothespins, we can always grow grass—but we cannot undo the way we have reared our children. Encourage them. Be positive with them whenever possible.

Take Time with Your Child

The third suggestion is to spend time with your children. One recent research study concludes that the average father of an infant spends roughly one minute a day relating to his baby, and that the average parent spends fewer than nineteen minutes a day talking to his or her child. A child may learn to hate the newspaper or an organization because the parent always seems to say, "Go away until Dad finishes the paper," or "Mommy has to go to the meeting now."

A family night once a week can help. Lunch occasionally with just one child can build a special relationship. Give your child the gift of time—quality time.

Understand Your Child's Point of View

The fourth suggestion is to try to understand the child's point of view. One way to communicate with a child is to kneel to the height of the child and discuss things eye to eye. We easily measure children by our own years and wind up nagging them. Somehow, we must neither expect them to become adults too soon nor try to keep them babies too long.

The father is both a companion to and an adult image for his son. If the father is simply a playmate, and the mother dresses and acts like a sister to her daughter, the child will miss the security which comes from being cared for by strong and effective adults. There may be too much democracy in the modern family. Children may be consulted on every issue, even matters far beyond their emotional maturity. Worries about money are discussed openly before very young children who cannot see the total perspective.

We may overgratify the child by centering the home completely on his wants and needs instead of educating the child to share, to work cooperatively, to have respect for the wants and needs of others. If there is a conflict over which television program to watch, we buy the child his own set. If an adolescent is monopolizing the phone, we provide another phone. The child later seeks a marriage partner who will gratify every wish, as the parents have done, rather than learn to consider the other person. The child needs to be understood but not pampered.

Shape Your Child's Values

The final suggestion is to introduce the child to God and his values. Children are naturally religious. They ask questions about the nature of reality. Parents are responsible to help the child learn what God would have him do with life. The most important thing in the world is to believe in God, to love and serve him. So many seem to decide, "I'm not going to influence my child in religion." But we influence them in everything else: what they are to eat, where they will go to school, what they will wear. To say that we are not going to influence them in religion is really to say that faith is not important. Children are gifts from God. We must do all we can to insure that the child grows up to be all that God intends him to be.

Let's help our children become children of God. This is done, Paul said, through faith, as we are baptized into Christ, thus putting him on (Gal. 3:26, 27).

The Valley of Jezreel

10   Mount Carmel

Mount Carmel refers to the mountain range jutting into the Mediterranean in the northwest section of the country. The Hebrew word *Carmel* means "Plantation," "garden land," "fruit of garden growth," or "vineyard of God." The word is even used several times in the Old Testament simply to refer to a fertile place where trees and gardens grow (II Kings 19:23; II Chron. 26:10). The Carmel area may be described as a triangle. One of the angles is the promontory extending into the Mediterranean Sea by the modern city of Haifa. One leg of the triangle runs southeastward for fourteen miles from the point where the mountain juts into the sea. Then the triangle has a right angle and the next leg of the triangle goes fourteen miles to the

Mediterranean Sea. The third side of the triangle then goes back north to the promontory or nose of the mountain, a distance of about twenty miles. The promontory reaches a height of 470 feet while the mountain range gradually climbs until it reaches 1,810 feet at the Druze Summit. The mountain is made of hard, porous limestone rock.

Several sites for the famous contest between Elijah and the prophets of Baal have been suggested. One is on the eastern height of Carmel where the Carmelite monks built a monastery in the sixteenth or seventeenth century A.D. The site towers over the river Kishon, which the text suggests was nearby (I Kings 18:40). Another site, much lower on the mountain, has also been proposed. Some argue that the slaughter of the prophets of Baal at the Kishon suggests a location very close to the river. Also, the fact that Ahab came and left in a chariot would suggest a place accessible to such transportation (I Kings 18:44). There is no indication in the text that the event was held on the mountain's top. In fact, after the event Elijah went up the mountain to pray and sent his servant on ahead to look out over the sea to see if there were rain clouds. It is not possible to know exactly where on the mountain the contest took place.

Elijah and Ahab

The idolatry of King Ahab (I Kings 16:29–34) had brought him into conflict with the prophet Elijah, who brought a drought on the land (I Kings 17:1–7). At one point they met and King Ahab greeted Elijah with the words, "Is it you, you troubler of Israel?" Elijah responded with a challenge for Ahab to gather his 850 prophets of Baal and the Asherah for a contest with the true God on Mount Carmel (I Kings 18:17–19).

All the people of Israel gathered with Ahab's prophets to hear Elijah offer the challenge, "How long will you go limping with two different opinions? If the Lord is God, follow him, but if Baal, then follow him." When the prophets of Baal erected their altar and placed the bull upon it, their cries to Baal to send fire from heaven went unheeded. When Elijah built his altar, placed the wood and the sacrifice upon it, and had doused it thoroughly with water, he prayed to God and fire from the sky consumed the sacrifice, the wood, the stones, the dust, and even evaporated the water in the trench around the altar. The people fell to the ground and said, "The Lord, he is God." Elijah and the people then seized the false prophets, took them to the brook Kishon, and killed them (I Kings 18:20–40).

After dealing with the prophets of Baal, Elijah told Ahab to eat and drink because rain was coming. Elijah then went to the top of Carmel and prayed fervently to God for rain. He sent his servant to look toward the Mediterranean Sea, but the servant saw no cloud. Elijah sent him seven times. The final time the servant reported a small cloud, no bigger than a man's hand. It was not long, however, before the sky was black and the wind brought a great rain (I Kings 18:41–46; James 5:17, 18).

The Cave of Elijah

Near the foot of the part of Mount Carmel which juts out into the Mediterranean Sea there is a Jewish shrine called the Cave of Elijah. The cave, which measures twenty-seven by forty-five feet, is located near a lighthouse. Tradition holds that the prophet Elijah took refuge here on one of his many flights from King Ahab. But there is no solid evidence to that effect.

From earliest times, the heights of Mount Carmel held altars to strange gods. The wooded ridges and slopes still contain remains of Canaanite shrines. Caves on the mountain offered solitude to hermits. Before becoming emperor, the general Vespasian offered sacrifice on Mount Carmel. Suetonius and Tacitus, Roman historians, reported that the mountain was thought of as a god by people of the land. The Crusaders used the mountain for military purposes and remains of their fortification have been found at several places on the mountainside.

Israel's main port and third largest city is Haifa, the center of the nation's heavy industry. It is not mentioned in the Bible but first appears in the Talmudic literature of the third century A.D. The town blossomed after the Muslim conquest of the land and resisted the Crusaders in A.D. 1100. In the early 1900s Haifa's port began to take business away from the older port of Acre—the large sea-going vessels needed the deeper water of Haifa.

Some twenty thousand members of the Druze community live in Israel in some eighteen villages. Two of the most prominent are on Mount Carmel. The Druze people have an independent status in Israel, holding to the Arabic language and to a religion that is an offshoot of Islam. The main principles of their faith are secret, passed by word of mouth from father to son. Their religion, which began in Cairo in the tenth and eleventh centuries, soon became closed to outsiders. Many adherents moved to Palestine in the thirteenth century. Their holiest figure is Jethro, the father-in-law of Moses. About 90 percent of the world's Druze population live in Syria and Lebanon. Their two villages on Mount Carmel are Isifia and Daliyat Ha Carmel.

Under the Broom Tree

Batsell Barrett Baxter

In ancient Greece there was a tiny kingdom of Epirus ruled by King Pyrrhus. We might never have heard of King Pyrrhus if it had not been for his ill-fated military campaign which was intended to put his kingdom on the map. At first his lightning war against his neighbors was a dazzling success.

He was celebrated throughout much of the ancient world as a military hero and genius. But then his troops were driven back as quickly as they had advanced, and his victory was short-lived. His name had been celebrated too soon. From this story of Pyrrhus there has come into the English language a new term—the "pyrrhic victory"—the victory which does not last.

For many people, the Christian life seems at times to resemble the career of Pyrrhus. There is a great beginning, there are great moments, but they are sometimes followed by difficult times, feelings of depression, and possibly even despair. For those who have entered the Christian life with great anticipation and hope, only to find that their moods sometimes change and there are extremely difficult hours, it may be helpful to review an event that occurred in the life of one of God's greatest prophets, Elijah.

From the Heights to the Depths

The eighteenth chapter of I Kings tells of the thrilling contest on Mount Carmel between Elijah and the false prophets of King Ahab and Queen Jezebel, in which God destroyed the forces of Baal. Strangely, it was after this great triumph, this extremely high moment in his life, that Elijah reached the depths. In I Kings 19 we read, "Then he was afraid, and he arose and went for his life, and came to Beer-sheba, which belongs to Judah, and left his servant there. But he himself went a day's journey into the wilderness, and came and sat down under a broom tree; and he asked that he might die, saying, 'It is enough; now, O Lord, take away my life; for I am no better than my fathers'" (vv. 3, 4). Elijah had given up in despair and had run away to the southernmost part of the land. Emotionally and physically exhausted he lay down to sleep.

At that point God sent an angel to bring sustenance for Elijah—a cake baked on hot stones and a jar of water. Elijah ate and drank, but lay down again to sleep. The angel brought food a second time, but after eating it and receiving strength, Elijah continued to run away, traveling forty additional days until he reached Mount Horeb in the Sinai desert, where he lodged in a cave. There the Lord came to him and said, "What are you doing here, Elijah?" Elijah responded, "I have been very jealous for the Lord, the God of hosts; for the people of Israel have forsaken thy covenant, thrown down thy altars, and slain thy prophets with the sword; and I, even I only, am left; and they seek my life, to take it away" (vv. 9, 10).

What Are You Doing Here?

At this point God called upon the elements to put on a spectacular show in order to awaken Elijah out of his depression. "A great and strong wind rent the mountains, and broke in pieces the rocks before the Lord, but the Lord was not in the wind; and after the wind an earthquake, but the Lord was not in the earthquake; and after the earthquake a fire, but the Lord was not in the fire; and after the fire a still small voice. . . . And behold, there came a voice to him, and said, 'What are you doing here, Elijah?' '' Elijah responded by making the same speech that he had made before. Then the Lord commanded, ''Go, return on your way to the wilderness of Damascus; and when you arrive, you shall anoint Hazael to be king over Syria.'' Then God added, ''Yet I will leave seven thousand in Israel, all the knees that have not bowed to Baal, and every mouth that has not kissed him'' (I Kings 19:9–18).

It is quite obvious that God's arithmetic was not the same arithmetic as that of Elijah. Elijah thought he was alone, yet God spoke of seven thousand who had been faithful. Notice especially, however, that God deals with this discouraged, despondent man by giving him work to do. He sends him back and gives him a task to perform. The result is that Elijah came out of his depression and continued to serve Jehovah in a fine way.

Causes of Depression

What caused Elijah to become so despondent? What causes us today to have our moods of depression? In this story there are several significant elements, which may also have a bearing on our lives. First, Elijah did much to cause the problem himself. He took his eyes off God and placed them on himself; thus he became fearful though he did not need to fear Ahab and Jezebel at all. As Elijah's gloom was due in part to his having run away from God, so also our low times may be a result of turning our backs on God.

Second, Elijah apparently expected too much of himself. He was intent on trying to be perfect, which inevitably leads to feelings of failure and inferiority. He said, ''I am no better than my fathers.'' This really means, ''I have accomplished no more than my fathers.'' When we realize that we are not what we want to be or ought to be, we may feel discouragement and depression.

Third, Elijah's depression came when he was tired and hungry. Our physical condition may be a major factor in our feelings of discouragement from time to time. Our physical feelings sometimes overpower our spiritual nature, so it is wise to take care of our bodies in order that our spirits may be in health.

Fourth, Elijah felt an overpowering loneliness. He somehow got the impression that he was the only one in all of Israel who was loyal to Jehovah. This may sometimes be the source of our frustration. We may become discouraged because of what we see as a lack of commitment on the part of the people of God around us. There were yet seven thousand who had not bowed the knee to Baal. Sometimes, we too need to open our eyes and see the many faithful ones about us.

Finally, Elijah's basic problem was a lack of trust in God. He took much upon himself, feeling that he was the one who had the responsibility of triumphing over the idolatrous people around him. If he had only trusted in God, realizing that while he himself was weak God was infinitely strong, this story would never have been written. Let us have patience when we are discouraged, remembering that God is still in his heaven and that his power is infinite.

The Ultimate Solution

The ultimate solution to Elijah's depression begins with "getting back to work." This is exactly what God called on him to do. He gave him a task and sent him back to accomplish it. Like Elijah, we may sometimes need to get away from our lonely brooding and back into the work of sharing the burdens and responsibilities of others and of helping them to know the joys and rewards of following Christ.

Even more basically, the solution involves trusting God. Without God and without Christ life inevitably becomes discouraging and dismal. There is no real ultimate purpose for living. There is no hope for the future. In order for our lives to be lifted from despair we need to believe in God, to believe in Christ as his divine Son, and them to make this faith meaningful by confessing our Lord as Savior, by committing ourselves to follow in his steps away from the sins of the world, and by being baptized, which symbolically suggests the death of the old person and the raising of a new person to live a new and better kind of life. Then, God has work for us to do which will help us to feel that our lives are meaningful rather than useless.

It is fitting to close with a few remarks of Donald Baillie: "Remember that what really matters in the Christian life is not our feelings, our emotions, our moods, but how we live, with dedicated wills, in faith and love. And thus we ought to be looking away from ourselves and our own feelings to God above us and our fellow creatures around us. A great many people make the mistake of judging their religious life by the state of their feelings. Our moods are sure to vary, just like the weather. But the Christian life must go on. . . . Let us remind ourselves that the great reality of God does not change with our changing moods. He is there . . . behold the clouds that hide him.''

Ruins of the Ancient Gates of Shechem

11 Samaria

The city of Samaria is located on a hilltop twenty-five miles from the Mediterranean Sea and forty-two miles north of Jerusalem. The site is six-and-one-half miles northwest of Shechem, the first capital of the northern kingdom of Israel. The Mediterranean Sea is visible from the site.

The name *Samaria* is explained in I Kings 16:24 as derived from Shemer, the name of the former owner of the land. The Hebrew word means "watch tower." Omri, king of Israel from 885 to 874 B.C., reigned for a total of twelve years, the last six from Samaria. He purchased the hill of Samaria from Shemer for two talents of silver and then began to fortify the hill. Much later Herod named the site Sebaste in honor of Augustus Caesar (Sebaste is the Greek form for Augustus). The hill is surrounded on three sides by fertile valleys and slopes. Omri's decision to build his capital here may have been prompted by the fact that the area is easy to defend, for no enemy can approach undetected. Today, the mound of ancient Samaria is oval and stands about 300 feet high. The spring for the city is about one mile away. The city comprised about twenty acres, large enough to hold the 27,290 people that Sargon deported, and the 40,000 people who were supposed to live in the city of Herod's day.

Samaria is also the name for the entire region, though the boundaries of the region are not defined in the Bible. It is generally considered to include the land occupied by Ephraim and the western portion of the land occupied by Manasseh. It comprises the area north of the road from Jericho to Bethel and south of a line of hills from Mount Carmel to Mount Gilboa, with the Jordan being the boundary on the east and the Mediterranean on the west. The area produced grain, olives, and other fruits. It was a prosperous area and also benefited from trade with Phoenicia. Samaria is mentioned 125 times in the Bible, mostly in the Old Testament. The word *Samaritan* appears three times in the singular and seven times in the plural.

King Ahab ruled Samaria from 874 to 853 B.C. He did much evil in the sight of the Lord, for he married Jezebel of the Sidonians and erected altars to worship Baal and the Asherah (I Kings 16:29-33). Ahab wanted the vineyard of Naboth in Jezreel, which was visible from his mountaintop palace, but Naboth refused to give it up since it was part of his family inheritance. Jezebel devised a plan whereby Naboth was falsely accused and as a result stoned. Ahab then took Naboth's vineyard. When Elijah the prophet met Ahab "in Samaria" he pronounced doom on the king (I Kings 21). This incident inflamed the intense rivalry between Elijah and Ahab, which is best represented by the contest between Elijah and the prophets of Baal on Mount Carmel (I Kings 18).

In prophecy against Israel, Samaria is often used to designate the entire northern kingdom (Isa. 7:9; 10:9; Amos 3:9; 8:14). It was the pride of Samaria that would doom her (Isa. 9:9), along with the graven images (Isa. 10:10) and the prophets of Baal (Jer. 23:13). The Samaritans had oppressed the poor and crushed the needy. Their women had said to their husbands, "Bring, that we may drink" (Amos 4:1). God's anger was kindled against the city, because it was full of wicked deeds (Mic. 1:1, 5, 6). The fall of Samaria was compared to the coming fall of Jerusalem. The sin of Judah was worse than her elder sister at Samaria (Ezek. 16:46). Samaria had not committed half of the sins that Jerusalem had. Better days would come again when men would plant vineyards in the mountains of Samaria and the fortunes of the area would be restored (Ezek. 16:53-55).

The Samaritans

There appears to be only one reference to Samaritans in the Old Testament. (II Kings 17:29) while they appear several times in the New Testament. In the Old Testament reference "Samaritans" designates Israelites who lived in the northern kingdom. The distinctive history of the Samaritans is difficult to write because of a lack of records. The Samaritans trace their beginning back to Adam. Their traditions run parallel with Jewish history until the time of Joshua. At that point, they have Joshua building a sanctuary on Mount Gerizim, which was the center of all Israelite worship. The religious break with the Jews came when Eli built a rival sanctuary at Shiloh. The two groups coexisted peacefully until the Philistines destroyed Shiloh and Saul later persecuted the tribes who descended from Joseph (the Samaritans).

When the Assyrians conquered the land, they deported only a small number of Samaritans. The Samaritans evidently intermarried with foreign peoples imported into their region. Jewish literature of the intertestamental period refers to the Samaritans as "no nation" and as "the foolish people that dwell in Shechem" (Ecclus. 50:25, 26). Negative feelings about the Samaritans are also reflected in Matthew 10:5–7; John 4:9; and 8:48. They are put in a positive light in Luke 10:29–37; 17:11–19. J. A. Montgomery, in writing of the Samaritans, says: "To sum up the witness of the New Testament: the Samaritan appears as an Israelite, but one whose religion is in the condition of ignorance and whose institutions are irregular."

There are five basic points in the Samaritan faith. (1) They considered themselves true worshipers of God. (2) Supreme authority was placed in the Pentateuch; the rest of the Jewish canon was rejected. They did look forward to the Messiah (John 4:25). (3) The text of the Samaritan Pentateuch in Deuteronomy 27:4 reads "Gerizim," not "Ebal," making Mount Gerizim the true place of worship. (4) They exalted Moses and gave him titles that Christians give to Jesus. (5) Circumcision, the Sabbath, kosher law, and a final judgment were part of their theology. Today Samaritans still live in Nablus and Jaffa and number about 355 persons.

Jesus and Samaria

In New Testament times, Samaria comes into the story of Jesus and the disciples prominently. For example, Jesus was in Samaria when he met the woman at the well and talked to her concerning worship (John 4). At another time a lawyer asked Jesus a series of questions to which Jesus responded by telling the story of a certain man traveling from Jerusalem to Jericho who fell among robbers and was left for dead. The hero of the story was a Samaritan

(Luke 10:25-37). While passing between Samaria and Galilee on a trip to Jerusalem, Jesus entered a village where he met ten lepers. He healed them all, but only one returned to express his gratitude. Jesus asked, "Was no one found to return and give praise to God except this foreigner?" (Luke 17:18). The grateful leper was a Samaritan.

Just before his ascension Jesus told the apostles that they would be his witnesses in Jerusalem, Judea, and Samaria, as well as to the ends of the earth (Acts 1:8). As the early Christians were scattered from Jerusalem, Philip went to a city of Samaria and preached the gospel with great response. One of the converts was Simon the sorcerer (Acts 8:4-25). On their way from the north to the Jerusalem conference, Paul and Barnabas passed through Samaria. They told the churches there of the conversion of the Gentiles and were received with great joy (Acts 15:3).

Modern archaeology has helped to fill out some of the history of the ancient Samaritans. For example references to Ahab's house of ivory (I Kings 22:39) and the beds of ivory (Amos 6:4) have been substantiated by the discovery of five hundred fragments of ivory, most of which were inlays from wooden wall panelings and furniture in Ahab's palace. According to Josephus, Herod loved Sebaste and erected a large beautiful temple on the city's summit for the worship of Augustus as a god. This was the same Herod who built the Jerusalem temple. The temple in Samaria had a forecourt which was about 240 feet square and was approached by a staircase 92 feet wide. An altar stood at the foot of the stairs and near it has been found a statue of a Roman emperor. A new city wall was installed measuring two miles in length. Herod also built a theater in Samaria. Many columns are still standing in the Roman forum constructed about 30 B.C.

Judging Themselves Unworthy

Batsell Barrett Baxter

There is a story told in the Gospel of Luke which is told nowhere else in the New Testament. It is found in the ninth chapter of Luke, and it is a brief story, comprising only verses 51 through 56. The setting is important. It happened in Samaria. Remember Samaria was the middle section of ancient Palestine, bordered on the north by Galilee and on the south by Judea. It was an area which measured approximately forty miles from north to south and thirty-five miles from east to west. The Mediterranean Sea was on the west and the Jordan River was on the east. More important than its area was the fact that it was populated by people who had once been united with the Jews, but now were deeply estranged from them. The Jews looked down upon the

Samaritans and the Samaritans hated the Jews. It is because of this situation that our text takes on special interest.

Rejection

The account reads, "When the days drew near for him to be received up [the end of Jesus' life was near], he set his face to go to Jerusalem. And he sent messengers ahead of him, who went and entered a village of the Samaritans, to make ready for him; but the people would not receive him, because his face was set toward Jerusalem. And when his disciples James and John saw it, they said, 'Lord, do you want us to bid fire come down from heaven and consume them?' But he turned and rebuked them. And they went on to another village."

The fact that Jesus was going directly through Samaria on his way to Jerusalem says something about Jesus. He was free of the ugly attitudes of discrimination felt by the people of his day. Although he was a Jew, he did not shun the Samaritans and was quite willing to lodge in one of their villages. The fact that he was going south from Galilee toward Jerusalem identified him in the minds of the people of Samaria as one of their traditional enemies. Hence, they refused to allow his group to lodge within their village overnight.

Apostles Are Human, Too

At this point we are a bit surprised at the behavior of James and John, who were two of the leading apostles. Jesus had chosen them nearly three years earlier and they had enjoyed a very close association with him for that interval of time. This means that they must have heard him teach on many occasions. They had observed the kindness and love of his life; but somehow, on this occasion at least, the attitudes which Jesus displayed were not their attitudes. When the Samaritan village would not welcome their Lord and themselves, they became angry and asked, "Lord, do you want us to bid fire come down from heaven and consume them?" Isn't that amazing? Imagine two of the apostles wanting to burn up the village, the babies, the old men and women, along with the rest. Yet, before we condemn these two men too harshly, perhaps we need to remember times when we also under some stress or strain have displayed some very unchristian attitudes. We, too, are never more vulnerable to temptation than when we are angry.

It is especially interesting to notice Jesus' reaction to the question. He showed no resentment toward the Samaritan village. Rather, he turned and rebuked James and John for so unworthy a suggestion as burning the village with fire. Jesus did not reprove the Samaritans who had affronted him, but his own apostles whose behavior was in contrast to everything that he taught. He made no comment about the Samaritan village, simply turning and going to another village.

Cursing Themselves

Before we turn from the story, let's spend just a moment thinking about the village which would not open its gates to Jesus. While he pronounced no curse upon them, they were cursed. They cursed themselves by not opening their gates to the One who could have blessed them so greatly. None of his miracles would be worked upon their lame or blind or deaf or dumb. None of the inhabitants of this village would hear his wonderful parables and his messages of hope and inspiration. His own personal example, which in a very real sense revealed the likeness of God, would be unseen by their eyes and unheard by their ears. No, Jesus did not judge them. They judged themselves unworthy of the blessings which Christ would have brought to them.

Because there is such a sadness in the story of the Samaritan village which would not receive Jesus, and because there is such a parallel with many who live today, let's explore this general theme and think of how it may apply to people of our time, and even perhaps to our own individual lives. Let's broaden the scene from the little area known as Samaria in the long ago to the whole world and let's include not just a few people in a small village but all the people of all the world.

The Good News

Now, with this broader picture, let's focus our attention on the Greek word *euangelion*. It was a word which the Greeks used to describe events which had a positive effect on everyone. They used the word when there was a birth in the royal family or when there was good news from the battlefront. The word was borrowed by the early Christians and has come into our language with the meaning of "gospel." When the early church told their story of the life and death of Jesus, they could think of no more suitable word to describe the story than "gospel," for this story was good news.

In fact, when you read through the narratives about Jesus you cannot miss this "good news" quality in the story. Everywhere Jesus went, lives were changed. Lepers were cleansed, the lame walked, and the deaf heard. People who had been turned into outcasts because of their sins suddenly found someone who understood and gave them a new chance in life. Jesus was good news. The good news was, of course, the fact that God has not left us like unwanted and unloved children. He has visited us in the person of Jesus Christ.

Indeed, when Jesus wished to describe what was happening, one of his favorite analogies was that of a wedding feast—a celebration. When asked why he did not fast, he replied, "Can the wedding guests fast while the bridegroom is with them?" (Mark 2:19). The kingdom was like a celebration following the return of a lost son, as in the story of the prodigal son (Luke 15). Or it was like a generous landowner who decided to pay his late-coming workers as much as he paid his people who had worked all day (Matt. 20). It was all incredible generosity. We speak of it as God's marvelous grace.

God's invitation calls us to believe in Jesus as the Christ, the Son of the living God. God's invitation also summons us to repent of the waywardness in our own lives. It calls us to make a new commitment of the central loyalty of our lives—a commitment to Jesus Christ and to God the Father. When that deep life-changing commitment is made we then must make it known to those about us as we confess Jesus before men and as we are buried with our Lord in baptism. That is exactly the way it was put on Pentecost when Peter answered the people's question, "Brethren, what shall we do?" Peter responded, "Repent, and be baptized every one of you in the name of Jesus Christ for the forgiveness of your sins; and you shall receive the gift of the Holy Spirit" (Acts 2:37, 38).

The Deepest Tragedy

The deepest tragedy known to man is to receive the invitation of Jesus Christ to a happier and better life here on the earth, and a still more wonderful life in the eternity to follow, yet to turn away judging oneself unworthy of eternal life.

One of the Sources of the Jordan River in Caesarea Philippi

12   Caesarea Philippi

Located on the southwestern slopes of Mount Hermon, some four miles apart, are Dan and Caesarea Philippi. The expression "from Dan to Beer-sheba" occurs often in the Bible (as in Judg. 20:1; I Sam. 3:20), and designates the northernmost and southernmost areas of the land of Israel. So, when Jesus visited Caesarea Philippi he was at the very northernmost tip of the land. The word *Dan* means "judge"; the city is located at Tell el-Qadi, which means "mound of the judge." Philip the tetrarch enlarged and beautified the city near Dan, changing its name from Paneas to Caesarea Philippi in honor of Tiberius Caesar and himself. Today it is known as Banias.

The city of Banias is located on a terrace 1,150 feet above sea level in a beautiful and luxurious area overlooking the fertile north end of the upper Jordan River Valley. The site is some fifty miles southwest of Damascus, and is on the highway connecting Acre on the Mediterranean with Damascus. Banias takes its name from the mythological god Pan, who was worshiped by some of the ancient peoples who lived in this area. The city is presently called Banias (instead of Paneas) because the Arabic language does not have a "p" sound.

Mount Hermon is the highest mountain in Syria and Israel. It reaches a height of 9,100 feet above sea level and its top is snow-covered much of the year. No trees grow above the snow line, but the lower slopes are covered with pine, oak, and poplar, along with vineyards. Wolves, leopards, and bears live in the forests. The word *Hermon* means "a consecrated place, a sanctuary." Today the Arabs call the height Jebel esh-Sheikh, "the mountain of the chief," or Jabel eth-Thalj, "mountain of snow." At the foot of Mount Hermon, two of the four sources of the Jordan River begin and flow south. The Leddan at Tell el-Qadi (Dan) and the Banias at Banias (Caesarea Philippi) originate in underground springs.

Biblical Events

Caesarea Philippi occurs in the Bible only at the time when Jesus and the disciples moved "into the district of Caesarea Philippi" (Matt. 16:13) or "to the villages of Caesarea Philippi" (Mark 8:27). It was here that Jesus asked his disciples what the multitudes were saying about him. The disciples gave several answers, repeating the words they had heard as they moved through the crowds following Jesus. Some thought he was John the Baptist, some Elijah, and still others Jeremiah or one of the other prophets. Jesus put a second question to them, "Who do you say that I am?" Peter answered, "You are the Christ, the Son of the living God" (Matt. 16:15, 16). Jesus responded by blessing Peter and then by telling the disciples that he would build his church upon the solid-rock foundation that he was the Son of God.

It is not absolutely clear whether Jesus and the disciples entered Caesarea Philippi or not. He may have had some reason to avoid such pagan Roman cities, or he may have come into Caesarea Philippi, the center of pagan worship, observing the useless gods of the heathen, much like Paul in Athens, when he chose to ask his disciples the crucial question about his own identity. With the appearance of the true Son of God, it is interesting to ponder the decline of the pantheon of gods and goddesses that were worshiped in thousands of temples throughout the Roman Empire. They are gone and all but forgotten; he rules in the hearts of millions of people throughout the whole world.

Dan figures in biblical history in the story of Jeroboam I (931–910 B.C.), the first king of the northern kingdom of Israel. He said to himself, "Now the kingdom will turn back to the house of David; if this people go up to offer sacrifices in the house of the Lord at Jerusalem" (I Kings 12:26, 27). So, he made two golden calves and spoke to the people, "You have gone up to Jerusalem long enough. Behold your gods, O Israel, who brought you up out of the land of Egypt" (I Kings 12:28). He set up one of the golden calves at Bethel and the other at Dan. He made houses of worship on the high places, appointed priests and feast days, and began the offering of sacrifices to the two golden calves.

Mount Hermon is mentioned occasionally in the Scriptures (Deut. 3:8, 9; Ps. 89:12; 133:3; Song of Songs 4:8). The territory came under the control of Herod the Great in 20 B.C. and was passed on to his son Philip the tetrarch at his death in 4 B.C. Philip ruled the area until A.D. 33. Titus and Vespasian camped their armies near Caesarea Philippi during the Jewish revolt of A.D. 66–70. Mount Hermon has been developed into a skiing center in modern times.

The Finality of Jesus Christ

Batsell Barrett Baxter

There is an important question in the early verses of the eleventh chapter of Matthew. John the Baptizer had completed his ministry and was in Machaerus prison, east of the Dead Sea. He had been unjustly accused and thrown into prison at the whim of King Herod. Languishing there, he evidently became concerned because Jesus, the Lamb of God for whom he had prepared the way, had not acted quickly enough and decisively enough, according to his thinking. John sent his disciples to Jesus to ask a significant question. The text reads, "Now when John heard in prison about the deeds of the Christ, he sent word by his disciples and said to him, 'Are you he who is to come [the Christ, the Messiah], or shall we look for another?' And Jesus answered them, 'Go and tell John what you hear and see: the blind receive their sight and the lame walk, lepers are cleansed and the deaf hear, and the dead are raised up, and the poor have good news preached to them'" (Matt. 11:2–5). John's question is supremely important. It is a question that men, for many different reasons, are still asking.

The Divinity of Jesus

Perhaps the most significant biblical passage on this subject of the identity of Christ is that found in Matthew 16, where we read, "Now when Jesus came into the district of Caesarea Philippi, he asked his disciples, 'Who do men say that the Son of man is?' And they said, 'Some say John the Baptist, others say Elijah, and others Jeremiah or one of the prophets.' He said to them, 'But who do you say that I am?' Simon Peter replied, 'You are the Christ, the Son of the living God.' And Jesus answered him, 'Blessed are you, Simon Bar-Jona! For flesh and blood has not revealed this to you, but my Father who is in heaven' '' (Matt. 16:13-17).

This revelation of the divinity of Jesus to Peter was confirmed by the sinless life which Jesus lived, by the unique quality of his teaching, by his miracles, and ultimately by his death, resurrection, and ascension. He was no ordinary man. He had all the earmarks of divinity. The disciples who knew him best were willing to give up everything that men normally hold dear and to invest their lives in their confident faith that Jesus was the Messiah.

Jesus of Nazareth is the central figure of all history. Every letter you write, every book you read, every significant event in your life (birth, graduation, marriage, death, and the like) is dated in relation to his life! All the armies that ever marched, all the navies that ever sailed, all the assemblies that ever met, and all the rulers that ever reigned put together have not affected the life of man upon the earth as powerfully as has the life of Jesus Christ!

The story began in the long ago when God had created man and man had rebelled against God. Man, estranged from God, needed to be redeemed. Because of his great love for man God inaugurated a plan for man's salvation which eventually led to the coming of Jesus of Nazareth. Even before he was born there were hundreds of prophecies about his coming.

The Word Became Flesh

In the fullness of time Jesus came to live among men, but that was not the beginning of his existence. Christ had existed before the world, in the beginning of time. At the outset of his account of the life of Christ John wrote, "In the beginning was the Word, and the Word was with God, and the Word was God. He was in the beginning with God; all things were made through him, and without him was not anything made that was made. In him was life, and the life was the light of men . . . . And the Word became flesh and dwelt among us, full of grace and truth; we have beheld his glory, glory as of the only Son from the Father" (John 1:1-4, 14). In later centuries we have called this the incarnation, the Son of God living in the flesh among men. This coming of the Messiah was the evidence of God's great love for men. "For God so loved the world that he gave his only Son, that whoever believes in him should not perish but have eternal life" (John 3:16).

When he had grown to be a man, Jesus began his public ministry. He went about teaching the people a new and better way of life. On one occasion there came officers who had been sent to arrest him, but instead of arresting him they reported to their superiors, "No man ever spoke like this man!" (John 7:46). They listened; they were impressed; and they went away empty-handed, "for he taught them as one who had authority, and not as their scribes" (Matt. 7:29). Jesus went about doing good: healing the sick, giving sight to the blind, restoring hearing to the deaf, working miracles, and performing signs. The people said of him, "What sort of man is this, that even winds and sea obey him?" (Matt. 8:27). He was like other men and yet he was unlike other men, for the things which he did were of God. In addition, he was "one who in every respect has been tempted as we are, yet without sin" (Heb. 4:15). He had the same inclinations of the flesh, the same temptations to live as the world lives, but in every instance he triumphed over them.

By his compassion he brought men from every walk of life to be his disciples. He attracted the sick and the well, the poor and rich, the unlearned and the wise. From every walk of life, from all age brackets, from all corners of mankind, men were impressed by the life of this Son of God. Even his enemies could find nothing evil in him. Yet, strange as it seems, the reception man gave this perfect life was murder on a cross.

Murder on a Cross

Yet, when he was murdered on a cross, it was not merely the murder of an innocent man. In its deepest significance it was the redemption of mankind from sin. "He was wounded for our transgressions, he was bruised for our iniquities" (Isa. 53:5). "God was in Christ reconciling the world to himself" (II Cor. 5:19). He transformed the shame of the cross into the glory of man's salvation. That which was ugly and despicable, the cross, was turned into the most glorious thing that has ever happened upon the earth—the salvation of man, made possible by Christ's death on the cross.

But Christ is not still hanging on the cross. That was only a moment in the life of Christ, and while it was a climactic moment, it was only for a little while that he hung on the cross and only for three days that he remained in the tomb. The real Jesus is alive, living forevermore. As the writer of Hebrews put it, "Jesus Christ is the same yesterday and today and for ever" (Heb. 13:8). He ascended into heaven and there reigns triumphantly. Not only does he reign in heaven but also in the hearts and lives of millions of people who have been blessed by him.

Who Is This Jesus?

Who then is this Jesus? Is he the humanistic Jesus of the play, "Superstar"? Is he the simplistic, emotional Jesus of the "Jesus-Freaks"?

Is he merely a great teacher and ethical guide, like Socrates? Is he simply the founder of a religion like Confucius or Mohammed? Or, is he uniquely the divine Son of God? His perfect life, his superior teachings, his genuine miracles, and his death and resurrection combine to prove that he was and is the Son of God.

Christ can make us over. He can take our old, sinful lives and make them clean again. Believe in the Lord Jesus with all your heart, announce that faith to those about you, repent of your past sins, and then enter into that wonderful new relationship with Christ that comes when you are baptized. He promises to cleanse you of sin and set you on a new road leading to eternal life in heaven. Ultimately, it is Christ or nothing at all. He is the last and best hope of earth.

Mount Tabor

13   Mount Tabor

Mount Tabor is located six miles east of Nazareth. Moshe Pearlman comments that it "squats placidly like a plump round loaf above the northern edge of the Valley of Jezreel." Shaped like an upside-down bowl, Tabor is one of the most interesting and lovely sites in the eastern part of Galilee. The mountain is not part of a chain, but stands in isolation.

Mount Tabor, whose name means "Mount of the height," rises 1,700 feet above sea level and 1,200 feet above the surrounding plain. Climbers report that Tabor can be climbed in less than an hour without the use of the road. One who climbs the mountain must come away impressed with the physical exertion required of Jesus on his various travels. The road up Mount Tabor contains twenty-nine 180° turns.

Located about twelve miles west-southwest of the Sea of Galilee, Tabor rises steeply from the Jezreel Valley. It curves gently to its roughly rectangular summit, which measures about a half mile east and west and nearly a quarter mile north and south. Whether standing on the plain looking up at the majestic lines of Tabor, or looking down from Tabor's heights to the beautiful expansive valley below, one can understand the psalmist's words of praise to a mighty and faithful God: "The heavens are thine, the earth also is thine; the world and all that is in it, thou hast founded them. The north and the south, thou hast created them; Tabor and Hermon joyously praise thy name" (Ps. 89:11, 12). Hermon refers to a mountain range on the northern border of Palestine with one peak reaching the 8,500-foot level.

The Period of the Judges

Mount Tabor was the place where the boundaries of the territories of Zebulun, Issachar, and Naphtali met (Josh. 19:12, 22, 34). The first major threat during the period of the judges appeared in the northern part of Israel. Jabin, king of Hazor, had nine hundred iron chariots which gave him superiority on the level plain of Jezreel (Judg. 4:1–3).

Deborah, the savior of her people, and the only woman judge, lived between Ramah and Bethel, some fifty miles from the scene of the decisive battle. Barak, chosen by Deborah to command the Israelite army, lived in Kedesh in Naphtali, about five miles northwest of Lake Huleh. Barak was told to gather the army together at Mount Tabor, a central meeting place. The Kishon, a rather seasonal river, very dry in the summer but a raging torrent in the winter and early spring, lies west of Tabor. Rain and the swelling river would make chariots useless as a force in battle.

Deborah's command, "Up! For this is the day in which the Lord has given Sisera into your hand," along with several lines from the poem in chapter 5, "The heavens dropped, yea, the clouds dropped water" and "the torrent Kishon swept them away, the onrushing torrent, the torrent Kishon," suggests that Deborah saw the approaching storm and gave order to attack (Judg. 4:14; 5:4, 21). Sisera fled on foot to the tent of Jael, the wife of Heber the Kenite. Heber had separated from the Kenites and had made an alliance with Jabin. Jael turned on Sisera, who sought safety in her house, by pounding a peg through his temple (Judg. 4:17–22).

The Transfiguration of Jesus

Although the identification is not certain, Tabor has been chosen as the traditional site for the transfiguration (Matt. 17:1–13; Mark 9:2–13; Luke 9:28–36). Both Matthew and Mark record that the event took place on "a high mountain apart.'' Luke records that it was a "mountain.'' Peter calls it the "holy mountain" (II Peter 1:18). Those who do not favor Mount Tabor usually suggest Mount Hermon as the mount of transfiguration. A church building was first erected on the summit of Tabor by Helena, the mother of Constantine, in A.D. 326. By the seventh century there were three shrines, dedicated to Jesus, Moses, and Elijah. Other churches and monasteries were built in the four centuries following, but all were destroyed by Saladin in A.D. 1187. His brother built a fortress on the hill in 1212. The fortress was soon destroyed and the summit abandoned for six hundred years.

Tabor Today

Late in the nineteenth century the Greek Orthodox built a monastery and church there. In the 1920s the Franciscans constructed a basilica on the foundation of a sixth-century Byzantine church and a twelfth-century Crusader church. Today a wall runs east and west across the top of Tabor, dividing the plateau into the southern part controlled by the Franciscans and the northern part by the Greek Orthodox.

The view from the top is beautiful. Carmel can be seen on the west, where Elijah contended with the prophets of Baal; and the mountains of Samaria can be seen to the south, including Mount Gilboa, where Jonathan and Saul met their death. The village of Nain (Luke 7:11) is also to the south in the valley. The mountains of Galilee stretch out to the north, the Sea of Galilee to the east, and off to the northeast is the towering snowy cap of Mount Hermon.

Some youth groups climb the mountain at night to catch the sunrise from its peak. Every year at Passover the Tabor Running Contest is held. Thousands of runners from all over the country run around the seven-mile circumference of the mountain's base.

Reflections on Authority

Harold Hazelip

Christopher Lasch, a contemporary American historian, has written that, just as students in the 1960s turned to various radical movements in order to "find themselves," the mood of the 1970s led people to turn inward in order to find themselves. One of the radical leaders of the 1960s has written, "In five years, from 1971 to 1975, I directly experienced est, Gestalt therapy, bio-energetics, Rolfing, massage, jogging, health foods ... Esalen, hypnotism, modern dance, meditation, Silva Mind Control . . . acupuncture, sex therapy.'' It was all an attempt to "find himself.'' He turned to one authority after another and found them unsatisfactory.

Just when we were being told that the human race had reached sufficient maturity not to depend on authorities, new cults began to spring up under the control of magnetic leaders. Seemingly mature and educated people turned their decision-making over to a cult leader who became the final judge of truth and falsehood. The popularity of these new cults suggests that people are often willing to turn themselves over to anyone who "speaks with authority."

But the fact that one "speaks with authority" does not make him the true authority for our lives. We must ask where he got his authority. Was it delegated by God? Is it attested by God? Does it conform to what God has already revealed about himself in his Word?

Freedom or Authority?

The twentieth century has been called the century of liberation. Ancient regimes which held millions of people in tyranny for centuries have ended. The emperor of China is gone; the monarchies of Europe have either disappeared or have been severely curtailed. Liberation has extended into the area of civil rights, with the insistence that everyone has a right to live a fully human life.

And we seek even more freedom: freedom from sickness, freedom from ignorance and falsehood, freedom to do something or to become somebody, freedom from hunger, freedom from war. We may decide that the greatest goal in life is unlimited freedom.

Jesus taught that true freedom comes in finding the right authority for one's life. He said, "If you continue in my word, you are truly my disciples, and you will know the truth, and the truth will make you free. . . . So if the Son makes you free, you will be free indeed" (John 8:31, 32, 36).

The early history of our nation illustrates this principle that freedom and authority go hand in hand. The aim of the founders of the United States was liberty. Patrick Henry put it, "Give me liberty or give me death." A revolution was fought and the colonists won their liberty. For a few years afterward, the new nation existed as a very loose coalition of separate states. But they soon found that if they were to survive and prosper as a nation, they would have to establish a stronger central authority which could protect the freedom they had won. Only then was the Constitution written as an effort to gain stability and organization.

How Does God Exercise Authority?

In what way does God exercise his authority over our lives? Several answers have been suggested. One response is: he exercises his authority through human reason. The human mind can boast remarkable achievements. But there are limits to what our intellects can do. We cannot enter into the secrets of another person's life unless that person chooses to reveal himself to us. We can know something about God through his creation but we cannot know his will until he reveals it to us. The prophet Jeremiah said, "I know, O Lord, that the way of man is not in himself, that it is not in man who walks to direct his steps" (Jer. 10:23).

A second option that has been suggested is that religious experience is our authority. When we know God, we have experiences and feelings which come through fellowship with him. But our experience is not the pathway to knowledge of God. We often have feelings about another person which turn out to be ill grounded and wrong. Rather than pointing to our psychological moods, Jesus said, "All things have been delivered to me by my Father; and no one knows the Son except the Father, and no one knows the Father except the Son and any one to whom the Son chooses to reveal him" (Matt. 11:27).

Sometimes the church itself is presented as the source of religious authority. It is argued that the church produced the Bible by bringing the authoritative books together in one collection. However, it is one thing to *bestow* authority upon the Bible and quite another to *recognize* the authority of the Bible.

The history of religious bodies does not encourage one to look to them for final authority. Their leaders have often reversed themselves. With all of her sin and schism, the church must be under an authority outside herself.

Only in Scripture

Only the Bible can claim to be the written record of God's conversation with his people over hundreds of years. Here and nowhere else do we have a record of the history through which God made himself known to man. Those ancient writings were addressed to particular situations, but their authority was not limited to that place and time. The ancient prophets were fully aware that they were spokesmen for God. More than three thousand times the Old Testament includes the formula, "Thus says the Lord." The only access we have to the mind of God is through his Word, the Scriptures.

The Scriptures drive home to us the authority of Jesus Christ as our Lord. Within a week of Peter's confession at Caesarea Philippi ("You are the Christ, the Son of the living God") Jesus took Peter, James, and John and went up into a high mountain to pray (Mark 9:2–8; Luke 9:28–36). On the mountaintop he was changed until he became a figure glowing with light. Moses and Elijah appeared and talked with him about his death. Peter proposed building three booths: one for Jesus, one for Moses, and one for Elijah. Mark explains that "he did not know what to say, for they were exceedingly afraid" (Mark 9:6). Then a cloud overshadowed and enveloped all of them, and out of the cloud there came the voice of God: "This is my beloved Son, with whom I am well pleased; listen to him" (Matt. 17:5).

The significance of this very unusual event is clear. Moses and Elijah were the two supreme figures of the religion of the Old Testament: Moses the lawgiver, Elijah the prophet. This was God's assurance that however much Jesus differed from the popular view of the Messiah, he was actually the fulfillment of all that the law and the prophets foretold.

Whereas Peter suggested that they remain longer in the glory of the mountaintop, Jesus' reaction was to come down from the mountain and enter again into the involvement of life. When Jesus withdrew to the mountaintops to pray, it was never an escape but always a preparation. Instead of remaining withdrawn, he returned to walk with determination the way that led to Calvary.

Today the world may well be disillusioned with those of us who claim to follow Christ, but our hope is that the world is not disillusioned with Christ. We fail him, we misrepresent him, but the light of authority still shines from Jesus Christ.

Augustine, who searched his way through several philosophies before coming to believe in Christ, said, "I found in my studies of Plato and Cicero many fine things acutely said, but in none of them did I find, 'Come unto me and rest.' "

It is not simply the beauty of Jesus' invitation that carries authority. God acknowledged him both at his baptism and at the transfiguration. His closing words in the Gospel of Matthew are, "All authority in heaven and on earth has been given to me. Go therefore and make disciples of all nations, baptizing them in the name of the Father and of the Son and of the Holy Spirit, teaching them to observe all that I have commanded you; and lo, I am with you always, to the close of the age" (Matt. 28:18-20). His is an authority that will not fail.

Ruins of Solomon's Stables in Megiddo

14 Megiddo

The mound identified with Megiddo is 130 to 200 feet above the surrounding Esdraelon Valley and covers an area of fifteen acres. It would be difficult to find a more strategic site than Megiddo. From the top of the mound the entire length of the Esdraelon Valley can be seen. To the east Mount Gilboa and Mount Tabor can be clearly seen. The western part of the Galilean hills is all that keeps the Mediterranean from sight.

The Via Maris, the "Way of the Sea," connected the lands of Egypt and Assyria. After passing along the Palestinian coast through Philistia and the Plain of Sharon, it crossed the Carmel range to Megiddo. Throughout its three-thousand-year history, Megiddo was located at an important intersection, one that brought much conflict and war.

Archaeologists have uncovered nearly twenty-five different layers dated from before 3300 B.C. until 350 B.C., when the city finally fell into ruins. The largest wall ever found at Megiddo was constructed in approximately the twenty-ninth century B.C. with a thickness of twenty-six feet. Made of brick, it is preserved to a height of thirteen feet.

The Israelite Kings

When the Israelites under Joshua invaded the land, they defeated the king of Megiddo (Josh. 12:7, 21), but they were unable to occupy the city at the time (Judg. 1:27) because the Canaanites had superior weapons, including chariots (Josh. 17:16). It is known that Solomon carried on extensive building projects there. The Old Testament says, "And this is the account of the forced labor which King Solomon levied to build the house of the Lord and his own house and the Millo and the wall of Jerusalem and Hazor and Megiddo and Gezer" (I Kings 9:15).

Upon being anointed king of Israel by a young prophet sent by Elisha, Jehu began a revolution. In about 842 B.C., he attacked Jehoram, the reigning king of Israel, who was recovering from wounds suffered in the battle against Hazael, king of Syria. Jehoram was killed in the attack by Jehu (II Kings 9:1-26). Ahaziah, king of Judah, had been an ally of Jehoram against Hazael and was visiting with Jehoram at the time of Jehu's attack. He fled with Jehu in pursuit, was shot in his chariot, and died at Megiddo. A chariot took his body to Jerusalem for burial (I Kings 8:25—9:28).

Josiah began to reign over Judah in 640 B.C. when he was eight years old. In his eighteenth year, he repaired the temple (II Kings 22:1-7). The book of the law was found and read to the king (II Kings 22:8-10). The king renewed the covenant with God and began a series of reforms in Judah. The Lord was still not pleased with Judah (II Kings 23:1-27). Josiah went to fight Pharaoh Neco, king of Egypt, who was on his way to fight the king of Assyria at Carchemish on the Euphrates River. Josiah intercepted Neco at Megiddo. The Pharaoh sent a message to Josiah, saying, "What have we to do with each other, king of Judah? I am not coming against you this day, but against the house with which I am at war; and God has commanded me to make haste. Cease opposing God, who is with me, lest he destroy you" (II Chron. 35:21).

Josiah would not turn away, but disguised himself for the battle. Egyptian archers shot Josiah. The wounded king told his servants, "Take me away, for I am badly wounded." He died shortly thereafter. He was carried back to Jerusalem in his chariot and buried.

The Place Called Armageddon

The New Testament mentions Megiddo only once and that in the form of "Armageddon," meaning "mountain of Megiddo." The text reads, "For they are demonic spirits, performing signs, who go abroad to the kings of the whole world, to assemble them for battle on the great day of God the Almighty. ('Lo, I am coming like a thief! Blessed is he who is awake, keeping his garments that he may not go naked and be seen exposed!') And they assembled them at the place which is called in Hebrew Armageddon" (Rev. 16:14–16).

The mention of "battle" and "Megiddo" in the same context calls to mind the several Old Testament battles fought in the general area. These include Deborah and Sisera (Judg. 4–5), Jehu against Ahaziah (II Kings 9), and Josiah against Pharaoh Neco (II Kings 23; II Chron. 35). Other noteworthy conflicts occurred nearby. For example, the battle between Gideon and the Midianite-Amalekite forces occurred in the Valley of Jezreel (Judg. 6–7), and the contest between the Philistines and Saul in which Saul died occurred on Mount Gilboa (I Sam. 31).

General Allenby defeated the Turkish army near Megiddo during World War I on September 19, 1918, and received the title of Viscount Allenby of Megiddo. One of the most interesting experiences the tourist can have today is a walk through the tunnel connected with the water system of Megiddo. Located on the west side of the tell is a shaft some 80 feet deep with steps cut out of the sides. At the bottom of the shaft is a tunnel which runs under the mound to a spring outside the walls. The tunnel, 230 feet long and 10 feet high, provided water to the city in time of siege. The spring was covered to prevent the enemy from detecting its location. The method of quarrying makes it clear that the tunnel was dug by cutting simultaneously from both ends in a manner similar to the Siloam tunnel in Jerusalem. The two passageways were just over three feet off when they met. The water system is dated variously from about 1200 B.C. to the time of Ahab (874–853).

The Battle of Armageddon
Harold Hazelip

The last book in the New Testament—The Revelation—is a book of hope. We cannot live long without hope. Pain is such a universal fact, tears pour down every cheek. The mortality rate in our world is 100 percent.

The communist dreams of a classless society. And many Americans dream of a technological solution to all of our problems. Thousands of years of human history indicate that we may dream of Utopia, but we build a tower of Babel every time.

These words strike a chord in our hearts: "I saw a new heaven and a new earth . . . . And I saw the holy city, new Jerusalem, coming down out of heaven from God . . . I heard a great voice from the throne saying, 'Behold, the dwelling of God is with men . . . . He will wipe away every tear from their eyes, and death shall be no more, neither shall there be mourning nor crying nor pain any more, for the former things have passed away'" (Rev. 21:1–4).

Who would not wish an end to death and pain and crying? Is this vision too good to be true? What is going on in the Book of Revelation? How do we reach this triumph for God's people?

Speculation About the End

There is a great deal of speculation today by futurists who use the Book of Revelation to try to predict a timetable for the end of the world. According to one popular book, the second coming of Christ should occur before 1988. The author has history coming to an end when only two great spheres of power are left on earth. These are supposed to be the revived Roman Empire and the Chinese. The Chinese are pictured as bringing 200 million soldiers across the dried-up Euphrates River for the battle of Armageddon. Total annihilation of the human race will be averted, according to this theory, only by Christ coming again and reigning on earth as a physical king for one thousand years.

The Message of Revelation

I believe this is a complete misunderstanding of the message of the Book of Revelation.

The problem the apostle John and his fellow Christians faced in A.D. 96, when the Revelation was written, was a decree of the Roman emperor Domitian which established Caesar worship throughout the world. The state itself was to be an object of worship, with the emperor being regarded as an incarnation of God. Christians believed emperor worship amounted to rank idolatry and blasphemy. They refused to bow the head or burn incense to the name of Caesar. The result was furious persecution. Revelation points to a decisive conflict between good and evil.

Admittedly, Revelation is a difficult book for the modern reader. It is apocalyptic literature—a cryptic message that was written during times of trouble. It had special symbolic meanings for the initiated but left the outsider baffled. The original readers were members of seven congregations of Christ's body in Asia Minor—"the seven churches in Asia" (Rev. 1:4–11).

The book opens with a vision of Christ in heaven. After brief letters to each of the seven churches (2-3), John was caught up for a heavenly vision (4:1). He saw a book, sealed with seven seals. When those seals were opened, terrible suffering occurred on the earth. In the following section of the Revelation, he saw seven angels as they sounded seven trumpets. Again, terrible suffering occurred on the earth. These two sets of symbols are probably referring to the same reality: God has forceful weapons with which to punish those who persecute his people—weapons such as military conquerors, famine, and death.

In chapters 12 through 14 a pure woman—obviously the church—is attacked by a dragon (the devil) assisted by two beasts. One of these beasts appears to be a political power, the other a religious power (he is also called the false prophet). The saints are encouraged to endure, and the section closes with a vision of divine judgment.

In chapters 15 and 16 seven bowls of wrath are poured out upon the earth, reminding us of the seven seals on the book being opened and the seven trumpets being sounded by seven angels in the earlier sections of Revelation. In chapters 17 and 18 the enemies of God's people are pictured as a great harlot city which falls suddenly. Then the consummation comes with the enemies of God's people being cast into the lake of fire (19-20) and the new Jerusalem coming down from God out of heaven (21-22).

What Does Armageddon Mean?

The only reference to Armageddon in the entire Bible is in Revelation 16:16, in connection with the sixth angel emptying his bowl of wrath on earth. The entire paragraph reads, "The sixth angel poured his bowl on the great river Euphrates, and its water was dried up, to prepare the way for the kings from the east. And I saw, issuing from the mouth of the dragon and from the mouth of the beast and from the mouth of the false prophet, three foul spirits like frogs; for they are demonic spirits, performing signs, who go abroad to the kings of the whole world, to assemble them for battle on the great day of God the Almighty. ('Lo, I am coming like a thief! Blessed is he who is awake, keeping his garments that he may not go naked and be seen exposed!') And they assembled them at the place which is called in Hebrew Armageddon" (Rev. 16:12-16).

What is the meaning of Armageddon? Although a great battle is mentioned in chapter 16, it is not fought until chapter 19. The three great enemies of the church which surfaced in chapters 12 though 14 were the dragon (Satan), a political power (the Roman Empire), and a religious power (the false prophet—probably the local council which enforced emperor worship). In chapters 19 and 20 these enemies are one by one cast into hell and the church is rewarded.

The message of Revelation is that Christ's cause will triumph over evil. Armageddon is not a physical battle but rather a spiritual conflict between the forces of good and evil. The mound identified with the hill of Megiddo today covers an area of only fifteen acres. We are not to envision a literal battle where one army of 200 million men comes against an opposing army (cf. Rev. 9:16). The hill of Megiddo and the valley alongside it were a very strategic site in many Old Testament battles, but the geographical area is too small for a battle involving hundreds of millions of soldiers.

But remember, the text of Revelation does not say that 200 million Chinese soldiers will fight with the armies of the revived Roman Empire at the hill of Megiddo, or Armageddon. This is speculation by interpreters who are seeking a timetable for the end of the world which the Bible does not give. Instead, the Bible allows Armageddon to stand for the final conflict between the forces of Christ and the forces of Satan. Megiddo was well known in Old Testament battles as a place where God intervened and helped when his people's resources had all been exhausted. The battle in the Book of Revelation is a spiritual battle, not a physical battle! And when the conflict is concluded, Satan is cast into the lake of fire (Rev. 20:10).

This highly controversial section of the Bible has a basically simple thrust. There will be alternate triumphs of good and evil, but Christ will ultimately overcome. This was the message needed by Christians facing death in the first century. And this is the message we still need today. Those who serve Christ will overcome.

The City of Nazareth in Galilee

15 Nazareth

The modern town of En Nasira in the northern section of Israel is generally accepted as the location of the Nazareth of the New Testament. Lying to the north of the Jezreel Valley in a basin that is open only to the south, it is about fifteen miles west of the south end of the Sea of Galilee and about twenty miles east of the Mediterranean Sea. Located about 1,300 feet above sea level, the city has a moderate climate. From the heights around Nazareth one can see south to the Jezreel, east to Mount Tabor, west to Mount Carmel, and north to Mount Hermon.

The meaning of the name *Nazareth* is uncertain, but it may be related to the Hebrew word meaning "separated," though some scholars relate it to the Hebrew words meaning "guard place, watchtower" or "sprout, shoot, branch." There is considerable discussion about the relationship of the town to the Nazirites, whose vows are mentioned in Numbers 6. Nazarene appears to mean "of Nazareth" in the New Testament and has no relationship to the Nazirites. Nazareth is not mentioned in the Old Testament.

Today, Nazareth has a population of between 35,000 and 40,000, including the largest Christian population in Israel except for Jerusalem. There are, in one sense, two Nazareths today. The older city is an important Christian center though it has a substantial Muslim population. The new Nazareth is a town of Jewish immigrants. Beginning in 1957 with 1,000 settlers, this area now numbers 17,000. Factories in the area produce cars, furniture, and textiles.

Biblical Events

The city of Nazareth became important to Christians of later times when the angel Gabriel visited the virgin Mary and said to her, "Hail, O favored one, the Lord is with you! . . . And behold, you will conceive in your womb and bear a son, and you shall call his name Jesus. He will be great, and will be called the Son of the Most High; and the Lord God will give to him the throne of his father David, and he will reign over the house of Jacob for ever; and of his kingdom there will be no end" (Luke 1:28–33). Mary replied, "Behold, I am the handmaid of the Lord; let it be to me according to your word" (v. 38).

Mary was betrothed, though not yet married, to Joseph, who was deeply disturbed by her pregnancy. The angel spoke to him, saying, "Joseph, son of David, do not fear to take Mary your wife, for that which is conceived in her is of the Holy Spirit; she will bear a son, and you shall call his name Jesus, for he will save his people from their sins" (Matt. 1:20, 21). This was a fulfillment of the prophecy in Isaiah 7:14, "Behold, a virgin shall conceive, and bear a son, and shall call his name Immanuel" (ASV). These events apparently took place in Nazareth (Luke 2:4).

Jesus was born in Bethlehem where Joseph and Mary had gone for the census of Caesar Augustus. After a brief sojourn in Egypt, fleeing from the threats of the bloody Herod the Great, Joseph and Mary brought Jesus back to Nazareth, where he grew to manhood.

At the age of thirty Jesus left Nazareth and went to the Jordan River to be baptized by John the Baptist (Mark 1:9). After beginning his ministry, Jesus returned to Nazareth, "where he had been brought up" (Luke 4:16), and as he usually did, he went to the synagogue on the sabbath day and took his turn in reading the Scripture. He read from Isaiah 61:1, 2 and ended by saying, "Today this scripture has been fulfilled in your hearing" (Luke

4:21). The people became disturbed, asking, "Isn't this Joseph's son?" They were angered to the point that they rose up and put him out of the city and would have thrown him over the brow of a hill had he not passed through their midst and escaped (Luke 4:16–30).

Joseph, his foster father, was a carpenter; Jesus apparently learned the trade himself. He had several brothers, James, Joseph, Judas, and Simon, and also several sisters whose names are not given in the Scriptures (Matt. 13:55, 56; Mark 6:3). After his rejection at Nazareth, he moved to Capernaum and centered his ministry there (Matt. 4:13; Luke 4:31).

Modern Nazareth

In modern Nazareth the Church of the Annunciation stands on the site where tradition places the appearance of the angel to Mary to announce the birth of Jesus. The church, built in 1730, was removed in 1955 and a new building was constructed and recently finished. It is one of the most expensive and most beautiful church buildings in the world. There is a cave under the altar and it is claimed that this is the site where the angel Gabriel appeared to Mary. There are many other sites that are confidently proclaimed by the local guides to be authentic, though most of them must be taken as mere traditions.

Among the various religious sites in Nazareth, the one with the most probable claim to authenticity is Mary's Well. The spring that feeds the well rises out of the ground above the Church of St. Gabriel and is piped down the hill to the current outlet, which was built in 1862. There are no remains in Nazareth from the time before the Crusaders came into the area.

Nazareth's market, no doubt, looks much today as it did in the time of Jesus, though the buildings themselves are of a much later date. The narrow, roofed streets, off limits to automobiles, are in the Oriental style. The food stalls and for other products recall what life must have been like in days gone by. Mary must have experienced a great deal in this town from the first announcement of the birth of Jesus to the day that he was cast out of the city's synagogue, having been rejected by his relatives and neighbors. Nazareth must have held many good memories and also some sorrowful recollections for this woman that God called "the favored one."

"According to Your Word"
Batsell Barrett Baxter

The opening chapter of the Gospel of Luke contains the story of the announcement to Mary that she would bear a child who would be the long-anticipated Messiah. Who in that day would have dreamed that an obscure Jewish girl from a peasant culture, from an unknown village, would be selected by God to be the mother of the Savior? Yet, that is the story. It happened not in Rome, nor Athens, nor Alexandria, nor Ephesus, not even in Jerusalem, but in Nazareth. The promise came not to the high-born nor wealthy nor famous, but to an unknown pure and innocent Jewish maiden. That's God's way. All people are important to him, even the unknown and unheralded.

The angel came to Mary and said, "Hail, O favored one, the Lord is with you!" The text continues, "But she was greatly troubled at the saying, and considered in her mind what sort of greeting this might be. And the angel said to her, 'Do not be afraid, Mary, for you have found favor with God. And behold, you will conceive in your womb and bear a son, and you shall call his name Jesus. He will be great, and will be called the Son of the Most High; and the Lord God will give to him the throne of his father David, and he will reign over the house of Jacob for ever; and of his kingdom there will be no end'" (Luke 1:28–33).

Mary's Response

Mary's response to all of this, which must be classed as overwhelming news, was simple and beautiful, "Behold, I am the handmaid of the Lord; let it be to me according to your word" (Luke 1:38).

God comes to those who least expect it. He comes to obscure and unimportant people and says, "I have a purpose for your life. I have chosen you to play an important role in my plan." That is the way God came to Mary, and that is the way he comes to us. In Mary God demonstrated once again that his blessings depend not on our fame or good works. They depend upon his love and goodness. Mary had found favor in God's eyes and he blessed her above all women.

There is a sense in which Mary is an example of all grace. She had done nothing to deserve the abundant favor which she found in God's eyes. Why then do we remember Mary with such fondness? One reason is her response to God's grace. She did not argue with the angel. She did not laugh at the news, as did Sarah long before. She did not reject God's promise. Rather, she said simply, "I am the handmaid of the Lord; let it be to me according to your word." Mary is a great example of what should happen when we encounter God's gifts. She willingly became an instrument in God's hands. Her song, which has come to be known as the "Magnificat" because in the Latin version this was the first word of the song, indicates further that she was a woman of faith and hope who announced the good news of salvation even before her son was born.

The Magnificat

It is most fitting at this point to read Mary's remarkable song, found in Luke 1:46–55. "My soul magnifies the Lord, and my spirit rejoices in God my Savior, for he has regarded the low estate of his handmaiden. For behold, henceforth all generations will call me blessed; for he who is mighty has done great things for me, and holy is his name. And his mercy is on those who fear him from generation to generation. He has shown strength with his arm, he has scattered the proud in the imagination of their hearts, he has put down the mighty from their thrones, and exalted those of low degree; he has filled the hungry with good things, and the rich he has sent empty away. He has helped his servant Israel, in remembrance of his mercy, as he spoke to our fathers, to Abraham and to his posterity for ever."

Mary's poem may be regarded by some as a museum-piece, but of little value to our generation. On the contrary, it has much to say to those who have lived down through the ages and to those of our modern twentieth century. "His mercy is on those who fear him from generation to generation" is as true now as it was then. Again, "he has scattered the proud in the imagination of their hearts, he has put down the mighty from their thrones, and exalted those of low degree." This has been demonstrated over and over again when the powerful and the mighty have fallen and the weak and defenseless have been exalted. Yet again, "he has filled the hungry with good things, and the rich he has sent empty away." This, too, has been demonstrated over and over. All the message of the Bible is here gathered together in this simple song, a song that rejoices and exults in God our Creator and our Sustainer.

C. S. Lewis has commented, "The Magnificat is terrifying. If there are two things in the Bible which make our blood run cold, [the Magnificat] is one; the other is that phrase in Revelation: 'The wrath of the lamb.' . . . There is no cursing here, no hatred, no self-righteousness. Instead there is mere statement. He has scattered the proud, cast down the mighty, sent the rich empty away. We have the treble voice, a girl's voice, announcing without sin that the sincere prayers of her ancestors do not remain unheard."

The good news, according to Mary, speaks not only of the tremendous mercy of God, but also of his rejection of every human pretension, his condemnation of our arrogance, our acquisitiveness, and our pride. Through this song we can almost hear the words which Jesus would later speak. This poem forecasts the plain language of Jesus about the dangers that beset the rich, the powerful, and the oppressors. It echoes his blessings on the poor, the meek, the oppressed, the workers for justice, and the pure in heart. The meaning of Mary's song is found most clearly in her Son, his life, and his teachings.

A Gigantic Reversal

The story we've been telling is the heart of biblical faith—the faith that God is the One who brings creation out of nothing, life out of death, promise out of hopelessness. In bringing Christ into the world through a humble peasant girl, God demonstrated his power to bring about a gigantic reversal in the affairs of men. Abraham had already learned that God could bring life out of what seemed to be barrenness. Israel had learned that God could choose a little nation, a nothing, and make it great, bringing its people out of slavery into freedom and opening the doors for them to come into fullness of life. Hannah had learned that God is the God of reversal, able to bring birth out of barrenness. The exiles knew that God could bring promise and freedom and hope out of captivity. So, Mary also learned that God could take herself, a little, insignificant vessel, and use her greatly. This is the faith that we find throughout the Scriptures and it is the faith that we must hold in our hearts. Our world has many evils and many difficult situations, but God is still the God of reversal who can make evil become good.

Shepherds' Fields, Bethlehem

16 Bethlehem

Bethlehem (the name means "House of Bread") lies five-and-one-half miles south of Jerusalem and about a mile east of the Hebron road. It lies off the main roads of antiquity.

There is no spring in the area so water was collected in cisterns. In the winter and spring the countryside is beautiful with the succession of vine, olive, almond, and fig-clad terraces.

The first mention of Bethlehem in the Bible is in relation to Rachel's death: "So Rachel died, and she was buried on the way to Ephrath (that is, Bethlehem)" (Gen. 35:19). Her tomb is by the roadside at the entrance to Bethlehem.

113

The inhabitants of Bethlehem were related to the family of Caleb, a descendant of Judah. The story of Ruth occurred in the Bethlehem area. Elimelech, his wife Naomi, and their two sons Mahlon and Chilion, were Ephrathites from Bethlehem. During the period of the judges they migrated to Moab, where the three men died. Naomi, with one of her Moabite daughters-in-law, returned to Bethlehem. Ruth, the Moabitess, worked in the field of a relative named Boaz. Boaz eventually married Ruth; their great-grandson was King David.

From David to Micah

After Saul's disobedience in the matter of Agag and the Amalekites (I Sam. 15), God told Samuel he would provide another king for Israel. Told to take a heifer for a sacrifice, Samuel went to invite Jesse the Bethlehemite to worship with him. When Samuel approached Bethlehem, the elders of the city met him, trembling with fear that he had not come in peace. Samuel merely wanted Jesse and his sons to sacrifice with him. One by one Samuel looked at Jesse's sons, but God rejected seven before choosing David, the ruddy shepherd boy. Samuel took his horn of oil and anointed David in the midst of his brothers (I Sam. 16:1–13).

When God's Spirit left King Saul, he was troubled and asked his servants to provide someone who could soothe him with music. One of the younger servants suggested a brave young man from Bethlehem who had developed expertise on the stringed instrument. When Jesse heard the request of the king, he sent young David to the king's house (I Sam. 16:14–23).

It was from Bethlehem that David took food and drink for his older brothers who were in the army and ended up doing battle with Goliath (I Sam. 17:12–54).

During the fighting with the Philistines, when David was in the cave at Adullam, and the Philistines were garrisoned in Bethlehem, David wished aloud for water from the well of Bethlehem. Three of his mighty men broke into the Philistine camp, drew water from the well next to the gate, and brought it to David. David refused to drink the water because they had risked their lives for it; he poured it out to the Lord (II Sam. 23:13–17).

The prophet Micah, from Moresheth-gath, about twenty-five miles southwest of Jerusalem, wrote in the latter part of the eighth century B.C., lamenting the sins of Judah. He wrote that the coming Messiah would be born in Bethlehem (Mic. 5:2).

The Birth of Jesus

Joseph, a descendant of David, was required to go to Bethlehem when the Roman emperor, Caesar Augustus, taxed the empire during the days of the

Syrian governor Quirinius. Joseph took his betrothed, Mary, with him. After finding no overnight lodging in the city they settled in a stable where she gave birth to a son (Luke 2:1-7).

The shepherds who were made aware of Jesus' birth by the appearance of a number of angels were near Bethlehem. They found the baby in the stable and worshiped him (Luke 2:8-20).

The Wise Men were led to Jerusalem. They asked King Herod the whereabouts of him who had been born King of the Jews. Herod deceitfully commissioned the Wise Men to seek the child in Bethlehem and report back to him, but they became aware of his trickery and did not do his bidding. Frustrated, Herod ordered all the male children under two in Bethlehem to be put to death (Matt. 2:1-18).

The works of Justin Martyr (died A.D. 165) speak of Jesus' being born in a cave near Bethlehem where Mary and Joseph had settled when unable to find a room. Origen of Alexandria (A.D. 185-254) states that even pagans knew the cave where Jesus was born. Constantine, at the suggestion of Marcaris, bishop of Jerusalem, constructed three imperial churches in Palestine, one over the cave of the nativity in Bethlehem. The construction began in A.D. 326. At the end of the fourth century, Jerome settled in Bethlehem and, together with others, founded two monasteries.

Modern Bethlehem

The church built by Constantine was destroyed during a Samaritan revolt in A.D. 529 and rebuilt by Justinian (A.D. 527-565). The present Church of the Nativity is basically the structure built by Justinian.

The traditional birth site is marked today by a grotto which measures ten by forty feet and is lighted by fifty-three lamps. The floor and walls are covered by fine white slabs of marble. On the east is the place of birth, marked by a silver star inscribed in Latin, "Here Jesus Christ was born of the virgin Mary." The star and inscription were installed in 1717.

A long feud has existed between the Greeks and the Franciscans for possession of the sanctuary. Dating from the sixteenth century, the conflict was exacerbated at the time of the Crimean War (1853-1856), when Russia fought Turkey, France, and Britain. The French, along with others, compelled the Greeks to allow a new Franciscan star to replace the old star which had worn out. On April 25, 1873, an armed band of Greek monks and others broke into the grotto, wounding eight Franciscans and pillaging the cave—even taking the marble slab covering the holy crib. Since then a policeman has always been on duty.

Modern Bethlehem is the combination of three towns: Bethlehem, Beit Jala and Beit Sahur. The population of the city has grown from 7,000 in 1948 to over 37,000, with a number of refugees adding to the population.

Few people work the land; most are involved in the tourist trade. The city serves as a market center for the Bedouin tribes in the area. Bethlehem is famous for its olive wood and mother-of-pearl souvenirs, the latter introduced by the Franciscans in the sixteenth century.

The Cradle and the Throne

Harold Hazelip

"And she gave birth to her first-born son and wrapped him in swaddling cloths, and laid him in a manger, because there was no place for them in the inn" (Luke 2:7).

"Therefore God has highly exalted him and bestowed on him the name which is above every name, that at the name of Jesus every knee should bow, in heaven and on earth and under the earth, and every tongue confess that Jesus Christ is Lord, to the glory of God the Father" (Phil. 2:9–11).

There seems to be no similarity between these two portraits of Christ. In the first, his humanity is very obvious. He is a helpless babe, lying in a manger. In the second, the whole universe bows in homage to him.

But there is an indissoluble connection between these two portrayals. One emphasizes the humanity of Jesus—he was one of us. If we forget this we lose sight of the love and purpose of God and of the nearness we may feel to Jesus at all times.

The other emphasizes his divinity—he was God the Son. If we forget this, we may admire him as a great leader in a bygone century, but we will fail to see his power as the ascended Lord at work in our lives today.

Jesus was both divine and human. Possessing all power in heaven and earth, how did he conduct himself among men? This is important. He is our model.

Who Are Our Models?

Our age is very conscious of power. We have become quite skillful in the use of power against others. Not only is this true of nations, it is also true of individuals.

We may be tempted to pattern ourselves after models in our own time. Stanley Kubrick, a very successful movie producer, has written about the influence of film and television. He says that the medium of television and film is like dreaming. The difference is that we can control the dream. But when a young person has watched fifteen thousand hours of television, and witnessed ten thousand murders by the time he is seventeen years of age, he may draw the conclusion, "Get what you want by whatever power you have."

This "power syndrome" in our culture is the exact opposite of the Christian faith. Paul urged Christians at Philippi, "Have this mind among yourselves, which you have in Christ Jesus, who, though he was in the form of God, did not count equality with God a thing to be grasped, but emptied himself, taking the form of a servant, being born in the likeness of men. And being found in human form he humbled himself and became obedient unto death, even death on a cross" (Phil. 2:5-8).

He Emptied Himself

Christ did not "grasp" or hold on to the power he had as the eternal Son of God. Instead, he "emptied himself." The form he took in his incarnation was that of a slave, a powerless one. He underwent the most shameful death possible.

If our value system says that "power is the name of the game," that we should get what we want by whatever power we have, by that standard Jesus Christ was a total failure. His whole life went in the direction of emptying himself. He emptied himself finally of his very life.

Perhaps this explains his birth in a stable. The way God did things is not the way we would have done them. "This will be a sign for you: you will find a babe wrapped in swaddling cloths and lying in a manger" (Luke 2:12). Isn't that the last place you would expect to find the Son of God?

Had we been planning Jesus' birth, we likely would have had him born in the palace of a king and arrayed in royal purple. A woman from the ranks of royalty would have been his mother. And his birthplace—Rome, or at least Jerusalem, the ancient capital of Israel, the site of the holy temple. Not Bethlehem, so "little" among Judah's thousands (Mic. 5:2). And we would have had the message sung to the Pharisees and Sadducees, the priests and Levites, not the shepherds.

Just before Jesus' public ministry began, he faced the temptations in the wilderness. Those temptations—to turn stones into bread, to jump from the pinnacle of the temple, to worship Satan for the sake of an earthly kingdom—were temptations to look out first for himself. They were temptations to find power and glory the way we often think power and glory are found. He could have gained the allegiance of people with an offer of daily bread. He could have dazzled the crowds with spectacular signs, such as jumping off the temple. He could have ruled by force. But he knew the lesson of history: those kingdoms will crumble. His temptations demonstrate once again the lesson of Jesus' self-emptying.

All through his ministry we find him among the lowly, the oppressed, the sorrowing, the ill, the lonely. And we hear him saying, "As you did it to one of the least of these my brethren, you did it to me" (Matt. 25:40). His entire life was of one piece—humility and service.

Then, on a low hill outside of an old city wall, a small crowd mills around a cross. There are hard breathing and excruciating pain. And mocking laughter and the dull thud of a hammer. Then an uneasy silence, and a voice, so dry and pained: "Father, forgive. . . . "

Winning Our Love

There is a legend of a prince who, on business in a poor section of town, saw a young girl. She was beautiful and he fell in love with her. He had a problem: How could a prince win the love of a peasant girl? There were several alternatives. Being a prince, he could say the word and she would be brought to the palace and made to marry him. That would not win her love. He could go to her and say, "I love you; will you marry me?" Maybe she would, but one might marry a prince for reasons other than love. He decided to lay aside his princely clothing. He moved into the neighborhood, took a job as a carpenter, worked hard during the day. At night he moved among the people, trying to get to know them, to understand them, to love them. In this process, he met the girl and was able to win her love. He did it by going where she was.

This is what God has done. In Christ he has come where we are. "Though he was rich, yet for your sake he became poor" (II Cor. 8:9). God sent "his own Son in the likeness of sinful flesh" (Rom. 8:3). During his human life Jesus cried aloud and wept "to him who was able to save him from death" (Heb. 5:7). "The Word became flesh and dwelt among us" (John 1:14).

At God's Right Hand

Yet, this is not the end of the story. If it were we might think of God as powerless in the presence of our agony and struggles. If he could only share our pain with no power to overcome it, we would have no reason to believe that the future is good.

But the good news is not only that he emptied himself and came to be born in a manger. It is that the very One who looks helpless on the cross is the One who is at God's right hand. He relinquished his prerogatives as God's equal, but God has decreed that every knee shall bend and that every tongue shall openly confess that Jesus Christ is Lord.

We are back to the question of ideals and models. What desire shapes your life? Is it the film and television model of those who look for power by destroying and belittling others? Or is it the story of Jesus Christ?

For Christians, the story of the cradle and the throne is not simply to entertain. It is meant to present us with a new model. "Have this mind among yourselves, which you have in Christ Jesus" (Phil. 2:5). Here is the key to real power in our lives. We can turn from selfishness and conceit (Phil. 2:3) and find our victory in following the One who emptied himself.

The way you become a Christian is such a beautiful, simple portrayal of what Christianity is all about. You begin with belief—childlike trust. And turn from selfish power-seeking toward a new purpose for life through repentance. You humbly submit to have your body buried in water as Jesus was buried in the tomb. You are raised from baptism to follow the example of the Servant-King.

The Jordan River

17 The Jordan River

Of the world's many great rivers, the Jordan is certainly one of the most famous. While it is neither as large as many of the others, nor as significant in producing power, nor as important for commerce, it has been of great interest to millions of people through thousands of years. The Great Rift, the deepest continental depression on earth, stretches from Syria to Africa. Central to the depression is the Jordan River Valley. The Dead Sea, some fifty-three miles long and eleven miles wide, occupies the deepest part of the rift.

Sources of the Jordan

Four sources found in the watershed of Mount Hermon form the Jordan River. The first stream begins in Banias, named after the pagan god Pan, and issues from a cave as a full-blown river. Beginning at the foot of Mount Hermon some 1,200 feet above sea level it is only six miles long. The Springs of Leddan, about four miles west of Banias, form the second source of the Jordan. The third river begins on the west slopes of Mount Hermon at about 1,700 feet above sea level and is known as the Hasbani. The fourth source is the river Bareighit which contains a beautiful waterfall. With the junction of the four sources the Jordan River flows seven miles before entering into what was formerly Lake Huleh, before it was drained some years ago. Only a marshy area remains today. Reeds, bulrushes, high grass, and papyrus flourish in the area, which is some 230 feet above sea level. The Jordan travels ten more miles to the Sea of Galilee which is 690 feet below sea level, dropping more than 900 feet in that short distance. The Sea of Galilee is about thirteen miles long and eight miles wide at its widest point.

The air distance between the Sea of Galilee and the Dead Sea is only sixty-five miles, but the meandering Jordan travels 135 miles between them. The Jordan drops 600 feet in its trip down the valley, from Galilee's 690 feet below sea level to the Dead Sea's 1292 feet below sea level. The average width of the riverbed is about ninety-eight feet, while the depth ranges from three to ten feet. The valley ranges in width from three to fourteen miles. During flood times, the Jordan swells to a width of one-half mile in certain areas.

The Jordan Valley

As the river approaches the Dead Sea, the Jordan Valley gradually develops into several levels. The lowest level, next to the river, is what the Arabs call the Zor. It has thickets of tamarisk, willow, poplar, cane, and reeds. Scripture calls this "the jungle of the Jordan." It is utterly desolate and nearly impenetrable. This jungle was the habitat of the lion in ancient times but none have been seen in recent years. On either side of the Zor are the Qattarah hills, desolate badlands of ash-gray marl appearing in different shapes and forms. The next level is the Ghor, forming the highest part of the valley. It is often a fertile area. In the area immediately south of the Sea of Galilee there are numerous kibbutzim with lush irrigated fields, fine orchards, and artificial fish ponds.

Several rivers join the Jordan on its trip between the two seas. The Yarmuk joins from the east just a few miles south of Galilee and nearly doubles the size of the Jordan. Near Beth-shan on the west the Jalud (Harod) joins the Jordan. Still later, the Jurm, Yabis, Kufrinjeh, Rajib, and Jabbok enter from the east while the Farah and Qelt join from the west. Nelson Glueck, the archaeologist, found over seventy sites in the valley, indicating a widespread occupation in ancient times, with the more prominent cities being Adam, Succoth, Jabesh-gilead, Pella, Jericho, and Gilgal.

The Jalud River entering near Beth-shan was the river where Gideon had his men drink so that he could determine which ones to choose for his army (Judg. 7:1-8). Even though some six bridges cross the Jordan today (not all are open), the first bridges on the river did not appear until Roman times. Remains of a Roman bridge can be seen at Damiya. There were also some fifty-four fords on the Jordan which were used in ancient times. The Jericho police searched for the Israelite spies all the way to the fords (Josh. 2:7). Jacob crossed the "ford of the Jabbok" (Gen. 32:22) and David crossed the "fords of the wilderness" (II Sam. 15:28; 17:16, 22).

Biblical Events

The Jordan River is mentioned some 195 times in the Bible with the bulk of the occurrences in the Old Testament. When Abraham suggested that he and Lot separate because of the strife between their herdsmen, Lot "saw that the Jordan valley was well watered everywhere" (Gen. 13:10) and so chose that area. It was at the Jabbok that Jacob wrestled with the angel (Gen. 32:22-31). The Israelites, waiting to enter the Promised Land, "encamped in the plains of Moab beyond the Jordan at Jericho" (Num. 22:1). The tribes were numbered as they camped by the Jordan (Num. 26) and not a man who had left Egypt was counted except for Moses, Joshua, and Caleb (vv. 63-65).

The Book of Joshua opens with God's command to Joshua, "Moses my servant is dead; now therefore arise, go over this Jordan, you and all this people, into the land which I am giving to them" (Josh. 1:2). When the people were prepared, the priests led the way across the Jordan, carrying the ark of the covenant. As they dipped their feet into the water, the water stopped flowing "and rose up in a heap far off, at Adam . . . and the people passed over opposite Jericho" (Josh. 3:16). Joshua ordered each of twelve men to take a stone out of the Jordan and set it up as a memorial. When the people had passed, the priests who were standing in the Jordan and holding the ark of the covenant came out of the dry river and the waters returned (Josh. 4:1-18). The stones were set up at Gilgal (Josh. 4:19-24).

Before crossing the Jordan and dwelling near the brook Cherith where he was fed by the ravens, Elijah warned Ahab about the coming drought (I Kings 17:1-7). Leaving Jericho, Elijah and Elisha came to the Jordan. "Then Elijah took his mantle, and rolled it up, and struck the water, and the water was parted to the one side and to the other, till the two of them could go over on dry ground" (II Kings 2:8). On the other side, Elisha asked Elijah for a double measure of his spirit and witnessed as a chariot and horses of fire took the old prophet into the whirlwind and on into heaven. Taking his companion's mantle, Elisha went back to the Jordan and parted the river to walk across (II Kings 2:9–14). A Syrian named Naaman came to Elisha to be healed of his leprosy. The prophet directed him to wash seven times in the Jordan River and promised that he would then be clean (II Kings 5:1–14).

Jesus' Baptism

John the Baptist preached in the wilderness of Judea and baptized in the river Jordan (Matt. 3:5, 6; Mark 1:5; Luke 3:3; John 1:28). Jesus came from Galilee from the city of Nazareth and requested that John baptize him in the Jordan River. After the immersion of Jesus, the Spirit of God descended upon Jesus and a voice from heaven spoke, saying, "This is my beloved Son, with whom I am well pleased" (Matt. 3:13–17; Mark 1:9–11; Luke 3:21–23). At least seven sites along the Jordan have been claimed as the location where Jesus was baptized; however, it cannot be known with certainty where that important event took place. John 3:23 indicates that John was baptizing at Aenon near Salim. The name *Aenon* means springs, though it is not known exactly which springs.

Jesus was often in the area of the Jordan during his public ministry. When he was at Jericho and at Caesarea Philippi, he was near the Jordan and may have crossed it on those trips. On his trips from Galilee to Jerusalem, if he bypassed ancient Samaria as many did, he may very well have traveled down the Jordan Valley (Matt. 19:1; Mark 10:1).

Archaeologists have added interesting information concerning the history of the Jordan. For example, skeletal remains of elephants and rhinoceroses have been found near Lake Huleh, while Kathleen Kenyon has shown that Jericho is one of the oldest cities in the world, claiming that she has found evidence that dates it to the eighth millennium B.C.

The Jordan River, as do many other of the sites where Jesus is known to have lived and worked, stirs the emotions of the traveler deeply. The Jordan has been mentioned prominently in sermons and also in songs. Among the latter are such songs as "On Jordan's Stormy Banks," "Jordan River, I'm Bound to Cross," and "There Is a Sea Which Day by Day." The Jordan has also been used to illustrate the life of a human being. Beginning small and fresh, it moves with great haste ultimately to bitterness and death. It has also been used as a figure of death, "passing over Jordan" suggesting the end of this earthly life and entrance into the life to come. All in all, it has been one of the most significant rivers in all history.

Jesus' Baptism and Ours
Batsell Barrett Baxter

One of the most beautiful pictures in the life of Jesus had as its setting the Jordan River, not far from where we now stand. It was here that Jesus was baptized. The scene is a beautiful one, for the Jordan is a lovely river of fresh water flowing along with deliberate speed to the sea below. There are trees growing along its banks and it affords a green oasis between arid lands on either side.

Here is the way that Matthew described that significant event in the long ago when Jesus was baptized in this river, "Then came Jesus from Galilee to the Jordan to John, to be baptized by him. John would have prevented him, saying, 'I need to be baptized by you, and do you come to me?' But Jesus answered him, 'Let it be so now; for thus it is fitting for us to fulfil all righteousness.' Then he consented. And when Jesus was baptized, he went up immediately from the water, and behold, the heavens were opened and he saw the Spirit of God descending like a dove, and alighting on him; and lo, a voice from heaven, saying, 'This is my beloved Son, with whom I am well pleased'" (Matt. 3:13–17).

Christ Our Example

Our Lord was baptized. Even though he was sinless, he insisted that he be baptized. He said, "Thus it is fitting for us to fulfil all righteousness." Surely if he submitted to baptism, we should. Over one hundred times in the New Testament the word *baptism* (or its cognates) appears. Those who believed in Christ were baptized in order to become Christians (Acts 2:38). Baptism *must* be important. It *is* important because of its deep symbolic meaning. But even if none of this were true, it would still be important because our Lord told us to baptize.

What is baptism? The Greek word is the word *baptizo*. We do not translate it into English; rather, we transliterate it. We simply pick it up out of the Greek and bring it over and print it in our language. So *baptizo* in the Greek is *baptize* in the English. The Greek lexicons are almost unanimous in defining it as meaning "to dip, to plunge, to immerse."

In Paul's writings to the Romans he gives us an idea of what baptism is supposed to mean. It is a beautiful act in which each follower of Christ does, symbolically, what Christ did for all mankind when he died, and was buried, and then was raised from the grave. In Romans we read, "Do you not know that all of us who have been baptized into Christ Jesus were baptized into his death? We were buried therefore with him by baptism into death, so that as Christ was raised from the dead by the glory of the Father, we too might walk in newness of life. For if we have been united with him in a death like his, we shall certainly be united with him in a resurrection like his" (Rom. 6:3-5).

Deep Spiritual Meaning

Baptism has meaning, deep spiritual meaning. Symbolically, the old sinful man is dead. We go through the act of being buried to signify that we have turned away from sin. Then a moment later we are raised to walk in a new kind of life, a life with Christ, a life of righteousness. It is a definite, concrete act, back toward which we can look for the rest of our days. It is an act that marks the dividing line between the old man of the world and the new man of God. Christ was baptized, not because he was a sinner, but as an example for us. We are baptized because we are sinners and in baptism we meet the cleansing blood of Christ which takes away our sins.

Baptism is the culminating act of being born anew. I do not say that baptism is being born again; I say it is a part of being born again. Being "born anew," the figure of speech that our Lord used in John 3, begins when his Word, the Bible, is preached and the message falls into some honest and sincere heart. The Word takes hold of the heart. After a while it creates belief in that heart; belief grows until one day there comes the hour of birth—baptism. Being born again is not something which happens in a moment. It is a process which starts when God's Word is preached and culminates when a person is baptized into Christ. The Lord's figures of speech are always beautiful and always rich in meaning. Being born again reminds us of a baby as it breaks forth into a world that it has never seen. When a person is baptized and comes from the water, he has been born again spiritually. That is what baptism means.

It's for All of Us

When Jesus had gone back to heaven and when Pentecost had come, Peter stood up and preached the first great sermon of the Christian era. He preached of Christ; when he had concluded the sermon, those who had heard "were cut to the heart, and said to Peter and the rest of the apostles, 'Brethren, what shall we do?' And Peter said to them, 'Repent, and be baptized every one of you in the name of Jesus Christ for the forgiveness of your sins; and you shall receive the gift of the Holy Spirit'' (Acts 2:37, 38).

As we turn through the pages of the Book of Acts we find one example of conversion after another. One of the clearest is found in Acts 8. It is the story of the nobleman from Ethiopia. There comes a point in the story where we read: ''And as they went along the road they came to some water, and the eunuch said, 'See, here is water! What is to prevent my being baptized?' And Philip said, 'If you believe with all your heart, you may.' And he replied, 'I believe that Jesus Christ is the Son of God.' And he commanded the chariot to stop, and they both went down into the water, Philip and the eunuch, and he baptized him. And when they came up out of the water, the Spirit of the Lord caught up Philip; and the eunuch saw him no more, and went on his way rejoicing'' (Acts 8:36-39).

Later on, in the Book of Acts, we read the story of the conversion of Saul of Tarsus. Acts 22:12-16 tells of the moment when God's preacher Ananias arrived to tell Saul what he must do. For three days Saul had been fasting and praying, after he had come to believe that Jesus was not an impostor, but the Christ. These are the preacher's words: ''And now why do you wait? Rise and be baptized, and wash away your sins, calling on his name'' (v. 16). Leafing through other books of the New Testament we find in I Peter 3:21 these words: ''Baptism, which corresponds to this, now saves you, not as a removal of dirt from the body but as an appeal to God for a clear conscience, through the resurrection of Jesus Christ.''

Born Anew

Finally, recall the words of Jesus from one of the early chapters of the Book of John. To Nicodemus Jesus said, ''Truly, truly, I say to you, unless one is born of water and the Spirit, he cannot enter the kingdom of God'' (John 3:5). These are only a few of the great passages in the New Testament which mention baptism. There are more than a hundred such passages.

Do not misunderstand what I have said to mean that baptism is the primary thing in becoming a Christian. It is one of several. I would not want you to understand that we earn salvation by being baptized. Salvation is a gift. Paul wrote to the Ephesians, ''For by grace you have been saved through faith; and this is not your own doing, it is the gift of God—not because of works, lest any man should boast'' (Eph. 2:8, 9). While salvation is his gift, God has laid down some conditions upon which he will give the gift. Faith is one of those conditions: without belief in Christ one will not be saved. Baptism is another condition: without giving oneself to the Lord in baptism, one does not have the promise of eternal life in heaven. Our Lord led the way by being baptized in order to fulfill all righteousness. We, as humble followers of our Lord, are baptized in order to obey his commandments and in order to be saved.

If you have never been baptized do not put it off longer. Out of your love for God, out of your love for Christ, do it immediately.

The Sea of Galilee

18 The Sea of Galilee

One of the most beautiful and most appealing bodies of water in the world is the Sea of Galilee. The earliest name for this freshwater lake was Chinnereth, a name which dates back to the fifteenth century B.C. The name is thought to mean "harp" and was probably chosen because the lake is harp-shaped or pear-shaped. Later the name *Gennesaret* was applied to the lake (Luke 5:1), and the New Testament also calls this body of water the Sea of Tiberias (John 6:1; 21:1). The best-known name, however, is the Sea of Galilee, a word which means "ring" or "circle."

The Sea of Galilee is 690 feet below sea level, thirteen miles long, eight miles at its widest, and some thirty-two miles in circumference. The greatest depth is about 170 feet. The lake is supplied by springs, but the majority of its water comes from the Jordan River, which enters on the north and leaves on the south. The waters are collected from Mount Hermon and flow through the Huleh marsh before reaching Galilee.

The Sea of Galilee is about sixty miles north of Jerusalem. The mountains of Galilee rise to the northwest to heights of about 4,000 feet above sea level while the hills immediately to the east and west of the lake rise 1,500 to 2,000 feet above sea level. This means that the drop from the heights to the lake surface is over 2,600 feet in some places. Several hot mineral springs are found on the southwest shore of the lake.

Concerning Galilee, Josephus wrote, "The land is everywhere so rich in soil and pasturage and produces such variety of trees that even the most indolent are tempted by these facilities to devote themselves to agriculture." Wheat, barley, figs, grapes, pomegranates, olives, and numerous vegetables grow well in the area because of the hot climate and the abundant water. The region around Galilee was known for its agriculture, dyeing, tanning, boat-building, fishing, and curing of fish. Over forty different kinds of fish are found in the Sea of Galilee.

Some maintain that in New Testament times, no fewer than nine cities grew up on the shore of the lake, each with a population of at least fifteen thousand. Ruins of palaces, hippodromes, theaters, and baths built by the Greeks and Romans also testify to the ample population in ancient times. During our visit, on a beautiful cloudless evening we were able to stand on the porch of the Chinnereth Hotel, which extends to the water's edge, and to observe the lights of fifteen different villages clustered about the lake. None of these, however, has a population even approaching fifteen thousand.

Situated in a deep valley protected on the east and west by high mountains, the lake is a likely place for storms. The cool air masses from the mountain heights rush down the steep slopes to the surface of the lake, causing the waters of the lake to erupt with sudden violent force. Such tempests are not infrequent and are extremely dangerous to small craft.

Christ and Galilee

The word *Galilee* appears in the Bible a total of seventy-three times, sometimes referring to the region and at other times to the lake. The Old Testament is virtually silent about the sea; but as a result of Jesus' moving his ministry to Capernaum after leaving Nazareth, the Sea of Galilee is very prominently mentioned in the New Testament.

When walking along the edge of the sea on one occasion, Jesus saw Peter, Andrew, James, and John mending their nets after a night of unsuccessful fishing. He borrowed one of the boats and from it preached a sermon to the people who stood or sat upon the sloping bank of the sea. Afterward, he called these men to be full-time disciples. They left their boats and followed him (Luke 5:1-11).

It was on one of the mountains overlooking the sea that Jesus preached the Sermon on the Mount (Matt. 5-7). It was around the shore of the sea that he presented his several parables concerning the kingdom of heaven (Matt. 13). Much of Christ's most meaningful teaching was done in his many travels about the Sea of Galilee.

Some ten of the thirty-three recorded miracles of Jesus took place around this beautiful body of water. On its shores he fed the five thousand (Matt. 14:13-23; Mark 6:30-46; Luke 9:10-17; John 6:1-15). At a later time he fed the four thousand (Matt. 15:32-39; Mark 8:1-9). At another time, when the disciples had rowed some three or four miles and the sea became very violent, Jesus walked upon the sea to them and then stilled the tempest (Matt. 14:22-36; Mark 6:47-56; John 6:16-21). Jesus also healed many who were ill, including Peter's wife's mother, the man with palsy who was let down through the roof of the house, and others who were deaf, blind, and lame.

It was also in this same area that Jesus sifted the multitude, offering them spiritual bread rather than the loaves and the fishes which they sought, ultimately finding that the multitudes turned away, leaving only the apostles with him (John 6). After his death and resurrection Jesus again visited the Sea of Galilee; he appeared one morning to seven of his disciples and prepared for them a breakfast of fish (John 21).

Herod and the Jews

Until his death in 4 B.C., Herod the Great, as king of Judea and governor of Galilee, ruled the territory which included the Sea of Galilee. His son Antipas took that part of his father's domain which included the sea and moved his capital to Tiberias. Antipas ruled the area during the entire life of Jesus, except for the first few years. When the Jews were expelled from Jerusalem in A.D. 70, the center of Jewish scholarship was transferred to Galilee. The Mishnah and the Talmud were later produced in Tiberias. The area was the home of the Masoretes, who worked on the Old Testament text. The Sanhedrin also was transferred to Tiberias.

Tiberias is mentioned only in John 6:23, where it is described as a place where boats following Jesus came from. The city was named in honor of Tiberius Caesar (A.D. 14-37) and was built by Herod Antipas (4 B.C.-A.D. 39). The city is located about five miles northwest of the place where the Jordan flows out of the Sea of Galilee. Herod's city included a stadium, and other Roman buildings constructed over ancient tombs. Some scholars suggest that the city had no Jewish population, but the presence of a place of prayer and the later prevalence of Jews in the area may suggest that Jews lived in the city at the time of Jesus. The tombs of Maimonides (twelfth-century Spanish-Jewish scholar) and of Rabbi Akiva (second-century scholar) are in the area. About three miles north of Tiberias is the site of Migdal, the ancient Magdala, the home village of Mary Magdalene.

Bethsaida is located on the northern shore of the lake. The word means "house of the fisher" or "house of the hunter." Bethsaida is called a city in Luke 9:20 and John 1:44, and a village in Mark 8:26. Philip, Andrew, and Peter were from Bethsaida though Peter had a house in Capernaum also (Matt. 8:14).

Altogether, the Sea of Galilee is one of the most rewarding experiences in a visit to Israel. We could be very sure that we were in the exact area where Jesus lived and worked. Cities change, but lakes and mountains remain much the same through the centuries. As we read again many of the familiar Scriptures concerning Christ's life and work, we felt very near to the Lord. Fishing is still a major activity on the sea and is done in much the same way as it was done in New Testament times.

"Put Out into the Deep"

Batsell Barrett Baxter

Sitting here, looking out over the Sea of Galilee, I am especially reminded of a passage of Scripture in the fifth chapter of the Gospel of Luke. Evidently in early morning Jesus came by a certain section of the lake where some fishermen were mending their nets, after having fished all night without success. The men had earlier come to know Jesus somewhat, but in this particular text we find that crucial moment when their lives made a 180° turn to move in a different direction.

But let us read the story from the opening verses of Luke 5: "While the people pressed upon him to hear the word of God, he was standing by the lake of Gennesaret. And he saw two boats by the lake; but the fishermen had gone out of them and were washing their nets. Getting into one of the boats, which was Simon's, he asked him to put out a little from the land. And he sat down and taught the people from the boat" (vv. 1–3). Let me interrupt here to say that we have no record in Luke concerning the content of the sermon preached. As important as Jesus' message must have been, its significance on this occasion was overshadowed by the event that was about to take place.

They Left Everything and Followed Him

We continue our reading, "And when he had ceased speaking, he said to Simon, 'Put out into the deep and let down your nets for a catch.' And Simon answered, 'Master, we toiled all night and took nothing! But at your word I will let down the nets.' And when they had done this, they enclosed a great shoal of fish; and as their nets were breaking, they beckoned to their partners in the other boat to come and help them. And they came and filled both the boats, so that they began to sink. But when Simon Peter saw it, he fell down at Jesus' knees, saying, 'Depart from me, for I am a sinful man, O Lord.' For he was astonished, and all that were with him, at the catch of fish which they had taken; and so also were James and John, sons of Zebedee, who were partners with Simon." Then, the story comes to its climax as Jesus says to Simon, " 'Do not be afraid; henceforth you will be catching men.' And when they had brought their boats to land, they left everything and followed him" (vv. 4–11).

Isn't that an impressive story? Here are four open-minded, rough fishermen who, when they come into intimate contact with Jesus, change the direction of their lives and follow him. The miraculous catch of fish is significant of course, for it convinced these men that Jesus was no ordinary man, but their Lord. However, the miracle was only a means to an end. The heart of this story is that some ordinary men change the direction of their lives and, to use the expression Christ used, "put out into the deep . . . ."

The Deeps of Life

Peter and the others had been living in the shallows of life—fishing, earning a living, establishing households, and all the rest of the things that people normally do. Of course, these are not bad things. They are just ordinary things. Then, when Jesus came into their lives, at first they literally "put out into the deep," and then symbolically "put out into the deep" with their whole lives. They left their boats and followed Jesus. Now, instead of the routine responsibilities of each day, the trivial conversations, the ordinary affairs of life, they were exposed daily to the spiritual influences which emanated from the Son of God. Three-and-one-half years later they were changed men. It was Peter, the humble fisherman, who was chosen to preach the first great full-gospel sermon on Pentecost, the day the church began. Having followed Jesus, he made his life count for something, while the hundreds of other Galilean fishermen are forgotten. The same was true of his fishing companions, Andrew, James, and John. From the shallows of life they moved out into the deep and moved on to greatness.

Do you remember the story in Acts 4 which tells of the arrest of Peter and

John by the Sanhedrin, the ruling body of the people? They were charged not to preach any more in the name of Jesus, to which they responded, "Whether it is right in the sight of God to listen to you rather than to God, you must judge; for we cannot but speak of what we have seen and heard" (Acts 4:19, 20). A little later Peter said, "We must obey God rather than men" (Acts 5:29). In this story there is this very revealing sentence, "Now when they saw the boldness of Peter and John, and perceived that they were uneducated, common men, they wondered; and they recognized that they had been with Jesus" (Acts 4:13). Following Jesus made a difference then, and makes a difference now.

The Shallows of Life

So many people live their lives in the shallows. Ultimately their lives add up to several thousand days spent in growing up, getting married, having children, buying a house, and a lot of other things: clothes, food, cars, gadgets, and all the rest. Usually there are involved the washing of mountains of dishes and heaps of soiled clothes, many mowings of the lawn, and the multitude of other ordinary things which go to make up daily living. Don't misunderstand me. All of these things are wholesome and fine and necessary, but they are not enough by themselves. There must be a higher center in life than these supporting activities. That is where Christ comes in.

There are shallows of thinking. So many people spend their time reading the current newspapers and magazines, which produce little that is of lasting significance. The great books of the world, containing the great ideas of thinking men through the ages, are all but unread. The great music that has lived on through generations is often almost unheard.

There are also shallows of social life. When men and women get together they talk of the weather, politics, sports, and the latest fads.

Spiritual Dimensions of Life

On the other hand, life can have its deeps. Thoughtful people seek for the reasons behind their existence, the why and wherefore of life. They ask questions like, "From where do we come?" "Why are we here?" "Where are we going?" To these deepest questions of life our political leaders, our business and industrial leaders, our educators, and our scientists have few answers. Only God can answer these deeper questions about the real meaning of life, the identity of man, the purpose for his living, and his eternal destiny.

God tells us that we are made in his own image, meaning that we are eternal spirits, not mere animals (Gen. 1:27). He tells us that our purpose in being is twofold: We are to love God and to serve our fellow men. God also tells us that our eternal destiny is a home in heaven with him, if we will only accept his invitation and let him guide our lives to that eternal destiny. It is in religion that we find the deeps of life.

It all begins when we hear the gospel of Christ preached and believe in him as the divine Son of God. Like the disciples of old, when we rearrange our lives so that Christ becomes the center, we turn away from our past sins, we confess Jesus as Lord, and then we "put on Christ," to use an expression of Paul. The passage is Galatians 3:27, which reads, "For as many of you as were baptized into Christ have put on Christ." Baptism is that ultimate act of obedience which brings us to the place where God adds us to his family, the church. Our new life in Christ is filled with the deeps of prayer, the deeps of Bible reading, the deeps of love for all mankind, and the deeps of trust in God in all our affairs. With Paul, we can have the confidence that we need not worry about anything. As he put it, "Have no anxiety about anything, but in everything by prayer and supplication with thanksgiving let your requests be made known to God. And the peace of God, which passes all understanding, will keep your hearts and your minds in Christ Jesus" (Phil. 4:6, 7).

May we "put out into the deep" with our lives, following Jesus wherever he leads! May we build our houses upon the solid rock of eternal truth which he taught and lived!

Tiberias

19 Tiberias

The city of Tiberias is located on the western shore of the Sea of Galilee where the coastline curves inward. Beautiful hotels afford rooms overlooking the sea. Looking southeast five miles one can see the outlet of the sea into the Jordan River. Nearly three miles north and a bit west is Magdala, located at the center point of the western coast. Across the lake some five miles to the north is Capernaum (visible because of the curvature of the coast); at the northern tip of the lake the site of Bethsaida is visible. In the far north Mount Hermon rises with its winter snowcap which supplies the water to the Jordan. Across the sea to the east are Gergesa, Hippos, and the mountains of the Golan Heights, with the kibbutz En Gev at the base.

Today Tiberias is the hub and capital of Galilee. It is nearly 700 feet below sea level and lies inside a great bowl of mountains.

The Sea of Galilee is five-and-a-half miles wide at Tiberias. Its greatest breadth is eight miles and its length is thirteen miles. A journey around the lake is some thirty-two miles in distance. The lake is about 170 feet deep at its lowest point.

The mountains immediately to the west rise 1,364 feet above the lake and block off the welcome western breeze. The hot sulphur springs in the area add to the heat. The climate is semitropical, humid, and oppressive at times.

The Founding of the City

There are two major theories concerning the date of the founding of Tiberias. Josephus mentions the founding of the city just after his discussion of the appointment of Pontius Pilate as procurator, a fact which suggests that Tiberias was founded in A.D. 25. On evidence from coins, George Adam Smith and others place the founding in the period A.D. 17–20. It may be significant that A.D. 18 was the sixtieth year of the emperor in whose honor the city was named.

Herod Antipas had ambitious plans for the city. The wall (from the shore in the north, around the city, and back to the shore in the south) was three miles long. The city included a forum and a stadium. Herod Antipas himself had a lakeside palace.

Herod Antipas located the city on Galilee to serve as capital of his tetrarchy of Galilee and Perea. The new site was more conveniently located than the old capital of Sepphoris, north of Nazareth, which he had built in 4 B.C. Both local and international roads passed through the area, making the choice even more propitious.

Josephus and the Talmud both refer to a legend that Herod Antipas built Tiberias on the site of an ancient city, including an old graveyard, making it off limits to Jewish people. However, after A.D. 135 Tiberias became a strong center of Jewish life.

The builder and founder of Tiberias, Herod Antipas, was the younger son of Malthace, one of Herod the Great's ten legal wives. He ruled Galilee and Perea from 4 B.C. until A.D. 39. His father, Herod the Great, who had ruled the entire land for thirty-seven years (40–4 B.C.), was hated by the Jews as a half-foreigner and friend of the Romans. His kingdom was divided among his sons, with Philip ruling the territory north and east of the Sea of Galilee, and Archelaus ruling Judea, Samaria, and Idumea. Archelaus' rule faced insurrection and he was soon banished (A.D. 6), with his territory being put directly under the rule of Roman governors.

Herod Antipas is remembered for his involvement in the imprisonment and death of John the Baptist (Matt. 14:3-12). He was also the one who tried Jesus in Jerusalem (Luke 23:6-12).

Tiberias in the New Testament

Tiberias, as a city, is mentioned only in John 6:23. The text reports that following the feeding of the multitude east of the sea (the disciples and Jesus having already left), some small Tiberian boats appeared at the eastern beach. The people left in them to go to Capernaum to find Jesus.

Since Tiberias did not exist during Jesus' childhood, and was populated with a large number of Gentiles, Jesus may not have visited the city at all. His ministry centered on Jewish people. Of the nine towns that once lined the shores of the Sea of Galilee, the smallest one with a population of about fifteen thousand (according to Josephus), only Tiberias has survived to the twentieth century.

Tiberias in Postbiblical Times

In A.D. 66 the Jewish revolt which was to result in the destruction of Jerusalem broke out. Many of the Gentile residents of Tiberias were sympathetic to the Jewish cause. Josephus, who was governor of Galilee at the time, destroyed the palace on the acropolis and strengthened the defenses of Tiberias. However, when Vespasian laid siege in A.D. 67, Josephus opened the gates and surrendered the city. The Jews rebelled in A.D. 132-135 and Jerusalem fell again. Tiberias then became a strong Jewish center. The Sanhedrin moved from Sepphoris to Tiberias in about A.D. 150. Shortly afterward schools of rabbinic study were established there. The Talmud reports there were thirteen synagogues at Tiberias.

Rabbi Judah (A.D. 135-219) copied down the oral tradition, which had become massive by his day, and organized it into sections. The result was the Mishnah. It has six orders which are further divided into tractates which have chapters and paragraphs. The work totals 524 chapters. As soon as the Mishnah (itself a commentary on the Old Testament) was finished, scholars began to study it and write down their own comments, which came to be called the Gemara. The Gemara, a commentary on the commentary, was produced in Tiberias by the end of the fourth century. The Mishnah and Gemara are together the Talmud, which means "teaching." The Palestinian Talmud, then, emanated from Tiberias.

Of the several famous Jewish leaders who lived in Tiberias, Maimonides was among the most influential. Born in Cordova, Spain, he lived from 1135 to 1204, and, according to tradition, was buried in Tiberias. He was a Talmudist, philosopher, and physician. According to some, he was the last product of the Golden Age of Spanish Jewry.

The Master's Men

Harold Hazelip

Every four years we elect a President of the United States. Between the election and the inauguration, nothing fascinates the news media quite so much as the question, Who will fill the important positions? Who will be the new Secretary of State? Attorney General? Secretary of Defense? Decisions in these areas will set the tone for the next years.

The names of the twelve apostles appear in all four Gospels. These were the people who were to represent Jesus both during his ministry and after his ascension. What kind of people were they? The New Testament does not give lengthy descriptions of them, but it provides some fascinating glimpses into their personalities and characters.

Those "Ordinary" Disciples

The Gospels record glaring failures in the lives of these disciples. Often they did not understand their mission. They failed Jesus at Gethsemane and at Calvary. Yet they went on to tell his story.

As we read the accounts of their successes and failures, we remember that Jesus still uses ordinary people to do his work. And we still fail him. But through our mixture of success and failure, his work goes on.

We are impressed by the ordinariness of Jesus' men. If we had wanted to choose twelve people at the beginning of a great movement, our list might look very different from the list in the four Gospels. There are no "superstars." There are no great orators; there is no "brain trust." They came mostly from Galilee—the most provincial and backward section of a very obscure country. They belonged to the class of craftsmen—we might call them the lower middle class.

We know very little about most of the apostles—only an isolated statement here and there about them. Some—Thaddeus, James the son of Alphaeus, Bartholomew—are only names to us. We may assume they went their own way in serving Christ while other apostles achieved more fame. Tradition indicates that these little-known disciples helped to bring the gospel to new places—India, Egypt, Ethiopia—and perhaps they did. They certainly remind us that the work of Christ is often carried on by those who receive no headlines. As they work quietly, lives are changed.

Thomas and Andrew

There are apostles about whom we know only one significant fact. There was Thomas, who had a disturbing struggle with doubt after the cross. His faith was shaken but he did not stop meeting with the other apostles. Nor did they give up on Thomas when he showed signs of doubt. Thomas later saw Jesus and exclaimed, "My Lord and my God!" (John 20:28).

There was Andrew, the brother of Simon. He is remembered most for the ones he brought to Christ. He knew when he found Jesus that he had found a treasure worth sharing. Not only did he bring his brother Simon to Jesus, he helped to bring several Greeks a short time before the crucifixion (John 12:20-22).

Four Events with Peter

We know a great deal more about Simon Peter. He was a fisherman who left his boat and his nets when Jesus called (Mark 1:16, 17). He had a home in Capernaum. Jesus healed Peter's wife's mother, who was sick with a fever (Mark 1:29-31).

Peter was a typical Galilean. Josephus, the historian who was governor of Galilee about a generation after Christ's resurrection, describes Galileans as "ever ready to follow a leader and to begin an insurrection." Recent historical study indicates that Galileans were despised by the more educated Judeans as "country folk" with their own distinctive accents and ways.

Four significant events emerge from Simon Peter's life. He was apparently the first to realize who Jesus was and to confess him openly. At Caesarea Philippi, he confessed, "You are the Christ, the Son of the living God" (Matt. 16:16).

There followed Jesus' great promise: "And I tell you, you are Peter, and on this rock I will build my church, and the powers of death shall not prevail against it" (Matt. 16:18). Peter's name, which meant "rock," was compared with the massive bedrock foundation of the church, the foundation which Peter had just confessed: the truth that Jesus is the Son of God.

Then there was a great rebuke. Peter was shocked when Jesus announced his coming death. When Peter said, "This shall never happen to you," Jesus replied, "Get behind me, Satan!" (Matt. 16:21-23). Peter was apparently presenting the same temptation that Satan had offered in the wilderness: the way of power and glory. Jesus rejected this way for the cross.

Finally, there is the great denial. Peter denied his Lord three times on the night of the trial. He was later reunited with Jesus and recommissioned with Jesus' words, "Feed my sheep" (John 21:17).

The Sons of Zebedee

We also know a great deal about James and John. They, along with Peter, belonged to the inner circle of Jesus' friends. They were with him at crucial moments—the transfiguration and the garden of Gethsemane. James and John were men of a stormy temper. Jesus called them "sons of thunder" (Mark 3:17).

James became the first to die a martyr's death for Christ (Acts 12:2). John, according to tradition, was the only apostle to die a natural death. He is described as being carried to church in his old age where he often said, "Little children, love one another."

James and John had been so immature as to go to Jesus and ask for the best seats in the kingdom. But they grew to the point that they could endure suffering for him.

A Zealot and a Publican

Perhaps the greatest contrast among the Twelve is to be drawn between Simon the Zealot and Matthew the tax-collector. The Zealots were fanatical nationalists. Utterly devoted to the law, they detested anyone who compromised with Rome. They believed God would intervene to help them if only they would take up arms against the foreign troops.

As a country under Roman rule, Palestine was always a sleeping volcano, ready to erupt in violence. In A.D. 6, the Romans undertook a census for taxation purposes. The Zealot Movement emerged when Judas the Galilean stormed the palace of Sepphoris, three miles north of Nazareth, broke into the arsenal, armed his followers, and launched a revolution. Roman power quickly destroyed his movement and crucified hundreds of his followers. But there continued to be Zealots who despised Roman power. We know nothing of Simon the apostle except that he was a Zealot.

Another apostle, Matthew, was a tax-collector. There was no class of men in the ancient world more hated than tax-gatherers. For strict Israelites, it was right to pay tribute only to God. They barred tax-gatherers from being either witnesses or judges, even from worship (Luke 18:13). Matthew was in the service of the Romans.

Jesus invited Matthew to leave his post and follow him. The first thing Matthew did was to give a feast in his own house for the only friends he had, his fellow tax-collectors and other outcasts. When Jesus was criticized for eating in such company, he replied, "Those who are well have no need of a physician, but those who are sick; I have not come to call the righteous, but sinners to repentance" (Luke 5:27-32).

Discipleship Without Questions

Given what we know about the apostles, their work together seems almost a miracle in personal relationships. If Matthew and Simon could live in peace within the apostolic group, then there is no breach between people which cannot be healed when we love Christ. These men are not mere pictures in stained-glass windows. They were very human—a fact easy to forget when they are called "Saint Matthew" and "Saint John."

When Jesus called them, they asked no questions. They dropped everything to follow him. They did not ask where the road would end. Discipleship has no conditions. They took up his cross, broke with their own families and friends, and became totally loyal to Jesus.

The demands of discipleship are still the same. If you and I are to follow Jesus, we must deny ourselves—that's the essence of repentance—and trustingly follow him. This life begins with a death to the old, marked by a burial in baptism, and a commitment to follow him wherever he leads.

Mount of Beatitudes

20 Mount of Beatitudes

The road from Tiberias to Metula skirts the northwest corner of the Sea of Galilee. The road branches at Tabgha. A church building known as the Church of the Loaves and Fishes appears to have been erected here in the fourth century. It is thought to be the site of the miracle of the feeding of the five thousand (Matt. 14:19–21).

Nearby is the Chapel of the Primacy, erected in 1943 by the Franciscans to mark the "Feed my sheep" episode of John 21:15–17. Capernaum is two miles further down the road.

Across the road from the Chapel of the Primacy, about two-and-one-half

145

miles northeast of Tabgha, is a hill which rises some 330 feet above the sea (which is itself 690 feet below sea level). This hill is known as the Mount of Beatitudes. A round chapel was built atop the hill in 1937. Tradition indicates that Jesus presented the Sermon on the Mount here (Matt. 5–7) and that it was on this same hillside that he called his apostles. Luke records: "In these days he went out into the hills to pray; and all night he continued in prayer to God. And when it was day, he called his disciples, and chose from them twelve, whom he named apostles" (Luke 6:12, 13).

Archaeological explorations-show that the Mount of Beatitudes was uninhabited until the Byzantine period. The implication is that Jesus would have found the mountain, with its numerous scattered rocks, available for his speeches to the large crowds.

From the Mount of Beatitudes one's panoramic view extends from the second-century synagogue at Capernaum to the city of Tiberias on the hillside west of the Sea of Galilee. The Church of the Beatitudes is entered through a lovely garden of olives, cacti, and palms, and is built on a foundation of basalt. It is unusual because of its white dome which is surrounded by a colonnade of marble columns. The windows are stained glass, depicting scenes from the life of Jesus, while the walls contain quotations from the Sermon on the Mount. The shrine is octagonal in shape. This commemorates the eight Beatitudes, one of which is inscribed on each of the windows. Symbols of the seven virtues (justice, charity, prudence, faith, fortitude, hope, temperance) are represented in the pavement around the altar.

A visit to this peaceful site helps one to understand the source of a number of Jesus' illustrations. The soft slopes carpeted in springtime with flowers call to mind the lilies of the field (Matt. 6:28). The active bird life recalls the "birds of the air" (Matt. 6:26). A number of cities visible from the mount almost seem to be "set on a hill" (Matt. 5:14).

Bolt, Beranek, and Newman, Incorporated, of Cambridge, Massachusetts, the same firm which analyzed the 18½-minute gap in the key Watergate tape and experimented with rifle shots at the site of the John Kennedy assassination in Dallas, has also participated in a study of the acoustics and crowd capacity of natural theaters in Palestine. One of the test sites was the cove near Capernaum where the road is about three hundred feed from the shoreline.

The specialists determined that speaking from the center of the cove, (i.e., from about thirty feet off the shore) would provide the best situation for clear communication. One of the experimenters suggested: "It is not unlikely that Jesus and other orators of his day were aware of these aspects of speech in an amphitheater. Thus, it is possible that he chose this particular site and sat in the boat away from the sloping audience for these reasons. There is no denying that speech communication would have been quite good inside this bowl."

The experimenters also suggested that as many as seven thousand people could have assembled in this sloping area next to the sea and have clearly heard a human voice originating from the center of the cove. The bowllike shape of the area would permit the speaker to be seen from almost any angle. It is entirely conceivable that the "great crowds" which the Gospel states that Jesus spoke to could have gathered here.

Happiness Is . . .

Harold Hazelip

Benjamin Franklin tells how he once tried to attain moral perfection. He drew up a list of twelve virtues which he thought embodied the essential traits of a good life. His program was to focus his mind on one virtue each week, keeping track of each daily violation. He worked through the list, thinking that since his conscience told him what was right and what was wrong he could accomplish the good and avoid the bad.

One day he showed his list to an older man of Christian principles who gently suggested that he had omitted the virtue of humility. Franklin immediately added it. His list then read as follows: temperance, silence, order, resolution, frugality, industry, sincerity, justice, moderation, cleanliness, tranquility, chastity, and humility. These virtues reflect Franklin's homely wisdom and they help in our relations with other people. But they are very different in spiritual depth and emphasis from Jesus' Beatitudes in the Sermon on the Mount.

The Pursuit of Happiness

The Declaration of Independence makes the pursuit of happiness an inalienable right. Malcolm Muggeridge complains that the "pursuit of happiness" is responsible for a good part of the ills and miseries of the modern world. He argues that to pursue happiness as a conscious aim is the surest way to miss it altogether, that the pursuit of happiness soon resolves itself into the pursuit of pleasure—a mirage of happiness.

How does one find happiness? On the surface, happiness seems to come from satisfying every wish. So we try! We acquire things, join clubs, accept positions of honor, indulge in new pleasures—all unsuccessfully. We can't control others' actions or our environment. We satisfy one desire and another breaks out.

Let's try a different approach. The Beatitudes which Jesus gave at the beginning of his Sermon on the Mount contain the most helpful clues for happiness ever written. The people Jesus dealt with were lonely, ill, care-worn, anxious, and guilt-burdened. The rules of life he gave them were new and totally different.

Emphasis on Inner Character

He began, "Blessed are the poor in spirit, for theirs is the kingdom of heaven." Many translators prefer "happy" instead of "blessed." The danger with "happy" is that in America today, happiness may be a martini before dinner—the "happy hour"—or a large bank account or a place in the sun. Christian happiness goes deeper than this. It is more lasting.

Jesus says the happy person, the "blessed" person, is the one who is poor in spirit. We may think the proud person is to be envied, but Jesus explains, "The person is happy who realizes his dependence on God." There is a paradox here: the more righteous one really becomes, the more unworthy he realizes himself to be. Real happiness begins with an awareness of our spiritual need.

Jesus' second clue in the search for happiness is, "Blessed are those who mourn, for they shall be comforted." His words are paradoxical again: This is like saying, "How happy are the unhappy!" From a human point of view, the happy person is the one who gets as much pleasure as he can. He isn't bothered by the world's needs. Jesus insists that real happiness comes through facing up to one's own sorrows, voluntarily sharing a neighbor's pain, mourning for our sins and the sins of others.

"Blessed are the meek, for they shall inherit the earth." The world's advice is that we "look out for number one," assert ourselves, gain power. Jesus, who was "meek and lowly in heart," counsels us to be submissive to God so that we can treat others with gentleness rather than claiming recognition for self.

The fourth Beatitude is, "Blessed are those who hunger and thirst for righteousness, for they shall be satisfied." The person may appear to be happy who puts up a good front and is self-satisfied. Jesus insists that the happy person is not satisfied as he is, but craves to be more like God as a starving person craves for food. What we most long for in life determines our priorities. Jesus recommends that we long to be filled with more and more of God's kind of righteousness.

Next, Jesus said, "Blessed are the merciful, for they shall obtain mercy." The human standard may be that we give as much mercy as we receive, that we show compassion to those who are kind to us. Jesus explained that happiness comes from giving mercy whether the recipient deserves it or not. When Jesus discussed the final judgment, mercy toward our fellow man was a heavy emphasis. His story of the rich man and Lazarus and his parable of the judgment, which noted that due to the efforts of the righteous the hungry were fed and the naked were clothed, both stress compassion toward others (Luke 16:19–31; Matt. 25:31–46).

"Blessed are the pure in heart, for they shall see God." Purity of heart involves chastity, but in the teaching of Jesus, it also involves singleness of motive. Purity of heart embraces honesty, truthfulness—all of our relationships with others. Having one single purpose—a desire for a deeper relationship with the living God—is the greatest test of our sincerity.

In these six Beatitudes—poverty of spirit, mournfulness, meekness, hunger for righteousness, a merciful spirit, purity of heart—the emphasis is on our inner character. Your happiness does not depend on your outward circumstances, Jesus is saying. Instead, it arises from true dependence on God, sincere concern over the wrongs in your life or others' lives, freedom from the drive for self-recognition, a real craving for uprightness, a willingness to show mercy whether it is deserved or not, and a pure motivation for life.

Working with God

The final two Beatitudes stress a second truth about happiness. Happiness comes from active participation with God in his world. "Blessed are the peacemakers, for they shall be called sons of God." We may decide to attend to our business and allow others to settle their problems. But Jesus encourages us to take the risks involved in being peacemakers. At school, in the office, at the plant, at home, or in church, there may be tense situations. Be the kind of person who prevents strife and overcomes alienation.

Finally, Jesus said, "Blessed are those who are persecuted for righteousness' sake, for theirs is the kingdom of heaven." It is human to think that popularity determines happiness. But Jesus urges us to have the courage to stand and be counted for the right, no matter what the cost. George Bernard Shaw wrote about one of John Bunyan's characters, Valiant-for-Truth: "This is the true joy in life, the being used for a purpose recognized by yourself as a weighty one . . . the being a force of Nature instead of a feverish little clod of ailments and grievances complaining that the world will not devote itself to making you happy."

To be used by God rather than to use him, to comfort rather than to seek comfort, to give love rather than to ask for love—this is the road to happiness.

How can you be happy? In his Sermon on the Mount, Jesus has given eight characteristics of the happy person. Happiness depends on your inner spiritual state rather than your outward circumstances. And happiness comes from cooperation with God in his great purposes for mankind—a willingness to serve and suffer for Christ's sake.

In your poverty of spirit, in your mourning for your wrongdoing, turn to Jesus Christ in obedience and submission. He promised, "He who believes and is baptized will be saved; but he who does not believe will be condemned" (Mark 16:16). Try his way of life!

Synagogue Ruins in Capernaum

21 Capernaum

Although Capernaum is derived from the Aramaic *Kepar Nahum,* which means "village of Nahum," there is no proof of any relationship between this spot and the Old Testament prophet Nahum. Located on the northern shore of the Sea of Galilee, the city lies along the coast on a narrow plain with ruins covering a strip nearly a mile long. It is located some two-and-one-half miles from the point where the Jordan River enters the Sea of Galilee.

Jesus' Home Town

Capernaum is mentioned some sixteen times in the Bible, all in the Gospels. The city is first mentioned after Jesus' temptation in the wilderness; hearing that John had been arrested, Jesus left Nazareth and moved to Capernaum. The text mentions that Capernaum is by the sea and in the territory of Zebulun and Naphtali (Matt. 4:12, 13).

We are not told why Jesus, early in his ministry, left Nazareth for Capernaum. It is the only place in the Gospels where Jesus is described as being "at home" (Mark 2:1). Following the miracle at Cana and before the cleansing of the temple, Jesus, his family, and his disciples went to Capernaum to stay for a few days (John 2:12).

Some have speculated that Jesus moved his residence to the seaside city because it was larger or because several of his disciples had their homes there. It was near this place that he called the fishermen (Simon and Andrew, James and John—Matt. 4:18–22) and the tax-collector (Matthew was sitting in the Capernaum tax office—Matt. 9:9). Matthew invited the tax-collectors along with Jesus and his disciples to dinner (Matt. 9:10–13).

Biblical Events

The centurion of Capernaum asked that Jesus heal his paralyzed servant without coming to his home. Jesus did so, being amazed that the centurion had the kind of faith that he had been looking for among the Jews (Matt. 8:5–13).

On one occasion when Jesus was returning from Jerusalem, he healed the son of a nobleman in Capernaum. The dying son was healed immediately as Jesus spoke, without requiring his physical presence. It was the seventh hour when Jesus told the nobleman that his son was healed; the man's servants later confirmed that it was the same hour that the boy began to mend. This is called the second sign after Jesus came from Judea to Galilee (John 4:46–54).

Jesus preached one sermon in which he was very critical of the cities which had refused to repent at his preaching. He included Bethsaida, Chorazin, and Capernaum. He compared his "home" to Sodom, saying that if the mighty works done in Capernaum had been done in Sodom, it would still be around. He indicated that Capernaum would be brought down to Hades and that Sodom would have a better chance in judgment (Matt. 11:23, 24).

It was also at Capernaum that Jesus went to Peter's house and healed his mother-in-law, who was sick with a fever. He touched her hand and the fever went away (Matt. 8:14–17; Mark 1:29–31). It may have been just outside this house that Jesus healed many others that evening, fulfilling the words of Isaiah, "He took our infirmities and bore our diseases" (Isa. 53:4).

Early in his ministry, Jesus was teaching in the synagogue at Capernaum on the Sabbath when a man with an unclean spirit challenged him. Jesus rebuked him and took the spirit out of the man. The people were impressed with his authority (Mark 1:21–28).

A bit later, Jesus crossed the Sea of Galilee and then returned to Capernaum. The people filled the house where he was, listening to him. A paralytic, carried by four men, sought access to Jesus. When they saw the crowd, they made an opening in the roof and lowered the man into Jesus' presence. Jesus forgave his sins. Then, to establish his power with the questioning scribes, he healed the man, who took up his pallet and walked away. It was in this house in Capernaum that the people said, "We never saw anything like this," and, "We have seen strange things today" (Mark 2:12; Luke 5:26).

Jesus was speaking to a crowd in Capernaum when a ruler of the synagogue named Jairus appealed to Jesus to lay his hand on his dying daughter. As Jesus was working his way through the crowded streets of the city, a woman with a bleeding problem which had afflicted her for twelve years, seeking to be healed, touched his garment. Jesus felt power leaving him and sought her out to note that a miracle had been performed.

After meeting Jairus' servants, who said the girl was already dead, Jesus continued to the ruler's house, where he saw flute players and a noisy crowd. He told them the twelve-year-old girl was not dead but sleeping. While they laughed, Jesus put the mob outside and raised the girl with the words, "Talitha cumi" (Mark 5:41). Jesus told those present to tell no one what had happened.

After feeding the five thousand, Jesus' disciples boarded the boat for the trip to Capernaum, only to run into a storm. Jesus walked the three or four miles across the sea to their boat, frightening them in the process. They took him into the boat and the boat was immediately at land (John 6:16–21). The people who had been fed on the other side of the sea, not able to find Jesus, got into boats the next day and headed toward Capernaum. They finally found Jesus at Capernaum and asked how he happened to be there. Jesus accused them of following him because of the free food. He then delivered his discourse on the bread of life: "I am the bread of life; he who comes to me shall not hunger, and he who believes in me shall never thirst" (John 6:22–40).

Following his transfiguration, as Jesus and his disciples worked their way back from the mountain, the disciples discussed who would be the greatest. Jesus took a child of Capernaum into his arms and began a lecture on humility: "If any one would be first, he must be last of all and servant of all" (Mark 9:33–37).

Also after Jesus' return to Capernaum following the transfiguration, the tax-collectors approached Peter about the tax which Jesus owed. Peter asked Jesus about it and a discussion followed. Jesus told Peter to take his equipment and catch a fish. In its mouth would be a coin which would pay the tax for both of them. Today a delicious fish called "St. Peter's fish" is served in restaurants near the Sea of Galilee. It is so named because of its wide mouth, giving rise to the tradition that it is the kind of fish Peter caught before paying the taxes (Matt. 17:24–27).

Remains at Capernaum

The synagogue ruins are the most interesting remains for visitors to Capernaum today. The longer archaeologists investigate Capernaum, the more recent the date attached to its synagogue. It was originally dated to the first century A.D. by Charles Wilson in 1806, but the date was later moved to the second century by H. H. Kitchener, and later to the third century. Several scholars today favor a fourth-century date, though not without argument. It is possible that the present synagogue rests on the remains of the synagogue which the centurion built (Luke 7:5) and in which Jesus taught.

Extensive house building occurred in Capernaum in the first century B.C. The residential area was built in eighty-foot squares. In each square were several houses complete with courtyards. The unroofed courtyards had grinding stones, outdoor ovens, and stairways leading to the flat roofs. Fish hooks found beneath the floors suggest that this was a fishing village.

Josephus, the Jewish historian, records that he was hurt near the Jordan while on a military activity: "The horse on which I rode, and upon whose back I fought, fell into a quagmire, and threw me to the ground, and I was bruised on my wrist, and carried into a village named Cepharnome, or Capernaum." He also writes a flattering description of the area around Capernaum as a place whose "nature is wonderful as well as its beauty," whose "soil is so fruitful that all sorts of trees can grow upon it."

The shore of the Sea of Galilee has a small inlet for boats at Capernaum, making this a pleasant place to relive biblical events.

Get This Habit

Harold Hazelip

The Gospel of Luke says of Jesus, "And he came to Nazareth, where he had been brought up; and he went to the synagogue, as his custom was, on the sabbath day. And he stood up to read . . ." (Luke 4:16). Why did Jesus have the custom or habit of attending the synagogue worship?

A college student commented recently, "I went to church as a child because my parents told me to go. I had never heard any other reason, so now I don't go anymore." How many times are those sentiments repeated? What is the sense of those regular meetings of Christians, with those regular acts of worship? I can remember as an adolescent feeling the attraction of the Christian way of life, the satisfaction of fellowship with God, and at the same time finding worship services often lengthy and tedious. Have you struggled with getting ready for church, sitting with a lot of people you scarcely know, listening to readings and prayers that seem remote from your concerns, and a sermon that may not hold your attention?

Without Public Worship

What does attendance at worship have to do with the Christian life? Can one live the Christian life without being a part of the worshiping congregation? The letter to the Hebrews deals with this question.

Among the readers of this letter there was a growing temptation to neglect the assembly. Hebrews 10:25 suggests that some had already done so. We cannot be sure what had caused this neglect. Perhaps it was the result of a general apathy. Or a feeling of *superiority* to the rest of the congregation may have led these Christians away from the public worship. Or there could have been the feeling that "nothing happened" at the public assembly. Whatever the cause of this neglect of public worship, the writer considers the matter serious enough to direct his readers' attention to the subject.

His comments suggest that something happens in worship which does not depend on the impressiveness of the sermon or the singing. We also conclude that attendance does not simply grow out of a strict sense of duty. Worship is important because "one loving heart sets another on fire."

The reason the Bible says so little about attending public worship seems to be that no one in those days would ever raise the question. In the Old Testament and in the young New Testament church, the believer was never on his own. He was incorporated in Israel—the people of God—in the Old Testament, and his private prayer was always enriched and supported by the common worship at the temple. It would never occur to an Israelite that he could cut himself off from the people of the covenant and develop a religion of his own.

Nor would the Christian have thought of cutting himself loose from the body. Can a soldier refuse the obligations and discipline of the army and go it alone?

Why Go to Church?

There are five reasons we should cultivate the habit Jesus had of attending the public worship of God regularly. First, we go to worship in order to honor and glorify God. Our English word *worship* is derived from a root which suggests "worth-ship." We ascribe supreme worth to God as our creator and sustainer.

The Book of Revelation contains some beautiful expressions of worship: "Worthy art thou, our Lord and God, to receive glory and honor and power, for thou didst create all things, and by thy will they existed and were created" (Rev. 4:11). "Worthy is the Lamb who was slain, to receive power and wealth and wisdom and might and honor and glory and blessing!" (Rev. 5:12).

Occasionally someone asks whether God needs our worship. A better question would be whether he is pleased with our worship. Suppose you have developed a rose garden with your own time, money, and effort. Every rose is already yours. But a child you love plucks a rose and brings it to you: "I picked this for you." Would you be pleased? Would you say, "They're all mine, anyhow?" You would be happy that the child's mind linked you with the beauty of nature. Jesus said the Father seeks true worshipers (John 4:23).

We participate in public worship also because of the fellowship we enjoy with other Christians. Human beings are gregarious. We need like-minded friends. Just as music needs an orchestra, learning needs schools, and baseball needs teams and leagues, Christians need congregations for fellowship with one another.

The earliest church—the congregation in Jerusalem from Pentecost forward—"devoted themselves to the apostles' teaching and fellowship, to the breaking of bread and the prayers" (Acts 2:42). We go to the praise service determined not only to get good from it ourselves but to make it easier for others to find God.

Even the memory of fellowship strengthens us. A man is far away from home, and he is sorely tempted. But he walks away, remembering the fellowship of his own home.

Power, Encouragement, and Forgiveness

A third reason to attend church services is to find strength for our weaknesses. Apart from what worship means to God, it means something important to us. As our minds contemplate the qualities of God's character, to some extent we become like him. When we express admiration for what God is, the admiration is strengthened. We tend to become like what we admire.

This complicated world is constantly challenging us. Bringing a child into the world almost takes away the breath of young parents as they realize the responsibility of rearing this child. When we have suffered a loss, a bereavement, when we are feeling the loneliness of growing older, or of serious illness, when we have disappointed ourselves and others, we need to be in God's presence in a special way.

There is spiritual power in worship. We learn to say with Paul, "I can do all things in him who strengthens me" (Phil. 4:13).

We also participate in worship to receive guidance and exhortation. The great principles of God are read and taught. The Bible contains hundreds of "case histories" selected for us by God to demonstrate the life he wants in us.

And we need exhortation because we often know the best course to take but fail to take it. Individuals do not inspire themselves to action. Love and good works are not produced in a vacuum. There is an infectious ability in the group to incite us to action.

A final reason for our public worship is that we seek forgiveness there. When all is said and done, sin is our problem. Our weak-willed, wayward hearts are so desperately undependable. There are the sins of the flesh and the more subtle sins of the spirit—our pride, envy, and hatred.

Unless we have a real sense of sin we will not appreciate the grandeur of God's offer of forgiveness. Even the gross sins—immorality, drunkenness—are "explained away" today. Only as we accept responsibility for our wrongdoing and turn to God will we be forgiven.

God is so often pictured as an indulgent, sentimental father, who pats us on the back and says, "There, there, I'm sure you didn't mean it." But in worship we are reminded of his holiness, and of the need to restore a broken relationship through his forgiveness. Paul wrote, "In him we have redemption through his blood, the forgiveness of our trespasses, according to the riches of his grace" (Eph. 1:7).

If you and I want to be among the "Christians-in-the-making," we have an obligation to worship God in his church. The life of worship begins with the obedient heart. Paul said, "If you confess with your lips that Jesus is Lord and believe in your heart that God raised him from the dead, you will be saved" Rom. 10:9). This faith, this confession, is sealed as we are baptized into Christ's body (I Cor. 12:13). If you are not regularly worshiping God with a congregation of his people, begin today.

Large Water Jugs

22 Cana

The name *Cana* probably derives from the Hebrew *kanah*, which means reed. There are two Canas mentioned in the Bible, one a village near Tyre (Josh. 19:28) and the other a village near Nazareth called "Cana in Galilee" (John 2:1; 21:2), to distinguish it from the northern city of similar name. The village in Galilee has been identified with two different places today, one a Kefr Kenna, located about four miles northeast of Nazareth, and the other a Khirbet Qana further to the north.

Kefr Kenna is some four miles northeast of Nazareth on the road to Tiberias. Many scholars believe this site was pointed out to pilgrims because it stood on the road from Nazareth to the Sea of Galilee and enabled the traveler to see another site without going much out of the way. A good spring is located in the area but there are no marshes or swamps which abound in reeds, as suggested by the name.

Located some eight or nine miles directly north of Nazareth is Khirbet Qana. Khirbet Qana is five to six miles from Kefr Kenna, and overlooks a marshy area where reeds are still plentiful. Like many other sites in Israel, it is not possible to be absolutely certain as to which is the true location. Fortunately, it does not greatly matter, for the biblical events which occurred in the area are the matters of primary significance.

The Wedding Feast

The wedding feast, especially Christ's miracle there, is the matter of greatest biblical interest. Jesus, along with his disciples and his mother, had been invited to a wedding feast in Cana of Galilee. During the feast a shortage of wine developed and Mary told her Son of the shortage. Jesus replied, "O woman, what have you to do with me? My hour has not yet come." Mary, however, told the servants of the host to do as Jesus bade them. At Jesus' suggestion six stone jars, each containing twenty to thirty gallons, were filled with water. Then Jesus miraculously turned the water into wine. This was Christ's first miracle, described by the apostle John as his first sign (John 2:1–11). As a result his disciples believed in him.

After being in Jerusalem for the Passover (John 2:13), where he cleansed the temple and talked with Nicodemus, and after baptizing in Judea, Jesus traveled back through Samaria, talking with the woman by the well; finally he arrived in Cana (John 4:46). An official from Capernaum, some sixteen miles from Khirbet Qana, hearing that Jesus had come down from Judea to Galilee, went to Cana to beg Jesus to go to Capernaum and heal his son, who was near death. After the official's earnest appeal, Jesus told him to go back home for his son would live. The man believed Jesus and began his journey home. On the way he was met by his servants who told him that his boy had been healed. He further learned that the boy began to mend at the very hour when Jesus said, "Go; your son will live." As a result of this encounter with Jesus, the official and all those in his house believed on Jesus. This was the second of Jesus' signs (John 4:46–54).

After his resurrection Jesus appeared to a number of the disciples along the Sea of Galilee. Included in the group were Peter, Thomas, the sons of Zebedee, two unnamed disciples, and Nathaniel from Cana in Galilee (John 21:1, 2).

Located in this general area, some two-and-one-half miles northeast of Nazareth, is Gath-hepher, the birthplace of Jonah the prophet (Josh. 19:13;

II Kings 14:25). The Horns of Hattin are also nearby. It was here on July 4, 1187, that the Crusaders met defeat at the hands of Saladin. Some twenty thousand believers in Christ died and another thirty thousand were taken captive. In the seventeenth century the spot was identified by some pilgrims as the Mount of Beatitudes. It is now generally thought that this was not the site of the Sermon on the Mount, but that Jesus delivered his masterful sermon on a hill closer to and overlooking the Sea of Galilee.

Joy in the Christian Life

Batsell Barrett Baxter

Sometimes people get the idea that Christianity is a sad, joyless way of life. The Puritans of Colonial days gave that impression. One prominent American was entirely alienated from religion because his family felt that way. He said that when he was a boy a pall settled over his household each Saturday evening and did not lift until Sunday was gone. Sometimes he and his sister were allowed a bit of recreation on Sunday afternoon—a solemn walk through the cemetery. Well, that is all wrong, for Christians are happy people.

Jesus once described his ministry as a wedding celebration. If Jesus' entire ministry was like a wedding feast, we are not surprised to find him enjoying the wedding at Cana. We can be grateful that this little moment of Jesus' life has been preserved, for it reminds us of Jesus' interest in the happy affairs of life. He was removed neither from the tragedies in the lives of people nor from the happier moments.

Attending a Marriage Feast

In the second chapter of the Gospel of John, we find the story about Jesus attending a marriage feast: "On the third day there was a marriage at Cana in Galilee, and the mother of Jesus was there; Jesus also was invited to the marriage, with his disciples" (vv. 1, 2). The story goes on to demonstrate that Jesus took a special interest in making sure that the celebration was a success. The wine gave out, we are told. This could have turned the wedding celebration into an embarrassment. At the encouragement of his mother, Jesus used this occasion to perform the first of his miracles, or signs. Jesus was not only present at the celebration; he turned the celebration into a great success. The story ends with the words, "This, the first of his signs, Jesus did at Cana in Galilee, and manifested his glory; and his disciples believed in him" (v. 11).

Throughout the ministry of Jesus, one of the most striking features, a feature which disturbed his opponents, was the sense of joy and celebration. Indeed, it is not accidental that in Jesus' parables of the lost sheep, the lost coin, and the prodigal son, the finale of the story always includes a celebration. In the story of the prodigal son the story ends with the killing of the fatted calf, merrymaking, and music. It is Jesus' way of saying, "I am celebrating God's lost sons who have returned." To follow Jesus is to have cause for happiness and joy.

A Religion of Joy

The religion of the Bible is a religion of joy. This is apparent long before the coming of Christ, in the Book of Psalms. "Be glad in the Lord, and rejoice, O righteous, and shout for joy, all you upright in heart!" (Ps. 32:11). How often the psalmist strikes this note, sometimes calling upon the whole of nature to rejoice. "Let the heavens be glad, and let the earth rejoice; let the sea roar, and all that fills it; let the field exult, and everything in it! Then shall all the trees of the wood sing for joy" (Ps. 96:11, 12). In the Book of Deuteronomy, God even commands man to rejoice, "You shall rejoice before the Lord your God, you and your son and your daughter, your manservant and your maidservant. . ." (Deut. 16:11).

When we come to the New Testament, we find that the word *joy* has become one of the key words of Christianity. It is a tremendous word. It means happiness of a very high order. It has more than the ordinary meaning of happiness. Happiness intensified is the idea contained in the word *joy*. God has always wanted his people to be happy. The word *joy* appears more than two hundred times in the Bible. Christ told his disciples, "Your sorrow will turn into joy" (John 16:20). In the Book of Acts we see how certainly that came true. Notice a few other New Testament passages: "Rejoice in the Lord always; again I will say, Rejoice" (Phil. 4:4); "Finally, my brethren, rejoice in the Lord" (Phil. 3:1); "Rejoice with those who rejoice . . ." (Rom. 12:15); "Rejoice always" (I Thess. 5:16); "But rejoice in so far as you share Christ's sufferings, that you may also rejoice and be glad when his glory is revealed" (I Peter 4:13).

Even Joy in Suffering

One of the truly great texts of the Bible is the beginning portion of the twelfth chapter of the Book of Hebrews. It comes immediately after the long roll call of worthies of the Old Testament who, because of their faith, are held up as examples to all subsequent generations. The next line reads:

"Therefore, since we are surrounded by so great a cloud of witnesses, let us also lay aside every weight, and sin which clings so closely, and let us run with perseverance the race that is set before us, looking to Jesus the pioneer and perfecter of our faith, who for the joy that was set before him endured the cross, despising the shame, and is seated at the right hand of the throne of God'' (Heb. 12:1, 2). It is a strange paradox that Christ, while dying on the cross, should have had joy in the act. It seems unbelievable that one who was being crucified should enjoy such a death, but such was the attitude of Jesus because of his great love for mankind.

What was the secret of the joy which the early Christians felt? How did they find it possible, and how is it possible today, for alert, responsible, warm-hearted people to be happy and rejoice amid the woes and sorrows of the world? How can a man facing all the uncertainties and dangers of life, surrounded by many who are carrying heavy burdens, keep on rejoicing?

The answer lies in the realization that God is in control of our universe and that his purposes will ultimately be served. Victory will ultimately belong to God, and to those who have been his faithful children.

Christ's purpose in coming into the world was to bring joy to all men, a joy that fades not away. It is interesting to notice, in the Book of Acts, as we read the stories of the conversion of various people, how often the story ends by mentioning that they went on their way rejoicing. Immediately after the church began, we read of the early Christians, "And day by day, attending the temple together and breaking bread in their homes, they partook of food with glad and generous hearts, praising God and having favor with all the people" (Acts 2:46, 47). Christians are a happy people.

Happiness Comes. . . .

Happiness in this world does not come when we go out selfishly to seek our own desires. Happiness comes when we renounce our own wills and submit to the will of God. When we go out to live as he wants us to live and to serve as he wants us to serve, there comes a happiness that will continue on and on, world without end, a happiness akin to the joy in the heart of Jesus our Lord. When we become Christians there is a deep inner joy. If you would know that great joy, believe in Christ as the divine Son of God, come to him in penitent faith, turning away from the world and its sinfulness. Confess Jesus before your fellow men and be baptized for the forgiveness of your sins. Like those who turned to Jesus more than nineteen hundred years ago, you will then go on your way rejoicing.

Jacob's Well, looking North from Mount Gerizim

23   Jacob's Well

Leaving Judea, on his way to Galilee, Jesus passed through the district of Samaria and came near the city of Sychar. He sat down at Jacob's well to rest. Jesus' disciples had gone into the city, which was not far away (John 4:8). A woman of Samaria came to the well for water and fell into conversation with him. She mentioned that the well was deep and alluded to Mount Gerizim where her fathers worshiped.

From Jerome (fourth century) on there is mention of a church building on the spot with the historic well inside. The building was apparently damaged in the Samaritan revolts (A.D. 484 and 529) and restored by the emperor

Justinian (A.D. 527-565). The Crusaders recorded the construction of a new building, which fell in A.D. 1187 to the Muslims. The Greek Orthodox acquired the spot in 1860. Work on a church building was begun in 1914 but has never been finished.

The Greek monk in charge of the site will let down a pail to show the depth of the well, which would be about fifty-eight feet if cleared of rubbish. The water is good and fresh in contrast to the bitter water from the abundant springs at the foot of nearby Mount Gerizim.

About 540 feet north of the well is Joseph's tomb, marked by a white dome. It was restored in 1868 and is accepted by Jews, Samaritans, Muslims, and Christians alike.

Old Testament Shechem

The name *Sychar* (John 4) does not appear elsewhere in Scripture. It has traditionally been identified with Shechem. However, excavations at Shechem indicate the area was not occupied in New Testament times, and archaeologists today tend to identify Sychar with El Askar, on the eastern slope of Mount Ebal, about a half mile north of Jacob's well.

Shechem is located about forty miles north of Jerusalem in the pass between Mount Gerizim and Mount Ebal. The main east-west and north-south roads converge here. The word *Shechem* seems to mean "shoulder" or "slope." A good water supply and a fertile plain east of the city combined to make the city wealthy and powerful.

Obeying God's command to move, Abraham came to Shechem, to the oak of Moreh, and built an altar. Before Abraham moved to the Bethel area, God said to him, "To your descendants I will give this land" (Gen. 12:7).

Jacob returned to Palestine following his marriages and the beginning of his family. After the meeting with Esau, the text states, "And Jacob came safely to the city of Shechem, which is in the land of Canaan, on his way from Paddan-aram; and he camped before the city. And from the sons of Hamor, Shechem's father, he bought for a hundred pieces of money the piece of land on which he had pitched his tent. There he erected an altar and called it El-Elohe-Israel" (Gen. 33:18-20).

Jacob's sons were pasturing their sheep near Shechem when Joseph was sent to check on them. Not finding them there he went to Dothan on the advice of a local man he had met wandering in the field around Shechem (Gen. 37:12-17). Later, Joseph's body was brought along on the exodus from Egypt and buried at Shechem when the people conquered the land (Josh. 24:32).

When the land was divided among the tribes, the boundary between

Ephraim and Manasseh passed near Shechem. Shechem also served as a city of refuge (Josh. 17:7; 20:7).

Joshua called an assembly of the tribes at Shechem following successes in the conquest of Canaan (Josh. 24:1). It was at Shechem that Joshua challenged the people with his last message: "And if you be unwilling to serve the Lord, choose this day whom you will serve, whether the gods your fathers served in the region beyond the River, or the gods of the Amorites in whose land you dwell; but as for me and my house, we will serve the Lord" (Josh. 24:15, 16).

After Solomon died, his son Rehoboam went to Shechem where the people had gathered to make him king. Jeroboam, hearing of Solomon's death, returned from Egypt and represented the people before Rehoboam. The people requested relief from the heavy burdens Solomon had placed on them. In return, they would be loyal to Rehoboam as king. Rehoboam rejected the advice of the older men and followed the counsel of his younger aides by continuing the burden.

The people refused to follow Rehoboam and his oppressive policy and quickly stoned Adoram, Rehoboam's taskmaster. Jeroboam was then made king of the ten northern tribes, leaving Rehoboam to flee Shechem for Jerusalem. Jeroboam rebuilt Shechem and then moved his capital to Penuel and later to Tirzah (I Kings 12).

Mounts Gerizim and Ebal

Gerizim and Ebal were the mountains on whose slopes the tribes of Israel assembled under Joshua, fulfilling Moses' command by hearing the curses and the blessings connected with the law. Gerizim was the mount of blessing, Ebal the mount of cursing (Deut. 11:29; 27:11–13; Josh. 8:33, 34). Simeon, Levi, Judah, Issachar, Joseph, and Benjamin were to stand on Mount Gerizim for the blessings; the other six tribes were to stand on Mount Ebal for the curses.

Gerizim is known in Arabic as Jebel et Tor, "the holy mountain." It rises some 2,849 feet above sea level. With Mount Ebal it commanded the entrance to the narrow valley of Shechem. Since this pass gave the only access from east to west into the mountains of Ephraim, and was situated on the main road from the north to the south, it was of strategic importance.

Mount Gerizim has been the spiritual and visible center of Samaritan worship since the beginning of the schism when the Jews returned from Babylonian captivity. The Samaritans erected a rival temple on Mount Gerizim where they continue to celebrate the Passover feast. The whole congregation (only about three hundred Samaritans are left) ascends the mount and spends an entire week there. The site of the celebration is a small trench about eight feet in length which they call the altar. They slaughter the seven Passover lambs there. Close to the altar is a pit which is used as the oven where the sacrifices are burned. The Samaritans also claim that twelve nearby rocks are the ones Joshua set up.

Mount Ebal, located north of and directly opposite Mount Gerizim, is 3,080 feet high. Nineteenth-century travelers frequently praised the view from Mount Ebal.

Modern Nablus

Some have thought that Old Testament Shechem is under the modern city of Nablus, but the results of excavations tend to disprove this. Nablus is the home of some ninety thousand people today and the headquarters of the Samaritans. The city was built in A.D. 72 by Titus, the Roman general. The small remnant of Samaritans, persecuted over the years, still live in Nablus and in a small community near Tel Aviv. In the Samaritan section, on the west side of Nablus, an ancient Pentateuch scroll is shown, which is the only Scripture accepted by the sect. Despite their claims for its antiquity, it dates no earlier than the tenth or eleventh century A.D.

A Word About Praising

Harold Hazelip

In his *Reflections on the Psalms*, C. S. Lewis tells about a problem he had as he was coming to believe in God. It had to do with praising God. People around him were urging him to "praise the Lord." He found the same emphasis in Scripture, especially in the Psalms. God himself seemed to demand praise.

Lewis explains that the whole idea troubled him. He had always been Uncomfortable with the kind of person who must be complimented. He suspected the motives of those who freely give praise to celebrities. An old maxim reads, "He who loves praise loves temptation." How could praise be so central to Christianity?"

Lewis explains that he could understand obedience to God, reverence, and gratitude. But a picture of God as "hungry for praise" and of his worshipers as flatterers disturbed him. Why did praising God so often consist in telling other people to praise him? Even the quantity of praise seemed to count. The psalmist wrote, "Seven times a day I praise thee" (Ps. 119:164). And again, "I will praise the Lord as long as I live; I will sing praises to my God while I have being" (Ps. 146:2).

I believe Lewis has voiced a problem many people have. I have known people who were concerned about heaven because the angels now, and men hereafter, seem to be permanently engaged in praising God. Does this mean that being in heaven is like being in church?

Jesus talked about worship with the woman at the well: "The hour is coming, and now is, when the true worshipers will worship the Father in spirit and truth, for such the Father seeks to worship him. God is spirit, and those who worship him must worship in spirit and truth" (John 4:23, 24).

Praise Is Spontaneous

How are we to understand God's desire for praise, or our responsibility to worship him? Lewis gives some helpful insights as he tells us the way he resolved this question. He admits that his original problem was a superficial understanding of the nature of praise. He had thought in terms of paying compliments, of flattery. When he looked more closely, he realized that praise involves a response to value. When we find ourselves in the presence of something beautiful, true, awe-inspiring, we spontaneously express our delight. Praise flows from us as naturally as a mirror reflects light.

Nothing is more natural to a human being than to praise that which pleases him. The lover praises the one he loves, a music lover praises a performance, a sports fan praises his hero. One of the marks of our humanness is that we can discern value and respond to it in this way.

And just as spontaneously, we want others to join us in praising the object of our adoration. "Isn't it beautiful?" "Isn't she pretty?" "Isn't that incredible?" When the psalmist tells everyone to praise God, he is doing what we regularly do when we tell others of something we care about.

Praise Completes Our Enjoyment

Our praise, then, is a response to the beauty and goodness of God. Another reason we love to praise what we enjoy is that praise not only expresses our delight but it completes our enjoyment. It's frustrating to experience great joy and not be able to respond to it. You see a beautiful view but there is no one present to share it. You enjoy a good meal but there is no one to tell how good it is. We instinctively want to say something when things thrill us, to share our joy with others. Our praise completes a delightful experience.

This deeper understanding of praise helps to explain the Bible's emphasis on praising the Lord. It isn't that God needs our praise. He says, "If I were hungry, I would not tell you; for the world and all that is in it is mine" (Ps.

50:12). Rather, we need to discern the "worthship" of God, and to respond to him. This is the way we grow.

And this helps us understand the meaning of heaven. We will be in God's presence, delighting in his love. Our praise now is never fully successful. We are pupils, learning to enjoy his presence and to glorify him. Just as we grow by the food we eat, our spiritual energy and growth come from what we take into ourselves. As we praise God, we are letting him do something for us more than trying to do something for him.

We often become negative about our world and complain about life. Worship calls us back to an awareness that life itself is a gift from God. Gratitude and praise are our proper response.

Reevaluating Our Praise

If our first duty as Christians is to praise God, are we fulfilling this responsibility? Think of your prayers. Are they absorbed with requests for things, with protests that life has not gone well? What of our hymns and songs? Is praise the keynote in them?

Perhaps the supreme value of the poetic books of the Old Testament is to train us in praise. There is Job, who is visited by one terrible blow after another until his whole life is reeling. His response? "Naked I came from my mother's womb, and naked shall I return; the Lord gave, and the Lord has taken away." And then follows praise: "Blessed be the name of the Lord" (Job 1:21).

Think of the Psalms. The psalmist faces every sort of bad experience—sickness, disappointment, death of loved ones, deep personal failure—and says repeatedly, "Praise ye the Lord!"

I think especially of Psalm 148. It is suggestive of a great conductor signaling one player after another in his orchestra until every instrument is brought into action at the climax of a piece of music. Psalm 148 seems to signal the whole universe to unite in God's praise. The psalmist calls on the sun, the moon and stars, "Praise him!" Then the mountains, the beasts, the kings of the earth, young men and maidens: "Praise him!" The whole universe seems to be shouting the praise of God.

In the New Testament, when little companies of redeemed people met together, we read, "The whole multitude of the disciples began to rejoice and praise God with a loud voice for all the mighty works that they had seen" (Luke 19:37). "And they returned to Jerusalem with great joy, and were continually in the temple blessing God" (Luke 24:52, 53). Early in the Book of Acts when Peter healed the lame man at the Beautiful Gate of the temple: "He stood and walked and entered the temple with them, walking and leaping and praising God'' (Acts 3:8). Their praises were the spontaneous outbursts of human gratitude for the wonderful works God had done.

The reason so much of our worship is dull and unfruitful may be that we have lost the essential note of praise. We *thank* God for all he gives us: our food, our clothing, our health, our families. But we *praise* God for who and what he is. Praise keeps us from merely thanking God for his material gifts. Praise can be the key to genuine worship. If we cannot praise God, or if our praise is shallow, our worship will lack power. But real praise is contagious. One song begets another. One person with praise to God in his heart will start others singing.

It is easy, once the practice of attending church has been established, to slip into a routine, to miss the real meaning in the various activities of the service. Jesus called on us to worship God "in spirit and truth" (John 4:24). Worship—this is more than just interaction with other human beings. We stand face to face with the God who has made us and proclaim his worth to him and to others. With the young Isaiah in the temple, we exclaim: "Holy, holy, holy is the Lord of hosts; the whole earth is full of his glory" (Isa. 6:3). And when God calls, "Whom shall I send, and who will go for us?" we respond again with Isaiah, "Here am I! Send me" (Isa. 6:8).

Have you placed yourself in God's service? Your whole life can ring with praise. Begin with faith in Jesus as Lord; turn from the desire to sin to a determination to do God's will. Your death and burial with him in baptism will begin your life as a new creature—with new motivation to praise the God who redeems you.

Ruins at Jerash

24 Decapolis

Just east of the Sea of Galilee is the area of ten Roman cities known as the Decapolis in Jesus' day. It was here that Jesus performed one of his most notable miracles: the casting of the demons out of a man named Legion, and sending them into a herd of two thousand swine which rushed down a steep area into the sea and were drowned. The miracle, recorded in Matthew 8:28–34; Mark 5:1–20; and Luke 8:26–39, obviously occurred along the eastern shore of the Sea of Galilee, the only place where the mountains approach the sea. Matthew speaks of the area as the "country of the Gadarenes," referring to the town of Gadara some thirteen miles south of the actual site, while Luke speaks of it as the "country of the Gerasenes," referring to the town of Gerasa, a city now known as Jerash, some forty miles southeast of the actual miracle site. Both references are correct, for the miracle occurred in the area dominated by these two Roman cities.

The word *Decapolis* is used only three times in the New Testament. It is used at the beginning of Christ's Galilean ministry, when the Scripture tells us that great crowds from Galilee, the Decapolis, Jerusalem, Judea, and from beyond the Jordan began to follow Jesus (Matt. 4:25). It was used again in the case of the casting out of the demons, mentioned above (Mark 5:20). It was mentioned a third time when Jesus returned from Tyre and Sidon, where he healed the daughter of a Syrophoenician woman, "through the region of the Decapolis" (Mark 7:31). The miraculous feeding of the four thousand with the seven loaves and a few fishes also occurred in the general area (Mark 8:1–10), though the word *Decapolis* is not used.

The historian Pliny listed the ten cities of the Decapolis as follows: Scythopolis, Hippos, Gadara, Pella, Philadelphia, Galasa (Gerasa), Dion, Kanatha, Damascus, and Raphana. Nine of these cities are east of Jordan. Only Scythopolis, the modern Beth-shan just south of the Sea of Galilee, is on the west side of the river. Following the death of Alexander the Great his successors established many Greek cities in the Near East, and these cities brought the Hellenistic or Greek influence into the areas. The Roman general Pompey put Palestine under Roman control and reorganized these cities, making them among the most advanced cities in the Roman Empire.

The Decapolis resembled a triangle, going southeast from Scythopolis to Philadelphia (the modern Amman, capital of Jordan), then northeast to Damascus, the third point of the triangle. Each city had its own council, control over the surrounding area, and the right of coinage and asylum. Each city had colonnaded streets, a forum, baths, theaters, temples, and an aqueduct.

In Jesus' Day

The Decapolis was flourishing at the time of the ministry of Jesus. Across the Sea of Galilee, the fishermen and farmers of the Jewish nation could see the Gentile world at its best. Centers of Greek and Roman culture could be found no more than ten or fifteen miles away. Perhaps the "far country" in the story of the prodigal son (Luke 15) was in this land where the swine grazed on the eastern shores of the Sea of Galilee and the cities could trap a Jewish boy looking for friends. A day's journey could bring such a lad back to the home of his waiting father. There are indications in the Gospels that many people living in the Decapolis heard about and followed Jesus.

The city of Jerash, located at an altitude of 2,000 feet above sea level some forty miles southeast of the site of Jesus' miracle, and some twenty-six miles north of the city of Amman, comes prominently into the biblical story when we read that the men tending the swine saw the remarkable event take place and then fled into the city to tell everyone what had happened. At that point, Luke 8:37 reads, "Then all the people of the surrounding country of the Gerasenes [Jerash] asked him to depart from them; for they were seized with great fear; so he got into the boat and returned."

Jerash was a remarkable city, being the hub of activity for a very prosperous province. It was a planned city, with the streets carefully laid out to convey traffic expeditiously. There was a systematic arrangement of the municipal, commercial, religious, and residential buildings. The city was surrounded by territory that was zoned to make the best use of the land, reserving certain areas for orchards, others for grain fields, and still others for pasture lands.There was an elaborate aqueduct system also. The city was adorned and embellished by Greek cultural objects and reflected the most advanced Greek and Roman influences. It was protected by a wall ten feet thick and with a circumference of two miles. Today, in the remarkable ruins of this ancient city, there are some 190 full columns still standing, with at least that many more partially broken off. There are remnants of two amphitheaters, a basilica, a temple, colonnades, large private homes, baths, and the aqueduct system.

George Adam Smith, in his *Historical Geography of the Holy Land,* wrote, "We cannot believe that the two worlds [the Jewish and the Roman], which this landscape embraced, did not break into each other.... The kingdom of God came forth in no obscure corner, but in the very face of the kingdoms of this world." We cannot know with certainty that Jesus visited any of these advanced Roman cities, though he was in the region, and he must have known a great deal about them.

Today, if one wishes to visit Jerash, he first goes to Amman, the capital of Jordan, and then within an hour's easy drive, he finds himself amid the extensive and very impressive ruins of a city of Jesus' day.

On Sending Jesus Away

Batsell Barrett Baxter

This message centers on the very meaningful story told in the fifth chapter of the Gospel According to Mark. It begins with Jesus' crossing the Sea of Galilee and entering into the area of the Decapolis, the ten Roman cities. The text reads, "They came to the other side of the sea, to the country of the

Gerasenes. And when he had come out of the boat, there met him out of the tombs a man with an unclean spirit, who lived among the tombs; and no one could bind him any more, even with a chain . . . . Night and day among the tombs and on the mountains he was always crying out, and bruising himself with stones. And when he saw Jesus from afar, he ran and worshiped him; and crying out with a loud voice, he said, 'What have you to do with me, Jesus, Son of the Most High God? I adjure you by God, do not torment me.' For he had said to him, 'Come out of the man, you unclean spirit!' And Jesus asked him, 'What is your name?' He replied, 'My name is Legion; for we are many.' And he begged him eagerly not to send them out of the country. Now a great herd of swine was feeding there on the hillside; and they begged him, 'Send us to the swine, let us enter them.' So he gave them leave. And the unclean spirits came out, and entered the swine; and the herd, numbering about two thousand, rushed down the steep bank into the sea, and were drowned in the sea.

"The herdsmen fled, and told it in the city and in the country. And people came to see what it was that had happened. And they came to Jesus, and saw the demoniac sitting there, clothed and in his right mind, the man who had had the legion; and they were afraid. . . . And they began to beg Jesus to depart from their neighborhood" (Mark 5:1-17).

A Strange Reaction

Here was a culturally superior, economically prosperous people, surprisingly asking Jesus, who had done a remarkable thing in their midst, to leave. As they had requested, Jesus left, never again to pass that way as far as the record indicates. Their first encounter with the Son of God was their last. He who had so much to give was not allowed to give it there. Jesus had demonstrated a concern for people, even ugly and unattractive and dangerous people. The residents of the area felt uncomfortable in his presence. Their concerns were not people, but fields and vineyards, prosperity and pleasure, buildings and possessions. Jesus' concern for people threatened their lifestyle. Hence, they wanted him to leave.

Perhaps it is good for us to pause and think about our own American way of life. This incident of long ago may have meaning for us. We are a prosperous and cultured people. We like fields and vineyards, prosperity and pleasure, buildings and possessions. And to our shame, as a nation we often overlook people, the kind who have special urgent needs somewhat as Legion had. The drunks and drug addicts, the hopelessly poor, the uneducated and unattractive, we often push out of sight. We are so busy with preserving our own lifestyle that we have little time for those in need. And in a very real sense modern man wants Jesus to go away, for he feels uncomfortable in the presence of Jesus. This is because modern man lacks concern for those in need and is preoccupied with material possessions, sensual pleasures, and his own achievements.

Jesus at Home in Nazareth

There is another story that is most appropriate to consider at this time. It is from the fourth chapter of the Gospel According to Luke. Beginning in verse 16, we find, "And he came to Nazareth, where he had been brought up; and he went to the synagogue, as his custom was, on the sabbath day. And he stood up to read; and there was given to him the book of the prophet Isaiah. He opened the book and found the place where it was written, 'The Spirit of the Lord is upon me, because he has anointed me to preach good news to the poor. He has sent me to proclaim release to the captives and recovering of sight to the blind, to set at liberty those who are oppressed, to proclaim the acceptable year of the Lord.' And he closed the book, and gave it back to the attendant, and sat down; and the eyes of all in the synagogue were fixed on him. And he began to say to them, 'Today this scripture has been fulfilled in your hearing'" (Luke 4:16–21).

Jesus had come home to Nazareth and gone to the synagogue. The text which he read (Isa. 61) was originally written to a people who had known the bonds of captivity under the yoke of a foreign power. Jesus read it to a people who were suffering under the bitter yoke of Rome. But the real significance of his reading was that he was announcing the basic purposes behind his own ministry in bringing good news to the poor, the ones who are largely deprived of the blessings of life. He also came to proclaim release to the captives. Babylonian captivity and Roman captivity were fresh in the minds of the people. Yet Jesus' release from captivity was far more than political. In some ways even more devastating in the lives of many is captivity to physical passions. Others are slaves of habits of thinking—racial prejudice, national hatreds, jealousies, and resentments. Some are prisoners of the aimless, purposeless, pleasure-centered way of life. Christ came to proclaim freedom to all captives of whatever kind.

Christ came to provide the recovering of sight to the blind. This includes those who are physically blind, but even more important, it includes those who are spiritually blind. He claimed to set at liberty those who are oppressed, including the many who are pushed down and trodden upon by those of wealth and power and position.

Another Strange Reaction

At first the message sounded very good to the people of Nazareth. But, as Jesus went on and reminded them of how their fathers had rejected earlier prophets and had thereby cursed themselves, the mood changed.

Eventually the story closes with the words, "When they heard this, all in the synagogue were filled with wrath. And they rose up and put him out of the city, and led him to the brow of the hill on which their city was built, that they might throw him down headlong. But passing through the midst of them he went away" (Luke 4:28–30). Once again, Jesus had come to bless, but the people drove him out.

Tragically, that same process is still going on. Jesus yearns to bless the millions of our day, too. Yet many, for one reason or another, turn away, asking him to leave them alone. A strange phenomenon, this. The Son of God, infinitely loving, infinitely kind, and intent only on blessing mankind, is pushed away by the people whom he loved enough to die for.

Don't let that describe you. If you have never yielded your life to the Lord and become a faithful follower, please don't let your opportunities slip away, as did the people of these cities in the long ago. While you still have the opportunity, seize it, by becoming a Christian. They way is simple: believe in the Lord Jesus Christ with all your heart, repent of your sins, confess your faith before men, and be buried with your Lord in baptism for the forgiveness of your sins. These are the simple conditions upon which he has promised to give you pardon and to add your name to the book of life.

Before you do anything else, ponder the fate of the people of Gerasa and the people of Nazareth who drove Jesus out of their borders and out of their lives. What a tragic mistake! A mistake that we must not make in our own lives!

Jericho Today

25   Jericho

Jericho was the major city of the southern end of the Jordan Valley. Located at the western end of the plain, Old Testament Jericho is identified with Tell es-Sultan on the northwest outskirts of modern Jericho. The mound contains about ten acres and is four hundred yards long from north to south. New Testament Jericho is located one mile west of the modern city.

Jericho is some ten miles from the point where the Jordan empties into the Dead Sea and about seventeen miles northeast of Jerusalem. A copious spring is located at the foot of the mound. Jericho is 820 feet below sea level.

Jericho is mentioned sixty-three times in the Bible, often with reference to the plains of Jericho. When Moses was taken up into the mountain to die, and was shown the land, the city of Jericho is specifically mentioned (Deut. 34:3). Jericho was on the border of Benjamin and Ephraim. Gilgal was located on the east border of Jericho (Josh. 4:19).

Israel Conquers Jericho

Joshua sent two spies to Jericho from his headquarters at Shittim. They lodged at the home of Rahab the harlot. Word reached the king of Jericho, who ordered the woman to hand over the men. She had hidden the men but told the king they had left at dark. She claimed not to know where they went but suggested that quick action might overtake them. Actually the two spies were hidden on Rahab's roof under the flax which was stored there.

The king sent men to search for the spies as far as the Jordan ford. Meanwhile, Rahab was bargaining with the spies. She had heard of the Red Sea crossing and the defeat of kings Sihon and Og. She asked to be remembered when the attack on Jericho came. The spies accepted her proposal, saying, "Our life for yours!" and promised that she and her relatives would be safe (Josh. 2:1-14).

Rahab let the spies down by a rope through her window. She advised them to go west for three days until the king's police came back. The men gave her a scarlet cord to tie to her window. This would afford her protection when the Israelites came against the city. As the men left, Rahab tied the cord in the window. The spies reported to Joshua, "Truly the Lord has given all the land into our hands; and moreover all the inhabitants of the land are fainthearted because of us" (Josh. 2:15-24).

As Joshua later stood by Jericho, the commander of the army of the Lord appeared to him. Joshua was told to take off his shoes because he stood on holy ground. He removed his shoes, bowed down, and worshiped (Josh. 5:13-15).

The city of Jericho was shut up as Israel approached. God commanded Israel to march around the city once each day for six days. Seven priests with seven trumpets of rams' horns were to go before the ark. In front of the seven priests were armed men, and the rear guard came after the ark, while the trumpets blew continually. For six days the people marched, retiring to their camp each night. Finally, on the seventh day, they went around the city seven times beginning at dawn. And they shouted and the walls of Jericho fell. The gold, silver, iron, and bronze were to go into the Lord's treasury. The people were to keep no spoil for themselves, but were to destroy the city, its men and women, and its animals. And the city was destroyed, except for the family of Rahab. The two spies who had met Rahab were charged with her rescue. She and her family were saved and went to live with Israel (Josh. 6:1-25).

After the destruction of Jericho, Joshua said, "Cursed before the Lord be the man that rises up and rebuilds this city, Jericho. At the cost of his first-born shall he lay its foundation, and at the cost of his youngest son shall he set up its gates" (Josh. 6:26). Years later during the reign of Ahab (874-853 B.C.) Hiel of Bethel rebuilt Jericho. Joshua's curse was fulfilled (I Kings 16:34).

As Joshua took other cities and kingdoms, it was often said that he did to the king of a certain city as he did to the king of Jericho (Josh. 8:2; 10:1, 28, 30).

From Jericho Joshua sent spies to Ai. They returned and told Joshua that two or three thousand men would be sufficient to take the city. Joshua issued the order, the army set out and attacked, but was repelled (Josh. 7:1-5). Joshua was driven to prayer and learned that the reason for the defeat was the presence of sin in the camp. It was finally learned that Achan had taken as spoil from Jericho a beautiful mantle from Shinar, two hundred shekels of silver, and a gold bar weighing fifty shekels (Josh. 7:6-26).

It is not clear when the people left Jericho. After their unsuccessful attack on Ai, the entire army went to the area and seized and destroyed the city. They built an altar at Mount Ebal (Josh. 8:30-35). Later, Joshua's headquarters were at Gilgal (Josh. 14:6) and then at Shiloh (Josh. 18:1). Whether some of the people camped at Jericho during the conquest of the land is not stated.

During the lifetimes of Elijah and Elisha, a school of prophets lived at the Jericho that Hiel built. While Elisha tarried at Jericho, the men of the city asked his aid because the water of the city was bad, making the land unproductive. Elisha asked for a new bowl with salt in it. He threw salt into the spring and said, "Thus says the Lord, I have made this water wholesome; henceforth neither death nor miscarriage shall come from it" (II Kings 2:4, 5, 15, 19-22). "Elisha's Spring" is pointed out to the modern visitor to Jericho.

Jericho in the New Testament

Herod the Great expanded the new Jericho, established some years before by Greek settlers, into a winter capital. Its climate is normally warm and pleasant, offering an improvement over the chilly, damp winters of Jerusalem.

Near Jericho a blind beggar by the name of Bartimaeus was sitting by the roadside when Jesus passed. The beggar heard a crowd passing and asked what was happening. He began to cry, "Jesus, Son of David, have mercy on me." Jesus heard him and told the people to call him. The blind man threw off his mantle, sprang up, and came to Jesus. Jesus said, "What do you want me to do for you?" Bartimaeus replied, "Master, let me receive my sight." Jesus told him to go his way for his faith had healed him. He received his sight and followed Jesus (Mark 10:46-52).

In response to a lawyer's question about the identity of one's neighbor, Jesus told a story of a man making a trip from Jerusalem to Jericho. The man was beaten, robbed, and stripped. His predicament was first witnessed by a priest and then a Levite. Both continued on their way without stopping. A Samaritan was the next to happen by. He had compassion on the man, dressed his wounds, administered medicine, and set him on his own beast. He paid the man's expenses at an inn and promised to check back. The neighbor in the story was the one who showed mercy (Luke 10:25-37).

Wealthy Zacchaeus was the head tax-collector in Jericho. When Jesus came to town the rather short Zacchaeus wanted to see the famous teacher. He went ahead of Jesus and chose a sycamore tree from which he could get a better view. Soon Jesus came to the tree where Zacchaeus was perched and spoke to him: "Zacchaeus, make haste and come down; for I must stay at your house today." Zacchaeus responded joyfully. The townspeople responded negatively. They thought it was terrible that such a good teacher was staying with such an evil man. Zaccaeus repented, repaid those he had cheated, and gave money to the poor. Jesus said, "Today salvation has come to this house, since he also is a son of Abraham. For the Son of man came to seek and to save the lost" (Luke 19:1-10).

Archaeological Work

At the Old Testament mound, nearly forty-five feet of current debris represents twenty successive levels of Jericho before the time of Joshua. Ernest Sellin and Carl Watzinger in 1907-1911 excavated the topmost layers of Old Testament Jericho before any accurate way of dating pottery had been established. John Garstang dug from 1929 to 1936, followed by Kathleen Kenyon from 1952 to 1961. It is generally held that today there are no remains at Jericho from the time of Joshua through the days of the judges and kings of Israel. Archaeologist James O. Kelso has written, "One of the major tragedies of Palestinian archaeology is that the Germans excavated Jericho when archaeology was still an infant science." The work of the Germans, along with the erosion caused by wind and rain over the centuries, has apparently prevented positive identification of any archaeological evidence dating from Joshua's conquest. Miss Kenyon's excavations have found evidence that the city existed in the eighth millennium B.C. Thus it is one of the oldest cities in the world.

The Roman road from Jericho to Jerusalem survives in places and a few of its milestones have been found.

The Christian View of Things

Harold Hazelip

Before the neutron bomb became a possibility, science fiction movies depicted the possibility of a "death ray" which could annihilate all human life and leave buildings intact. Viewers soon realized that all of the wealth of this planet could not make one happy if he were utterly alone. He might be free to live in any house, possess any object, go anywhere he pleased. But there is no real joy unless it can be shared with others.

Money is a problem for most people. For many, the difficulty is not having enough. But if money suddenly becomes plentiful, there are new difficulties: how does one conserve, invest, and use his money wisely? As strange as it may seem to the poor, the rich have problems too.

Jesus was on his way to Jerusalem from Galilee. He had just had an interesting encounter with a rich man who was saddened when Jesus told him to give his possessions to the poor and follow him (Luke 18:18-30). Jesus told this rich young ruler, "It is easier for a camel to go through the eye of a needle than for a rich man to enter the kingdom of God" (Luke 18:25). Those around Jesus were amazed at his statement and asked, "Then who can be saved?" Do you remember Jesus' answer? "What is impossible with men is possible with God" (Luke 18:26, 27).

Encounter with Zacchaeus

Then Jesus came to Jericho, where he encountered another rich man, Zacchaeus, a tax-collector. Zacchaeus is so fascinating that we want to analyze him politically, socially, and psychologically. But the Gospel doesn't tell us much about him. Was he unhappy? Did he have a complex because he was short? Why was he so anxious to see Jesus? The truth is, we don't know.

What the Bible does say is that he was "a chief tax collector and rich" (Luke 19:2). Most of his contemporaries were angered by the presence and the actions of the Roman conquerors. Zacchaeus managed to turn this situation to good advantage. The Romans needed Hebrew IRS men. They needed someone who spoke the language, who heard the gossip, who knew who traded for a new donkey every year, and who threw the best parties.

Zacchaeus was their man. But when Jesus invited himself to be a guest in

Zacchaeus' home, Zacchaeus "received him joyfully." Before Jesus left him, Zacchaeus was saying, "Behold, Lord, the half of my goods I give to the poor; and if I have defrauded anyone of anything, I restore it fourfold" (Luke 19:8). He was talking about his money, but if we think only of money, we will miss the full implication of his commitment.

Zacchaeus' money represents his work. His commitment will shape the way he handles his business. His whole lifestyle will be changed. How he cares for and uses his money will demonstrate what has happened to him because he knows Jesus. Everything is different. Knowing Jesus will turn Zacchaeus toward other people.

The response of Zacchaeus to Jesus illustrates the way Jesus taught people to treat things and other persons. More than once Jesus insisted that material things will not satisfy our deepest longings. He saw a real competition in our souls: shall we accumulate more things or shall we share what we have with others? He said, "No one can serve two masters; for either he will hate the one and love the other, or he will be devoted to the one and despise the other. You cannot serve God and mammon" (Matt. 6:24). Mammon was the Aramaic word for money. Actually, money is neutral in the teachings of Jesus—it is neither good nor bad. The question is whether it will be master or servant.

Material Values Are Temporary

So, Jesus' recommendation was, "Do not lay up for yourselves treasures on earth, where moth and rust consume and where thieves break in and steal, but lay up for yourselves treasures in heaven, where neither moth nor rust consumes and where thieves do not break in and steal. For where your treasure is, there will your heart be also" (Matt. 6:19-21).

Jesus indicated two reasons why laying up treasures for ourselves on earth will never satisfy us. First, material things are only temporary. Time and decay erode them, thieves may steal them. Garage sales are popular in our neighborhood. One person's junk may be another person's treasure; have you noticed as you cleaned out your closet or attic, how many things were once precious to you and are now worthless? When you first saw that piece of furniture, that dress, that set of golf clubs—you had to have them. You acquired them at considerable sacrifice. But now, as Jesus predicted, moth and rust, time and custom, have done something to them. What you once thought you had to have, you now do not even want to keep.

What is now an old junk car may have been the very model you once wanted so much. Look what twenty-five short years have done to your "treasure." This is Jesus' point. Material things do not have the power to hold their value.

Our Needs Are Personal

The other reason for Jesus' warning about our use of money is that we are personal beings: "Where your treasure is, there will your heart be also." Things—houses, cars, furs, diamonds—cannot love us, listen to our heart throb, or speak back to us. Thomas Kelley wrote in his *Testament of Devotion,* "The deepest need of man is not food and clothing, important as they are. It is God." And Victor Hugo in *Les Miserables:* "The supreme happiness of life is the conviction that we are loved; loved for ourselves—say rather, loved in spite of ourselves. . . ."

We are personal in nature, and personal in need. We hunger most for personal qualities: warmth, tenderness, understanding, sharing. These are the very things a material object can never give us.

So Jesus offered an alternative. We can use material things to serve the needs of others. This is the way we lay up treasure in heaven. This is the point of Jesus' exchange with the rich young ruler. His heart was hungry for something meaningful. Jesus said, "Go—sell—give—come—follow." He did not say that money is inherently evil. His words were not, "Go destroy your possessions so they will not harm anyone else." Rather, he insisted that possessions must become the means by which we and others live, not the end for which we live.

This is Jesus' view of material things. The rich young ruler rejected Jesus' words with sadness. Zacchaeus was changed by them. You and I are in the process of making our decision. Too many of us are like Augustine, who at one point in his life said, "God, make me a Christian—but not yet." Today is the day. Make your choice. Live for God. Serve people. Use things. Demonstrate your love for Christ by obeying. He commands repentance—that you turn from sin. He commands baptism for the forgiveness of your sins. And his promise to you is, "You will have treasure in heaven" (Luke 18:22).

A Home Among Bethany's Oldest Buildings

26   Bethany

The meaning of the name *Bethany* is uncertain. Some suggest that it means "house of dates" or "house of figs." John 11:18 indicates that Bethany was fifteen stadia (1⅞ miles) from Jerusalem. This means that Bethany was about half-an-hour's walk from the city of Jerusalem. Bethany is located on the eastern slope of the Mount of Olives on the road from Jerusalem to Jericho. Its modern name is el-'Azariyeh, obviously referring back to the fact that the home of Lazarus, Mary, and Martha was in Bethany. The present village, numbering from one thousand to fifteen hundred people, is entirely made up of Muslims.

In the famous story of the resurrection of Lazarus (John 11) Jesus was beyond the Jordan when word came that Lazarus was gravely ill. It was not until four days after the death of Lazarus that Jesus came and met with Mary and Martha and afterward raised Lazarus from the dead. The miracle was unexpected by the two sisters and was also very impressive to the townspeople, who believed on Jesus as a result of the miracle.

The Final Week

Toward the close of Jesus' life he came to Jerusalem at Passover time. Apparently he stayed in Bethany during the week preceding Passover, for Luke says, "And every day he was teaching in the temple, but at night he went out and lodged on the mount called Olivet" (Luke 21:37). Since Bethany was located on the eastern slope of the mountain, it is logical to assume that his lodging was in that village. At one point Jesus was in Bethany at the house of Simon the leper. A woman who had an alabaster jar of very expensive ointment came to Jesus and poured it out on his head while he was sitting at the table (Matt. 26:6-13; Mark 14:3-9). The conversation in which Martha chided Jesus for allowing Mary to sit at his feet and listen to his teaching while she had to prepare the meal alone had also occurred in Bethany (Luke 10:38-42). Moreover, the Scriptures tell us that Mary took a pound of precious ointment and poured it on the feet of Jesus and wiped it off with her hair (John 12:1-8). It is interesting to compare with this story a similar, but different, story found in Luke 7:36-50.

On the first day of the Passover week Jesus called two of his disciples to him and sent them to a nearby village to secure an ass and her colt upon which he would ride into Jerusalem. This took place to fulfill the prophecy spoken by the prophets Isaiah and Zechariah (Matt. 21:1-11; Mark 11:1-10; Luke 19:29-44).

The Ascension

After his crucifixion and resurrection, Jesus spent some time with his disciples, assuring them by his presence that he had been raised from the dead. Finally he "led them out as far as Bethany, and lifting up his hands he blessed them. While he blessed them, he parted from them" (Luke 24:50, 51). This is the simple account of his ascension into heaven. Acts records the event as taking place on the Mount of Olives (Acts 1:9-12).

Visitors to the general location of ancient Bethany have their credulity strained somewhat by some of the claims of the present inhabitants and the tour guides. The ruins of the house of Simon the leper are shown, as are also the ruins of the house of Lazarus, Mary, and Martha. The tomb of Lazarus is also displayed. Its entrance is at the bottom of twenty-four well-worn steps and consists of an antechamber about ten feet square, with three more steps leading to the tomb itself, which is seven-and-a-half feet long and eight feet wide. Nearby is a mid-twentieth-century church which appears to have been built upon foundations of earlier churches of the fourth, fifth, and twelfth centuries. Another church has been built over the exact spot, so it is claimed, where Mary went forth to meet Jesus when he came to raise Lazarus from the dead. While all of these places are of interest and in all probability are somewhere near the sites of the ancient events which they commemorate, it is unlikely that any of them are authentic.

In this connection it is interesting to note that at Citium on the island of Cyprus tourists are shown the tomb of Lazarus, suggesting that the risen friend of Jesus met his second death there. Another legend, dating back to the eleventh or twelfth century, places Lazarus in France. On the Sunday prior to Passover each year a procession begins near Bethany and makes its way to Jerusalem to St. Stephen's Gate, in commemoration of Christ's triumphal entry.

The Resurrection and the Life

Batsell Barrett Baxter

The Gospel According to John features seven major miracles of Jesus, each of which is referred to as a sign. Each of these miracles was a sign of the divinity of Jesus Christ, part of the overwhelming evidence that he was no mere human being. The last of these miracles is the raising of Lazarus of Bethany from the dead. Brother of Mary and Martha, Lazarus was a good and respected man. While Jesus was far away beyond the Jordan River, word was sent that Lazarus was seriously ill. After a time Jesus made his way to Bethany.

At this point let us pick up the story as it is found in the eleventh chapter of the Gospel of John: "Now when Jesus came, he found that Lazarus had already been in the tomb four days . . . . When Martha heard that Jesus was coming, she went and met him, while Mary sat in the house. Martha said to Jesus, 'Lord, if you had been here, my brother would not have died. And even now I know that whatever you ask from God, God will give you.' Jesus said to her, 'Your brother will rise again.' Martha said to him, 'I know that he will rise again in the resurrection at the last day.' Jesus said to her, 'I am the resurrection and the life; he who believes in me, though he die, yet shall he live, and whoever lives and believes in me shall never die. Do you believe this?' She said to him, 'Yes, Lord; I believe that you are the Christ, the Son of God, he who is coming into the world' " (John 11:17-27).

Raising the Dead

Subsequently Mary also came and talked with Jesus. The Lord was deeply moved by the sorrow of the two sisters and in the account of the story we read, "Jesus wept" (John 11:35). He then asked to be taken to the place where Lazarus had been buried. At that point we read, "Then Jesus, deeply moved again, came to the tomb; it was a cave, and a stone lay upon it. Jesus said, 'Take away the stone.' Martha, the sister of the dead man, said to him, 'Lord, by this time there will be an odor, for he has been dead four days.' Jesus said to her, 'Did I not tell you that if you would believe you would see the glory of God?' So they took away the stone . . . . He cried with a loud voice, 'Lazarus, come out.' The dead man came out, his hands and feet bound with bandages, and his face wrapped with a cloth. Jesus said to them, 'Unbind him, and let him go' '' (John 11:38–44).

On two other occasions Jesus had raised someone from the dead, according to the Gospel record. The first occasion to be mentioned was the raising of the daughter of Jairus, a ruler of a synogogue, described in the fifth chapter of the Gospel According to Mark. In the seventh chapter of Luke we read another tender story of Christ's compassion as he raised from the dead the only son of a widow who lived in the little village of Nain. Jesus happened upon the funeral procession carrying the boy to a place of burial and was so concerned that he stopped the procession, touched the coffin, and raised the boy to life again. The third account mentioned in the Scriptures is the resurrection of Lazarus.

Christ, the First Fruits

More significant than these temporary resurrections (each of these died again) was the resurrection of our Lord himself. After he had lived a third of a century and had been nailed to the cross God raised him up out of the grave. Much later, the apostle Paul spoke of Christ's resurrection in these words, "But in fact Christ has been raised from the dead, the first fruits of those who have fallen asleep. For as by a man came death, by a man has come also the resurrection of the dead. For as in Adam all die, so also in Christ shall all be made alive" (I Cor. 15:20–22). Christ's resurrection is the foundation for one of the central promises of Christianity. When we die it is not all finished. We will live again.

Moving from I Corinthians to the Book of Ephesians, notice the highlights in a paragraph in the first chapter of the book: "For this reason . . . I do not cease to give thanks for you, remembering you in my prayers, . . . that you may know what is the hope to which he has called you, . . . according to the working of his great might which he accomplished in Christ when he raised him from the dead'' (Eph. 1:15-20). This is a paragraph of tribute to Christ; it is an exaltation of Christ. At the heart of this exalting of Christ is the phrase, ''which he accomplished in Christ when he raised him from the dead.''

Moving into Ephesians 2, we find that the subject is changed from the resurrection of Christ to the resurrection of man. But it is not the same kind of resurrection. Man was dead in sin; Christ was dead only physically. Jairus' daughter, the boy at Nain, and Lazarus were raised from the dead physically, as also was Christ. But when we come to this chapter the subject is different, though the same word is used. Now the subject is raising men who are spiritually dead. Men without Christ are dead men. When Paul went to Corinth, when he went to Rome, he saw dead men. They were alive, of course, for they had eyes and they used them to see. They had tongues and they spoke. They had hands and they worked. But they were dead men. They were dead in sin.

Dead in Sin

Note the opening paragraph of Ephesians 2: ''And you he made alive, when you were dead through the trespasses and sins in which you once walked, following the course of this world, following the prince of the power of the air . . . . Among these we all once lived in the passions of our flesh . . . . But God, who is rich in mercy, out of the great love with which he loved us, even when we were dead through our trespasses, made us alive together with Christ (by grace you have been saved), and raised us up with him'' (vv. 1-6). So far as you and I are concerned this resurrection is a thousand times more important than the resurrection of physical bodies. The resurrection of man from his sinful, dead condition means that salvation is possible.

In Paul's earlier writings he had said to the Romans, ''None is righteous, no, not one. . . . All have sinned and fall short of the glory of God'' (Rom. 3:10, 23). There is no one on earth who has not sinned. The story of Cornelius is a case in point. Cornelius was a devout man who feared God with all his house, gave much alms to the people, and prayed to God always, but he was lost. As good as he was he was lost, because he was not a Christian. He was dead until the day when Peter came and preached to him, dead until he heard the gospel of Christ, dead until he obeyed it. Then he was raised from the death of sin.

The Life-giving Word

The whole spirit of the New Testament emphasizes the urgency of getting the gospel to the people. Why? Because people are dead, dead in sin. In the inspired Scriptures we have the life-giving Word of God. Until the blood of Christ, our Savior, our Redeemer, cleanses us from our sins, we are all dead men.

Model of Herodian Jerusalem

27 Jerusalem

The word *Jerusalem* is used over eight hundred times in the Bible. This suggests the great importance of the city in biblical history. It is called Urushalim or Urusalim in ancient Egyptian texts, and Salem or Jebus in certain Old Testament passages. Other names applied to the city are Moriah, Zion, City of David, and Ariel. The word *Jerusalem* probably means "foundation of Shalem," though traditionally it is taken to mean "city of peace."

Jerusalem is located thirty-three miles east of the Mediterranean Sea and fourteen miles west of the Dead Sea at an elevation of 2,500 feet. It sits on top of a ridge which reaches from Mount Gilboa in the north to Hebron in the south. It enjoys a protected location and is on the major north-south highway in central Israel.

Hills and Valleys

Jerusalem consists of five once sharply distinguished hills separated by valleys. Erosion and building have altered the hills, while debris and sediment have filled the valleys. On the west and south is the Valley of Hinnom and on the east the Kidron Valley, also known as the King's Valley. The interior of the city was divided by a ravine called the Tyropoeon (cheesemaker's) Valley, which ran from the present Damascus Gate through the city and out the Dung Gate, passing the Wailing Wall in the process.

Between the Tyropoeon and Kidron Valleys lie three mountains. The southernmost was called Ophel and was the lowest with an elevation of only 2,000 feet. It was the site of the earliest city and because of its sharp drop into the valleys was the easiest to defend. Just north across what was once a slight depression is Mount Moriah. It was originally a threshing floor but was designated by David as the place of sacrifice. It was the site of the three Jewish temples and now holds the Dome of the Rock. The third hill is Mount Bezetha just to the north of the temple area. Herod expanded the temple platform northward and covered the ravine which once separated Moriah from Bezetha.

Between the Tyropoeon and Hinnom Valleys lie two mountains. To the south is Zion, the highest of the five on which Jerusalem was built. A smaller hill or spur occupies the section north of Zion. Jerusalem was not taken by Israel during the conquest, but was later conquered by David, who made it his city. It was to this city that the exiles returned. Jesus often visited the city and the early church was very strong in Jerusalem.

Old Testament History

Archaeological finds date the beginning of Jerusalem in the fourth millennium B.C. or earlier, with a walled city during the Early and Middle Bronze periods (3150–1550). Abraham is connected with the city twice, once when he visited Melchizedek of Salem in Genesis 14 and again when he prepared to offer his son Isaac in the land of Moriah. Perhaps it should be mentioned that neither of these events is assigned by all scholars to Jerusalem. Joshua fought with and slew Adoni-zedek, king of Jerusalem, but did not take the city (Josh. 10). During the period of the judges, the city is mentioned only in passing; it was held by the Jebusites (Judg. 19:10–12).

After being anointed king over all Israel, and after reigning in Hebron for seven-and-one-half years, David took the city of Jerusalem, making it his capital. David accomplished this by challenging several of his strongest military men to take the city, promising the captaincy of his army to the one who was successful. Joab led the way, probably entering the city through the Jebusite shaft—the channel through which a spring outside the northern wall flowed into the city.

David built a palace and the Millo. II Samuel 5:9 reads, "And David built the city round about from the Millo inward." The word *Millo* comes from the Semitic root which means "filling." This suggests to some the filling of the ravine separating Mount Ophel from Mount Moriah. Kathleen Kenyon, as a result of excavations, suggested that Millo refers to the rock terraces constructed on the east side of Ophel to provide more room and to fill up the area on the side of the hill which led to the city wall.

David brought the ark to the city and during the years 1003–970 B.C. took concubines and wives who bore him eleven sons (II Sam. 5–6). It was also here that he committed adultery with Bathsheba and was punished (II Sam. 11–12). David's son, Absalom, fled from the city but later returned and drove out his father (II Sam. 13–15). After Absalom's death, David returned to the city and made elaborate preparations for the construction of a temple to God on Mount Moriah, the threshing floor of Araunah the Jebusite (II Sam. 24; I Chron. 21). David died in Jerusalem and was buried there (I Kings 2).

Solomon followed his father David on the throne and also lived in Jerusalem. Solomon built the temple and an elaborate palace (I Kings 5–8). The temple construction began in April/May 966 B.C. and was completed in October/November 959 B.C. (I Kings 6:1, 38). Israel provided the labor for the temple construction but the Phoenicians of Tyre provided the timber (I Kings 5:6–12; II Chron. 2). The construction of the temple forced the expansion of the city walls to the north (cf. I Kings 3:1). Solomon's complex presumably included stable facilities (I Kings 9:19; 10:26), the "House of the Forest of Lebanon" (150 by 75 feet, built on forty-five columns of cedar in three rows), and a large palace (I Kings 7:2–8). After the completion of his building projects, Solomon hosted the queen of Sheba, took many foreign wives, and built altars to foreign gods (I Kings 10–11). Solomon ruled Jerusalem for forty years from 970 B.C. to 930. He died and was buried in the city of David.

Hezekiah, who began to reign by himself in 725 B.C., instituted a series of reforms in Jerusalem, including reopening of the temple (II Chron. 29:3). casting down the pagan altars, and burning the religious paraphernalia that had been brought in by some of his predecessors. During his reign, Hezekiah strengthened the walls of Jerusalem as Sennacherib the Assyrian threatened the city (II Chron. 32). Hezekiah also diverted the water from

Gihon Spring so that the enemy's besieging army would not have access to it. He built a conduit, now known as Hezekiah's tunnel, to bring the water into the city. The ministry of the prophet Isaiah also centered in Jerusalem.

Josiah (640–609 B.C.) was another king who led in reforming the nation after others had carried it into idolatry. Josiah decided to repair the temple and carry out thorough religious reforms. In repairing the temple, he found the book of the law. It was used as a guide for Josiah's work of reform (II Kings 22–23; II Chron. 34–35).

There were four deportations into Babylonian captivity: 605, 597, 586, and 581 B.C. Jerusalem remained the hope of those in exile (Ezek. 34:13; 36:38). Some maintained the practice of praying toward Jerusalem three times each day (Dan. 6:10). Cyrus issued a decree in 538 B.C., authorizing the Jews to return to Jerusalem and to reestablish services at the temple (Ezra 1:2–4). The rebuilding of the temple soon began (Ezra 3–5). A second major return to Jerusalem took place in the summer of 458 B.C. under Ezra (Ezra 7:7). A decade later a third return was led by Nehemiah, who made a nighttime tour of the city just three days after his arrival, then led in the rebuilding of the walls in a period of fifty-two days (Neh. 2, 4–6).

Jesus and Jerusalem

The Roman general Pompey conquered Jerusalem in 63 B.C. and made it subject to Rome. Tacitus indicates that Pompey entered the Holy of Holies and was surprised to find it empty. Herod the Great made the right political moves and with the support of Rome ruled Jerusalem from 37 B.C. to 4 B.C. Herod's most famous building project was the temple. Herod extended the temple platform both to the north and south, making the area some 2,500 feet from north to south and 1,000 feet from east to west. Of the temple itself, not a stone remains; but the sacred area today remains much as it was when Herod built it. The famous Wailing Wall on the west and other portions on the east and south sides of the platform can still be seen. Construction of the temple began in 20 B.C. and was not completed until A.D. 64, six years before its destruction in A.D. 70. The date of the statement made to Christ in John 2:20, suggesting that the temple had been under construction for forty-six years, must have been A.D. 27.

Jerusalem figures in the stories of Jesus' birth as the home of Herod (Matt. 2:1–12), the place where Zechariah (the future father of John the Baptist) had his vision (Luke 1:5–23), and the scene of the presentation of the infant Jesus at the temple (Luke 2:22–38). At age twelve, Jesus attended the Passover feast and stayed behind to speak with the teachers (Luke 2:41–50). After his fast in the wilderness, he was brought to the pinnacle of the temple where Satan tempted him to cast himself down (Matt. 4:5-7). John recorded two trips to Jerusalem for the Passover; during the first of these visits Jesus cleansed the temple and talked with Nicodemus (John 2:13-22; 3:1-8). Jesus also journeyed to Jerusalem for the Feast of Tabernacles; on this occasion he taught in the temple, forgave the woman caught in the act of adultery, healed the man born blind by telling him to wash in the pool of Siloam, and gave his discourse on the good shepherd (John 7-10). Jesus was in Jerusalem at other times as well, and during the last week of his life he was in Jerusalem daily. He was also there after his resurrection until the time of his ascension from the Mount of Olives (Luke 24:44-53).

The apostles and others remained in Jerusalem after Christ's ascension, and were there for the beginning of the church on Pentecost (Acts 2). Many of the important events connected with the beginning and growth of the church occurred in Jerusalem, until the members generally were scattered (Acts 8). The apostles remained in Jerusalem.

Archaeological Studies

More than forty-four archaeological enterprises have been conducted in Jerusalem since 1863, many of which included several prominent archaeologists. Few if any other cities in the world have been subjected to such archaeological scrutiny. The most recent finds suggest that the ancient city of David probably included about 12 acres. While modern American cities have about 50 to 80 persons per acre, ancient cities had closer to 160 people per acre. Given that figure, the population of Davidic Jerusalem was no more than 2,000. Solomon's city included about 32 acres. The estimated population of the walled city of Jerusalem during his reign would be 4,500 to 5,000. In the seventh century B.C. the city is thought to have expanded, adding an additional 125 acres, with the possibility that the population inside the walls then reached 25,000. There are no known archaeological remains of David's city. Very little from the time of Solomon remains and nothing has been found of Solomon's temple except for a pilaster, a rectangular support or pier that was part of a wall.

A line of cemeteries stretching from Akeldama in the south around the east side of Jerusalem has recently been excavated. Most tombs have a central room with niches in which ossuaries (pottery vessels in which the bones are put after a body decays) were placed. Many of these tombs date to the first century A.D. A great deal of excavation and writing has been done trying to locate the walls of the ancient city of Jerusalem. This is extremely difficult since the walls were expanded from time to time, taking in additional territory. The present walls were built by Suleiman II (or Solyman), sultan of Turkey. Known as Suleiman the Magnificent, he lived from 1494 to 1566. At its largest, it is thought that the city comprised about 230 acres. This would mean a possible population of 40,000 people. Josephus, whose figures are generally regarded as unreliable, indicates that the population of Jerusalem at the beginning of the third century B.C. was 120,000 and that 1.1 million Jerusalemites were killed by the Romans in A.D. 70.

The modern visitor to Jerusalem is greatly assisted in his understanding of the ancient city by visiting a model of Jerusalem on the grounds of the Holy Land Hotel. A scaled-down version of Jerusalem as it was in A.D. 66, some thirty-six years after the time of Jesus, the model is about 95 feet wide and 130 feet long. It represents a city that would have been nearly a mile wide from east to west and a mile-and-a-quarter from north to south. Built under the guidance of the late Michael Avi-Yonah of Hebrew University, the model is revised from time to time as archaeological discoveries are made.

Jerusalem is a city rich in meaning not to just one religious faith, but to three—Jews, Muslims, and Christians. It is extremely difficult to separate facts from traditions. Many of the buildings in Jerusalem could not possibly be authentic, due to the fact that the present-day streets of Jerusalem are in some areas ten or twenty or even thirty feet above the level of the streets on which Jesus walked. Pointing out a particular building as the site of the upper room in which Jesus and the disciples ate the Last Supper is obviously a relatively recent tradition. The burial site for King David on Mount Zion is likewise questionable. Two tombs recently excavated on Mount Ophel within the ancient city of David are much more likely to be the burial sites of David and Solomon. In spite of the false claims and late traditions, it is a moving experience to visit the city that has a biblical history all the way from Melchizedek and Abraham down to Christ and the beginning of the church.

"O Jerusalem, Jerusalem"
Batsell Barrett Baxter

During the last week of Christ's life on earth he apparently spent the nights at Bethany just outside of Jerusalem on the eastern slope of the Mount of Olives. Each day he would go into Jerusalem, walk among the people, and teach them. Sometime during that week Jesus cast his eyes across the city and thought of its people. It was then that he said, "O Jerusalem, Jerusalem, killing the prophets and stoning those who are sent to you! How often would I have gathered your children together as a hen gathers her brood under her wings, and you would not! Behold, your house is forsaken and desolate. For I tell you, you will not see me again, until you say, 'Blessed is he who comes in the name of the Lord' " (Matt. 23:37-39).

Christ's Purpose

In order to feel the full impact of the disappointment which Jesus registered, we need to remember the purpose for which he came into the world. The angel announced to Joseph, "She will bear a son, and you shall call his name Jesus, for he will save his people from their sins" (Matt. 1:21). Or, as Jesus himself put it, "For the Son of man came to seek and to save the lost" (Luke 19:10). Jesus came to his own and his own received him not. At least the religious leaders, who should have been most sensitive to his message, and the masses, for whom his heart especially yearned, seemed not to be willing to accept his salvation.

The lamentation over Jerusalem occurred sometime in the middle of that last fateful week in the life of Jesus. Let's go back to the Sunday which began that important week. Jesus called two of his disciples to him and said, "Go into the village opposite you, and immediately you will find an ass tied, and a colt with her; untie them and bring them to me" (Matt. 21:2). The prophet Zechariah had written centuries earlier, "Behold, your king is coming to you, humble, and mounted on an ass, and on a colt, the foal of an ass" (Matt. 21:5; cf. Zech. 9:9). The disciples did as Jesus had directed them to do and immediately the scene was one of great excitement. "Most of the crowd spread their garments on the road, and others cut branches from the trees and spread them on the road. And the crowds that went before him and that followed him shouted ... 'Hosanna in the highest!' And when he entered Jerusalem, all the city was stirred, saying, 'Who is this?' And the crowds said, 'This is the prophet Jesus from Nazareth of Galilee' " (Matt. 21:8-11).

Excitement was obviously running high, for the people saw in Jesus the fulfillment of their hopes for a leader that would come and break the yoke of Roman bondage and lead them into the era of prosperity of which they had dreamed for centuries. The Old Testament prophets had written of a Messiah who would come and save his people. The nation of Israel had misunderstood those prophecies, thinking they were referring to a physical, earthly kingdom, whereas they actually were referring to the spiritual kingdom which Jesus came to establish. On this day excitement was running high, as it does on great festive occasions, and the natural excitement of Passover week was heightened by the appearance of this one whom the people thought might be their long-anticipated emancipator. Everyone grabbed something, branches from the trees, clothing from their backs, and threw it down upon the road as a carpet in his path. Something amazing was about to happen, they thought.

A Different Messiah

Then, something unexpected happened. The great expectations of the people somehow failed to materialize. There was the tremendous build-up followed by an equally tremendous let-down. What happened? The account of the story in the Gospel of Luke explains it. Luke wrote, ''And when he drew near and saw the city he wept over it, saying . . . 'The days shall come upon you, when your enemies will cast up a bank about you and surround you, and hem you in on every side, and dash you to the ground, you and your children within you, and they will not leave one stone upon another in you; because you did not know the time of your visitation' '' (Luke 19:41–44).

From that moment on the story is not a simple story of delirious crowds welcoming their hero as the promised Messiah who would establish his earthly kingdom. The story takes on a deeper meaning, one that has important implications for our time as well. Christ had taken great care to prepare his entrance into Jerusalem. But he was a different Messiah from the one the crowds thought they were welcoming with psalms and hosannas. He was calling people not to a kingdom of great military power, great economic wealth, and abundant physical pleasure. He was calling people to a better kingdom, a spiritual kingdom, one that would satisfy the deeper needs of their souls.

Ways of Looking at a City

There are different ways of looking at a city—any great city—Jerusalem, New York, London, Paris, Rome, or other cities with which we are more familiar. When William Wordsworth saw London, he wrote poetry. When Thomas Carlyle saw the city, he philosophized. When Jesus saw Jerusalem, he wept over it.

Jesus wept over Jerusalem. This ought to have meaning for us. How do we see a city when we come to visit? Is it made up of people to be manipulated and used. . . or to be avoided . . . or to be joined in their vices? Or do we see a city in terms of its needs, needs which we can help to fulfill?

A friend of mine spoke of flying on one occasion into a great city and instead of saying, ''It was a city of three million people,'' he described it as ''a city of three million souls.'' In that simple description, I think he had caught the essence of Christ's way of looking at a city.

An Unresponsive People

Jesus wept over Jerusalem, for they were misguided and their goals and desires were ultimately empty and meaningless. On the deepest level, here was the Son of God, who had come to the earth to guide men to a better way of life—a happier, purer, spiritual way of life; but they would not hear him. They turned away for mere baubles, when they could have had an eternal home in heaven.

Does this say anything to us about how we need to look at our cities and the people in them? Does it also say something to us about how we ourselves live in our cities? Are we like the people of ancient Jerusalem, looking for the material, impermanent things of life, overlooking the greater spiritual values that are within our reach? There were some in ancient Jerusalem who saw more clearly than the others and realized that Jesus was the Christ and Savior of the world. They followed him to happiness and salvation. May each of us have that same insight and turn toward the better way, and may we also bring others with us as we turn.

I leave you with those haunting words of Jesus, "O Jerusalem, Jerusalem . . . . How often would I have gathered your children together as a hen gathers her brood under her wings, and you would not!"

The Old City of Jerusalem

28   The Upper Room

What we today call the Old City of Jerusalem was built during the Arab domination following the Crusades. The traditional site of the upper room and David's tomb is located outside the Old City's Zion Gate. The site of the upper room, however, was actually inside Herod's city, as parts of the first-century walls have been found further toward the Valley of Hinnom. The Valley of Hinnom makes a sharp turn near the site of the upper room and can be reached by going either west or south from there.

Two different Greek words lie behind the English phrase, "the upper room." One is *anagaion,* which means "room upstairs"; it is used in the description of the Lord's Supper (Mark 14:15; Luke 22:12). The other word is *hyperōon*, which means "upstairs" or "under the roof"; it is used in reference to the gathering place of the apostles (Acts 1:13) and the deathbed of Dorcas (Acts 9:37–39). Jerome rendered both words in his Latin translation as *coenaculum*, which has aided the supposition that the upper room of the Lord's Supper and the gathering place of the apostles were the same. Although it is possible that the two rooms were the same, the fact that Luke uses different words strongly suggests that the place of the Last Supper and the place of receiving the Holy Spirit and choosing the new apostle (Matthias) were different.

The Last Supper

On the first day of unleavened bread, Jesus sent Peter and John to make preparations for the Passover feast which they would celebrate together. He told them to go into the city of Jerusalem, where they would meet a man bearing a pitcher of water, and to follow him until he entered a house. They were to speak to the master of the house, inquiring where the guest chamber for the Master's use was located. Jesus said the man would show them a large upper room, furnished and ready. It was that evening that Jesus and the Twelve gathered in that room (Luke 22:7–14).

Jesus realized that he was in the final hours with his apostles and that Satan had entered into Judas. Jesus finished his meal, removed his outer garments, wrapped a towel around his waist, and poured water into a basin. He then washed the feet of his disciples one by one. Peter refused the washing, but after a brief discussion with Jesus, he submitted. Jesus finished the task and dressed before sitting down to drive home the point of his lesson: "A servant is not greater than his master; nor is he who is sent greater than he who sent him" (John 13:1–20).

Jesus then predicted that one of the Twelve would betray him. This greatly troubled the group. John was leaning against Jesus and Peter told him to ask Jesus which one would betray him. Jesus replied that it was the one to whom he would give a morsel after he dipped it. He gave it to Judas. At this point Judas left, some thinking he had financial matters to attend to (John 13:21–30).

Some of the apostles then began arguing about who would rise to the top in the movement Jesus had started. Jesus responded by saying that in other organizations some men would exercise lordship over others, but it was not to be so among his followers (Luke 22:24–30).

At this point, Jesus took the bread, blessed it, broke it, and distributed it to his eleven followers. He did the same with the fruit of the vine which was included in the Passover meal. By this he established a simple supper that represented the covenant he was making. They sang a hymn together and then went to the Mount of Olives (Matt. 26:26–30).

Postresurrection Appearance

After the resurrection, on the evening of that Sunday, Jesus' disciples were shut up in a room where Jesus came and appeared to them. Jesus gave them peace, the Holy Spirit, and the power to forgive sins. Thomas was not present on that occasion, but eight days later Jesus' disciples were again in the house." This time Thomas was there to feel the hands and sides of Jesus (John 20:19–29). While the text does not specify that this place was the upper room, it was a house in Jerusalem and is traditionally taken to be the same upper room where the Lord's Supper was instituted and the disciples waited for Pentecost. It may be that it was to this very room that the two disciples who had been walking on the Emmaus road returned when they "found the eleven gathered together and those who were with them" (Luke 24:33).

Postbiblical History of the Site

The specific house(s) in which the celebration of the Lord's Supper and the discussions of the apostles before Pentecost took place is (are) unknown. It could have been anywhere among the maze of streets in the general area. The hall shown today as the place of the Last Supper was built by the Franciscans in the fourteenth century on Crusader foundations. According to ancient traditions the early Christians met there before Pentecost.

After one enters the alleged tomb of David, a pair of stairs on the left lead to the top. The arched ceiling reflects the Gothic architecture characteristic of Crusader buildings, though it dates from the fourteenth century. The columns are reused Byzantine works while the stained-glass windows are Muslim additions (they contain sentences from the Koran). In addition to the room which is said to be the upper room, there is, toward the back, directly over David's tomb, another room honoring David.

Epiphanius, a native of Palestine (A.D. 310–403), wrote of events of which he had learned from older documents. According to him, in A.D. 130 "Hadrian found the city razed to the ground and the temple of God destroyed and trampled upon, with the exception of some houses and a certain small church of the Christians, which had been constructed in that place, in which the disciples, after the Savior was taken up to heaven from Mount Olivet, betaking themselves, mounted to the Cenacle." *Cenacle* is from the Latin word for dining room and came to refer to the upper room.

This church building was restored by Massimus in the fourth century.

Pilgrims to the church mentioned seeing the column of the flagellation (scourging), the horn for anointing the kings (including David), the crown of thorns, the lance used to pierce Jesus' side, the stones used to stone Stephen, and the chalice used by the apostles. The church was burned by the Persians in 614 and rebuilt by Modestus in 634. After other destructions and rebuildings the present room, as we have seen, was built in the fourteenth century; it was taken over by the Muslims in the sixteenth century and made into a mosque. After 1948, the building was handed over to the Jews (downstairs) and Christians (upstairs).

The present upper room is empty. It is interesting to try to estimate whether 120 people could gather in the room. From the roof of the building which houses the tomb of David and the upper room, one has a good view of the Old City from the Zion Gate to the Dome of the Rock.

The Towel and the Cross

Harold Hazelip

Reading the Gospels can sometimes be like standing in front of a full-length mirror. We see ourselves reflected clearly.

Jesus and the Twelve had returned from Caesarea Philippi, where Jesus' messiahship was openly discussed and confirmed. A week later Peter, James, and John had seen his glory in the transfiguration. They did not understand what he meant by his coming sufferings but it was obvious that some crisis lay ahead.

Struggle for Greatness

Soon thereafter, "an argument arose among them as to which of them was the greatest" (Luke 9:46). They knew Jesus was going to establish the kingdom of heaven, but they did not understand the nature of that kingdom. Their speculation about the glories of the coming era evidently led them to vie for the most influential, honorable positions.

Shortly before Jesus' death, the subject arose again. Jesus explained to the apostles, "You know that the rulers of the Gentiles lord it over them, and their great men exercise authority over them. It shall not be so among you; but whoever would be great among you must be your servant, and whoever would be first among you must be your slave; even as the Son of man came not to be served but to serve, and to give his life as a ransom for many" (Matt. 20:25–28).

Then the hour for the Last Supper arrived. Jesus and the apostles were in a large upper room in Jerusalem where they were to observe the Passover meal. In those days most of the roads were unsurfaced and people wore open sandals. Any home expecting guests would keep a water pot at the door. Normally a servant would take a basin and towel and wash the feet of guests as they came into the house.

A towel and a basin were present in the upper room. But tempers may have still been aroused over the dispute about the greatest places in the kingdom. Competitive pride apparently kept any of the apostles from being willing to wash the feet of Jesus and the others.

"Let's Talk About Me"

But let's move from the first century to the twentieth. Thomas Wolfe coined the expression *the Me-Decade* to describe the 1970s. He argues that everyone is preoccupied with the "Me." The major appeal of encounter sessions, meditation practices, and other "find yourself" movements of the 1970s was that they all said, "Let's talk about me."

Christopher Lasch argues that one significant change in the mentality of our era is that the concept of "making it"—success—has changed between the 1950s and now. In the 1950s "making it" involved competitiveness, a struggle against poverty, until one gained wealth and honor. The "Organization Man" symbolized the 1950s. The ideal of today, he tells us, is the person without commitment. Heavy emphasis is placed on clichés like "you owe it to yourself" and "self-realization at any cost."

Lasch then describes the man who will be successful in the modern office. He does a quick reading of the centers of power in the office. He cultivates his standing and his opportunities with the persons of power. He "looks out for number one." He "pulls his own strings." He "wins through intimidation." He sees a "virtue in selfishness." Self-love is exalted above love for others.

We can easily allow our culture's values to dominate us. Who are our heroes today? Do we look to the model on television or in the movies? The pleasure-seeker whose commitment is only to himself? The politician whose commitment can change with any new tide of opinion? Or do we still find heroes who have commitments beyond themselves? Who give up promising personal careers in order to make commitments to others?

The Man for Others

Jesus has appropriately been called "The Man for Others." He took a towel and a basin in the upper room, but this was only the first step. We must never forget or ignore the fact that Jesus came as a servant. For hundreds of years God's people had anticipated the "suffering servant" who would give his life on behalf of the people. Jesus identified himself as that suffering servant: "But I am among you as one who serves" (Luke 22:27). "This is my blood of the covenant, which is poured out for many for the forgiveness of sins" (Matt. 26:28).

Years later Paul was reminding the church at Philippi of the dangers of selfishness and egoism. He told of the One who "was in the form of God, [but] did not count equality with God a thing to be grasped, but emptied himself, taking the form of a servant, being born in the likeness of men. And being found in human form he humbled himself and became obedient unto death, even death on a cross" (Phil. 2:6-8).

Jesus clearly rejected the temptation to found a hierarchy. He had come as a slave to the Father's will and he intended this lifestyle for his church. If you should be in Jerusalem on Thursday before Easter, you might observe a somewhat theatrical reenactment of the washing of feet. The higher-ranking prelate washes the feet of lower-ranking clergy, often to the accompaniment of flash bulbs. But Jesus wanted selfless service in his name, not ceremony or ritual. He took an old word which others despised, and told his disciples that the sign of discipleship was in service.

Someone has suggested that the towel may be a more appropriate symbol of the Christian life than is the cross. The cross reminds us of the sacrifice which made the Christian life possible, but most of us are called upon to live for him rather than to die for him. The towel suggests the service of a person whose body has become a living sacrifice to God (Rom. 12:1).

Free to Serve

How can we move toward Jesus' frame of mind concerning service and greatness? We feel the need to establish our own worth, to make our mark. The narrative of his washing the disciples' feet in the upper room is prefaced by the apostle John's comment, "Jesus, knowing that the Father had given all things into his hands, and that he had come from God and was going to God, rose from supper, laid aside his garments, and girded himself with a towel" (John 13:3, 4). Jesus knew who he was; he did not have to vie with others for greatness. He knew that greatness is the gift of God.

You and I were created by God. We are the objects of his love and grace. The heart of our problem is that we forget how God feels about us. We have heard his words intellectually, but we may not have realized them emotionally. "See what love the Father has given us, that we should be called children of God; and so we are" (I John 3:1).

Jesus was completely free as a person. He could serve others; he was not constrained to exalt himself. He knew that he had come from the Father and was going to return to the Father. You and I often relate to other people by conforming to their wishes—we want them to like us. Or we try to overpower them by our strength and make them like us. If, like Jesus, we could realize how the Father feels about us, we would not have to establish our greatness. We would be free to serve others.

When Jesus began his public ministry to others, he started at the river Jordan. He could not repent of sins, for he had no sins. But he convinced John the Immerser that he should make an exception and baptize him, even though he was sinless. He explained, "It is fitting for us to fulfil all righteousness" (Matt. 3:15).

You and I are sinners. But we too begin our lives of service by fulfilling the Father's commandments. We turn from our sins, confess our allegiance to Jesus as Lord, and submit completely to him in the humbling act of baptism. We become "Christ-Ones"—we belong to him. And the life of service gets underway!

The Valley South of Jerusalem

29 The Akeldama

The term *Akeldama* is used only once in the New Testament, where it means "Field of Blood" (Acts 1:19). Today the site is known as Hakk ed-Dumm, "the price of blood."

Eusebius in his fourth-century work on biblical geography, *Onomasticon*, lists Akeldama twice. He places it on the north of the city but Jerome later corrects this statement to read "south." Arculf, a pilgrim from the seventh century, placed it on the city's south side, where the present Akeldama is located at the east end of the Hinnom Valley.

Marking the Site

A long, low building occupies the site today, serving as the home of the Greek Convent of St. Onuphrius. The convent is built over a labyrinth of rock tombs which contain the bones of medieval pilgrims. The largest vault among the tombs is called the Apostles' Cave, since tradition indicates this was the place where the apostles hid during the trial of Jesus. The soil contains a kind of clay which some say is suitable for use in making pottery, suggesting a possible connection with the name *potter's field* (Matt. 27:7).

God told Jeremiah, "Go, buy a potter's earthen flask, and take some of the elders of the people and some of the senior priests, and go out to the valley of the son of Hinnom at the entry of the Potsherd Gate" (Jer. 19:1, 2). The Potsherd Gate is mentioned only here in Scripture and may be the same as the Dung Gate of postexilic times (Neh. 2:13; 3:13; 12:31). The gate, now lost, appears to have given access to the pottery works in the Valley of Hinnom. Jeremiah visits the potter and his house in Jeremiah 18:1, 2. In all probability the present site of Akeldama overlooks this area.

Pilgrims were buried in a cemetery here until the seventeenth century. During the Crusader period (twelfth century) a Church of St. Mary was constructed on the site. The Latins had taken the area from the Syrians. It passed to the Armenians in the sixteenth century, the Greeks in the seventeenth century, and back to the Armenians again, before the Greeks built the present convent in 1874.

Judas Betrays Jesus

Matthew cites the events surrounding the betrayal of Jesus, the subsequent suicide of Judas, and the purchase of the potter's field with the blood money as fulfillment of a prophecy of Jeremiah (Matt. 27:9, 10). The words quoted are from Zechariah 11:12, 13, though there is no reference to "field" in the passage. Some students have suggested that the reference to a field comes from Jeremiah 32:6-9, where the prophet is reported to have purchased a field from his cousin; others suggest allusions to Jeremiah 18:2-12 and 19:1-15.

The biblical events leading to the purchase of the "field of blood" began just before the Passover when the elders and chief priests called a meeting in the high priest's palace. With the high priest Caiaphas they discussed the possibility of and problems involved in arresting Jesus. They decided not to do it during the feast because of a possible revolt among the crowds (Matt. 26:1-5; Mark 14:1, 2; Luke 22:1, 2). A bit later, one of the twelve apostles, Judas, approached the chief priests and captains, seeking payment for turning Jesus over to them.

It was agreed that Judas would betray Jesus at a time when there were no crowds around him. The officials gladly gave Judas thirty pieces of silver for his treachery. It was because Satan entered into him that Judas watched for an opportunity to betray Jesus.

After completing the feast in the upper room, where Judas was excused from the company by Jesus (John 13:27–30), Jesus and the remaining disciples went across the Kidron Valley to a place called Gethsemane where Jesus prayed. After his prayer, as he was talking to his disciples, Judas came leading a small army of police and officials who carried swords, clubs, and lanterns.

Judas had prearranged a sign so that the officials would know who Jesus was with the least amount of difficulty. Judas would kiss Jesus. Upon entering the garden, Judas said, "Hail, Master," and kissed Jesus.

Jesus asked the officials for the name of the one they sought and they replied, "Jesus of Nazareth." Jesus confirmed the sign by acknowledging his identity (John 18:4, 5). Peter tried to defend Jesus by cutting off the ear of Malchus, a slave of the high priest, but Jesus immediately restored it. The band of soldiers with their captain and the Jewish officials seized Jesus and took him to the Jewish high priest. All of his followers, except a partially naked young man, who followed from a distance, ran away into the darkness (Mark 14:43–52).

Seeing the consequences of his act and feeling the condemnation upon him, Judas tried to return the thirty pieces of silver to the officials, confessing his wrongdoing in the process. Their response was to assume a "hands-off" position. Judas threw the money on the temple floor in their presence and committed suicide by hanging himself. The officials gathered up the money and, realizing that it could not be put into the temple treasury, finally decided to buy the field which was to become the "wayfarers' cemetery" (Matt. 27:3–10).

The Mystery of Judas

Harold Hazelip

In Leo Tolstoy's *Anna Karenina,* Anna is the wife of a high government official. Her position places constant demands on her in the name of propriety. Bored with her marriage to an austere state official, she becomes infatuated with a young army officer. Anna finally leaves her social position and her husband and lives openly with a man who is not her husband. In this situation she gives birth to a daughter.

At first she thought "love would conquer all." Her love for the young man was so great that she would withstand being totally ostracized from society. But finally, the pressures of being an outcast became too heavy. There was no place to which she could go. She was jealous when her lover would leave on business trips, because she remained confined to the house.

Finally, when Anna could see no future at all in her existence, she threw herself in front of a moving train and was killed. She had woven a web for herself. Her tragic suicide was the only logical recourse, it seemed, since there was no way to start all over again.

Why Was Judas Chosen?

Is this what happened to Judas Iscariot? Judas was certainly not a puppet, a victim of divine predestination. He was a human being, made in the image of God, free to make decisions. There is no reason to believe he had always been evil. Luke says that he "became a traitor" (Luke 6:16).

Jesus freely chose Judas to be an apostle, just as he chose the others, after he had spent all night in prayer to God (Luke 6:12). Judas was sent out on the preaching missions with the other apostles, and there is no indication that he was a failure in those missions. Nor is there any evidence in the Gospels that Jesus chose him because he needed someone to betray him.

We are able to see some deterioration in Judas' character in the Gospels. John tells us that when many shallow disciples turned away from following Jesus rather early in his ministry, Jesus knew that Judas would betray him (John 6:64–71). When Mary, the sister of Lazarus, anointed Jesus' feet, Judas complained that the costly ointment could have been sold and the money given to the poor. John comments that Judas did not really care for the poor. Rather, he was in charge of the moneybox for Jesus and his disciples, and was stealing from it (John 12:1–8).

On the night of Jesus' Last Supper with his disciples, Judas went out to fulfill the bargain he had struck with the chief priests (Matt. 26:14–16; John 13:21–30). He would deliver Jesus into their hands for thirty pieces of silver. "The one I shall kiss is the man; seize him" (Matt. 26:48).

The next morning, when Judas fully realized his responsibility in Jesus' impending death, he took back the thirty pieces of silver and said, "I did wrong in betraying innocent blood." "What does that matter to us? . . . it is your affair, not ours," was the response (Matt. 27:4, Moffatt). Judas went out and hanged himself.

Why Did Judas Betray Him?

What happened to Judas? We have to begin by considering what Judas could have been. Jesus saw that Simon could become a rock (Peter). He knew that John, whose stormy temper led Jesus to call him a "son of thunder," could become an apostle of love. He knew that Saul, fiery persecutor of the church, could become an apostle to the Gentiles. And he saw potential in Judas. But Judas made choices which led him on a different course.

Why did Judas betray Jesus? Several theories have been suggested. Judas was the only one of the Twelve who was not a Galilean. Did he feel left out or rejected by the other apostles? Did he betray Jesus for the money? Was his heart so set on earthly position that he was disappointed in Christ when it became apparent that Christ's kingdom was not of this world? Or did he intend to put Christ to the test by forcing him to use his power to avoid death? If Jesus did nothing, and was killed, Judas would be through wasting time following an idealistic preacher. On the other hand, if Jesus exercised divine power to overcome his captors, and inaugurated an earthly kingdom, Judas would have set the activity in motion.

Judas Could Have Been Forgiven

As attractive as some of these theories may be, the Bible does not give us a full explanation of Judas' motivation. Perhaps the most important lesson we can learn from the mystery of Judas' behavior is that his story did not have to end as it did. Judas was not the only one who failed Jesus in those final hours. "All the disciples forsook him and fled" (Matt. 26:56). Simon Peter completely crumpled under the taunts of a mere slave girl. He denied his Lord three times, reinforcing his denial with oaths. Then he fled in disarray into the night.

But in the depth of his failure, Peter remembered what Jesus had taught—a message of grace and forgiveness. He remained with the other disciples and eventually had his opportunity to be forgiven and recommissioned by Jesus. Jesus called on him to confess his love for him three times, as he had denied him three times. Each time the Lord said, "Feed my lambs ... Tend my sheep ... Feed my sheep" (John 21:15-17).

Or think of Saul of Tarsus as he sat in Damascus, waiting for the arrival of Ananias, who would give him the Lord's instructions. Surely his life passed before him as he thought of innocent lives which he had helped to destroy. Years after his conversion he recalled in a speech, "In every synagogue I imprisoned and beat those who believed in thee. And when the blood of Stephen thy witness was shed, I also was standing by and approving, and keeping the garments of those who killed him" (Acts 22:19, 20).

There was no sense in which Paul could bring Stephen back to life. It seemed that there was no way he could undo the harm he had done. He might easily have followed the example of Judas. He could have committed suicide in bitter remorse. But instead, a door was opened for him to give his life for the cause he had tried to destroy. He did not have to go on "bearing the luggage of the past." There was a future.

If only Judas had returned to Jesus and asked his forgiveness. The Gospel of Matthew says, "When Judas, his betrayer, saw that he was condemned, he repented and brought back the thirty pieces of silver to the chief priests and elders, saying, "I have sinned in betraying innocent blood'" (Matt. 27:3, 4). There is much that is commendable about that confession. There was no attempt to escape the blame. He did not, like Pilate, wash his hands of the whole affair. But he saw that he could not undo his wrong. The chief priests and the elders responded to his confession of sin, " 'What is that to us? See to it yourself.' And throwing down the pieces of silver in the temple, he departed; and he went and hanged himself" (Matt. 27:4, 5). I believe the ultimate tragedy in Judas' life was not the betrayal, but what he failed to do when the moment of truth dawned on him. If he had only remembered what Jesus had taught throughout his ministry, instead of hanging himself, he would have gone outside the city wall to "the place of a skull" and have pleaded his case to the One on the middle cross. But Judas did not seek grace and forgiveness.

Let's not remove Judas too far from life. You and I betray our Lord too. Then we align ourselves either with Judas on the one hand or with Peter and Paul on the other. Peter, and later Saul of Tarsus, remembered Jesus' words and deeds of grace and forgiveness and, as the writer of Hebrews puts it, found "grace to help in time of need" (Heb. 4:16). Judas succumbed to despair.

Which will you and I do? With the guilt of your wrongs upon you, are you going to give in to despair? Or will you, with Saul of Tarsus, believe in Jesus as Lord, make an about-face in your lifestyle with determination to do his will, and then be baptized to wash away your sins (Acts 22:16)? No matter how terrible your sins are, if you turn to him, you will find "grace to help in time of need."

Olive Trees in Gethsemane

30   The Garden of Gethsemane

The Garden of Gethsemane is located at the foot of the western slope of the Mount of Olives in the Kidron Valley. The name *Gethsemane*, found in Matthew 26:36 and Mark 14:32, means "oil press." The name of the site probably came from an olive oil press located on the hillside at some point in history. It is altogether natural that such a press would be located on a mountain that abounded in olive trees, as suggested by the name *Mount of Olives*.

The Kidron Valley, which is only three miles long, separates Jerusalem on the west and the Mount of Olives on the east. The actual bed of the valley today is thought to be some ten to fifty feet above the level of the valley in ancient times due to the accumulation of debris over the centuries. Two springs provide the valley with water, the Gihon and the En-rogel.

The Davidic kings owned property in the Kidron Valley; this led to its being called the King's Valley. David crossed the valley when he fled from Absalom (II Sam. 15:23). Absalom set up a monument for himself in the King's Valley (II Sam. 18:18).

In Jeremiah 31:40 the prophet looked forward to the day when the city would be rebuilt and even the places of burial would be sacred to God. The verse reads, "The whole valley of the dead bodies and the ashes, and all the fields as far as the brook Kidron, to the corner of the Horse Gate toward the east, shall be sacred to the Lord. It shall not be uprooted or overthrown any more for ever." G. A. Barrois wrote that this passage "opened the way for all sorts of symbolic interpretations." Key among these was the interpretation of Kidron as the Valley of Jehoshaphat. This identification results from such passages as Joel 3:1, 2 which states, "In those days. . . . I will gather all the nations and bring them down to the valley of Jehoshaphat, and I will enter into judgment with them there, on account of my people and my heritage Israel, because they have scattered them among the nations, and have divided up my land." Verse 12 reads, "Let the nations bestir themselves, and come up to the valley of Jehoshaphat; for there I will sit to judge all the nations round about." The tradition arising from this interpretation can be traced back to the fourth century A.D. It has led many to believe that the final judgment will take place at this site. It is for this reason that many have wished to be buried in the area, thinking that there will be some special advantage on the great judgment day.

A Garden of Prayer

Our interest in this area is based on evidence far more solid than these traditions. The Scriptures plainly declare that on the night of Christ's betrayal Jesus and the faithful apostles left the upper room and went out to the Mount of Olives (Matt. 26:30; Mark 14:26), as was his custom (Luke 22:39). The site was located just across the Kidron Valley (John 18:1) where there was a garden known by the name *Gethsemane*. The Synoptic Gospels give the impression that the area was large enough for the apostles and Jesus to be a good distance from one another. Leaving the group, Jesus took Peter, James, and John with him a bit further into the garden; then he left them and went still further to pray alone. It was here that he prayed, "Father, if thou art willing, remove this cup from me; nevertheless not my will, but thine, be done" (Luke 22:42; cf. Matt. 26:39; Mark 14:35). Luke records that his agony was so intense that his sweat was like great drops of blood. When he came back to his apostles, he found them sleeping. He left them a second and a third time, praying earnestly that the cup of suffering might pass from him; each time when he returned he found them asleep (Matt. 26:42–46). Soon Judas came leading a multitude, carrying swords, clubs, and lanterns, and guided the officials to Jesus, whom he identified with a kiss. Jesus readily admitted his identity, was arrested, and led away to be subjected to a series of hastily arranged, illegal trials. His followers left him and fled (Matt. 26:47–56).

The Crucial Decision

It was in the Garden of Gethsemane that the Son of God made the final decision which made possible the eternal salvation of the entire human race. It is awesome to contemplate the magnitude of this decision: "My Father, if this cannot pass unless I drink it, thy will be done" (Matt. 26:42). The quiet beauty of the garden today, amid the centuries-old olive trees, belies the titanic struggle which took place there nearly two thousand years ago. Even then, outwardly, it was a pleasant, restful place where Jesus frequently retreated for prayer and for private sessions with his apostles (Luke 21:37; John 18:2).

The Bible does not give enough information to pinpoint the exact location of the garden where Jesus prayed. Only that it was on the west side of the Mount of Olives seems clear. Today the uncertainty is illustrated by the fact that four different sites are revered by leading religious groups: the Russians, the Armenians, the Greek Orthodox, and the Roman Catholics. Josephus indicates that the area east of Jerusalem was cleared by the Romans, who "cut down all the trees there were in the country that adjoined to the city, and that for ninety furlongs round about" when they besieged Jerusalem during the first century A.D. at the time of the Jewish revolt. If this is true, the present-day ancient gnarled olive trees, while quite old, do not go back to the time of Jesus.

The Christian who visits the western slope of the Mount of Olives today finds the rival claims concerning the exact site of the Garden of Gethsemane somewhat disquieting. The commercialism that has grown up with the tourist trade and the elaborate, ornate church buildings and memorials which have been erected seem out of place. He finds himself wishing for a period of uninterrupted quiet in which to meditate upon the fact that somewhere on this hillside the spiritual destiny of the human race hung in the balance as Jesus prayed and then submitted his will to the will of God.

"This Cup"

Batsell Barrett Baxter

Matthew, in his account of the life of Jesus, describes the agony of the final night of Jesus' life in this very place, the Garden of Gethsemane, in these words, "Then Jesus went with them to a place called Gethsemane, and he said to his disciples, 'Sit here, while I go yonder and pray.' And taking with him Peter and the two sons of Zebedee, he began to be sorrowful and troubled. Then he said to them, 'My soul is very sorrowful, even to death; remain here, and watch with me.' And going a little farther he fell on his face and prayed, 'My Father, if it be possible, let this cup pass from me; nevertheless, not as I will, but as thou wilt.' And he came to the disciples and found them sleeping; and he said to Peter, 'So, could you not watch with me one hour? Watch and pray that you may not enter into temptation; the spirit indeed is willing, but the flesh is weak'" (Matt. 26:36–41).

Luke adds an additional comment, "And being in an agony he prayed more earnestly; and his sweat became like great drops of blood falling down upon the ground" (Luke 22:44). The writer of Hebrews adds still more, "In the days of his flesh, Jesus offered up prayers and supplications, with loud cries and tears, to him who was able to save him from death, and he was heard for his godly fear. Although he was a Son, he learned obedience through what he suffered" (Heb. 5:7, 8). While in the agonies of crucifixion, Jesus called out, "My God, my God, why hast thou forsaken me?" (Matt. 27:46).

"Thy Will Be Done"

As we think of the agony through which Jesus went as he anticipated the cross and as he underwent the excruciating pain of crucifixion, we are deeply impressed that he spoke out, not to his disciples or others who were about him, but only to God. And even more importantly, we notice that as he addressed God it was not in an attitude of rebellion or rejection of God, but as an obedient and accepting son. He cried, "*My* God, *My* God." Even though he felt forsaken, he still held on to God. Someone was there to whom he could say, "Father."

Even after all these centuries we find it very difficult to understand why Christ had to die on the cross. Why should he who was sinless die for our sins? Was there not some other way? Could not our guilt have been erased without the divine Son of God dying so ignominiously in so horrible a way? Yet, we recognize that our eyes are blinded by our own sins. We also recognize that we do not have the divine perspective to see how terrible sin is. In trusting faith we accept the fact that there was no other way for the salvation of our souls. Only by his death on the cross could we be cleansed from our sins and made whole.

To the limits of our ability to feel gratitude we are thankful for God's love and for the love of Christ as demonstrated on Calvary. The eternal fate of the world hung in the balance that night in Gethsemane when Jesus said, "Not my will, but thine, be done." The salvation of all mankind was made possible the next day when Jesus willingly submitted to the cross and paid the price for our redemption. It was there that he became the Savior of the world. The least that we can do is to allow him to be the Lord of our lives now.

The Value of Suffering

Are there other meanings for us that come from the cross? Could it be that Jesus' hour of agony might also be designed to remind us of what it means to suffer? Could it be that he was telling us that when we suffer, as inevitably we do in life, we can look back to the One who suffered infinitely and who found strength to triumph over suffering by his appeal to God?

Could this be part of the reason that the inspired writers did not gloss over the agony of Jesus in Gethsemane and at Calvary? They could easily have minimized the feelings of anxiety which Jesus felt in the garden. They could have softened the agony of the cross. They might have pictured Jesus as triumphantly playing the role of some superman, but they did not.

One of the most impressive statements of all is that sentence in Hebrews 5:8, 9, which says, "Although he was a Son, he learned obedience through what he suffered...." Think of that for a moment. Then, listen to the rest of the sentence, "...and being made perfect he became the source of eternal salvation to all who obey him." Suffering was a learning experience even for the Son of God! This statement is past our comprehension, but it helps us to some extent to understand the value of suffering in our own lives.

Later in the Epistle of Hebrews, the author tells his readers that their own suffering is nothing other than the "discipline of the Lord" (Heb. 12:3–7). In other words, suffering is not shameful. It is a learning experience. Perhaps in this we can understand at least partially why we are told that the Son of God "learned" from suffering. He was sharing our situation. Even our worst suffering can be a part of God's plans to help us learn to develop the most valuable qualities of life.

We're Not Made Yet

George MacDonald in one of his books tells of a woman who met a sudden sorrow. She exclaimed bitterly, "I wish I'd never been made!" A friend replied, "My dear, you're not made yet. You're only being made—and this is the Maker's process." In one of Ibsen's plays, a character asks another, "Who taught thee to sing?" The answer came back, "God sent me sorrow." In the producing of life's deepest and profoundest qualities, suffering has a positive and creative function to fulfill.

It was Martin Luther who said, "My temptations have been my masters in divinity." William James, the Harvard psychologist, once commented concerning the famous painting by Guido Reni in the Louvre in Paris which shows Michael with his foot on Satan's throat, "The world is all the richer for having a devil in it, so long as we keep our foot upon his neck." James, in the Scriptures, wrote, "Count it all joy, my brethren, when you meet various trials, for you know that the testing of your faith produces steadfastness" (James 1:2, 3). Hardships, temptations, and discipline help us to develop the qualities of character that are imperative if we are to be God's people.

Who are the men whose names stand in the honor roll of faith in Hebrews 11? Are they men whose lives were happy and unclouded, peaceful and serene, or were they men who became victors by the challenges which they met and by the sufferings which they underwent? Consider this, "They were stoned, they were sawn in two, they were killed with the sword; they went about in skins of sheep and goats, destitute, afflicted, ill-treated—of whom the world was not worthy—wandering over deserts and mountains, and in dens and caves of the earth" (Heb. 11:37, 38).

Our Lord Led the Way

Nineteen centuries ago our Lord suffered the agony of the cross. In his suffering we find great encouragement and strength, as we in a far lesser way must also suffer from time to time in our lives. It helps to know that he led the way and that through suffering even the Son of God developed strength. He also points the way to the source of strength for us, as we follow in his steps in turning to God in times of difficulty and anxiety.

Far more important, however, his suffering on the cross made possible our salvation. Had it not been for his willingness to die, we would still be in our sins, hopelessly, eternally lost. How wonderful it is to have the gift of salvation, paid for by his death, freely offered to us, no matter who we are or where we are. How tragic that some turn away from Christ's offer of freedom from the guilt of sin and let his sacrifice go unappreciated and unused.

If you have never come to Christ in obedient faith, you are among those for whom he died but who have not yet claimed their gift. Believe in him as the divine Son of God, make a deep commitment of heart to turn away from the sins of the world, let those around you know of your faith in Christ openly and gladly, and then put on Christ in baptism, by being buried in a grave of water out of which you will be raised to live a new kind of life. This is the simple, yet profound, plan by which Christ calls all men to come to him and to salvation. As you do this you will become a part of a great host of millions of others who have been redeemed by the blood of Christ, freely given on the cross of Calvary, for the redemption of mankind.

The Sheep Gate, Jerusalem

31 The Via Dolorosa

The Via Dolorosa, or "Way of Sorrows," is the traditional path followed by Jesus from his condemnation by Pilate until his death on the cross. The present ground level is many feet above what it was in the first century. Accordingly, the sites we see today do not date back to the time of Jesus. Excavation, however, has uncovered some first-century remains.

From Gethsemane to Calvary

After his arrest Jesus had been taken first to the house of Annas, the father-in-law of the high priest Caiaphas. Before Annas, Jesus was asked

225

about his disciples and his teaching. When he answered, Jesus was struck by one of the soldiers standing near. Annas sent him bound to Caiaphas (John 18:12-27).

Jesus was then tried before Caiaphas, the high priest, and before the scribes and elders that were gathered. To accuse him they hired false witnesses, but unfortunately for them, the testimony of the witnesses was contradictory. Unable to make their case with false witnesses, they began to question Jesus. His replies threw them into a frenzy. They decided he had blasphemed and was worthy of death. They spat in his face and beat him with the palms of their hands. They hit him and then asked him to identify the person who had done the striking (Matt. 26:57-68).

The next morning Jesus' accusers took him to Pilate the governor. They did not want to enter the hall because they would defile themselves for the Passover. Pilate came out to them and exchanged remarks concerning Jesus; finally, he told them to try Jesus themselves. They replied that he deserved death and this required Roman approval. At this point, Jesus was asked by Pilate if he were the king of the Jews. During the ensuing conversation Pilate asked his famous question, "What is truth?" After the examination, Pilate told the Jews outside he could find no reason to condemn the man (John 18:28-38).

When Pilate learned that Jesus was from the northern part of Palestine, he sent him to Herod, who happened to be visiting in Jerusalem. Herod was glad to see him because Jesus had acquired a reputation and Herod wanted to see a miracle. Herod also had a number of questions for Jesus, which Jesus refused to answer. All during the trial the Jews kept up a steady stream of accusations. Soldiers mocked Jesus, dressing him in royal robes (Luke 23:6-12).

Jesus was sent back to Pilate, who announced that he had decided Jesus was innocent and that Herod agreed. He indicated that Jesus would be chastised and then released (Luke 23:13-16). Since the governor usually released one prisoner at Passover, Pilate offered the people a choice between the notorious Barabbas and Jesus. He knew the accusations were brought against Jesus because of the envy of the Jewish leaders (Matt. 27:15-18).

About this time, Pilate's wife sent a message that she had had a bad dream about Jesus and warned Pilate against harming him. Jewish officials stirred up the crowd, and when Pilate made his offer, the people asked for Barabbas. When Pilate asked what to do with Jesus, the crowd ordered him to be crucified (Matt. 27:19-23). Pilate made his appeal three times, but the crowds were insistent that Jesus should be killed (Luke 23:22-24).

Pilate saw that a riot was developing, so he took a bowl of water and symbolically washed his hands of the affair in full view of the crowds. Pilate then had Jesus scourged and taken into the palace. The soldiers on duty stripped him and put on him a scarlet robe and a crown made of thorns. They placed a reed in his right hand, mockingly bowed in front of him, spat on him, and hit him with the reed (Matt. 27:24-31).

Pilate went back out to the crowd and indicated that he had found nothing wrong in Jesus. The soldiers brought Jesus out and Pilate presented him: "Behold the man!" During Pilate's conversation with the crowd, he became aware of the fact that Jesus was claiming to be the Son of God. This worried Pilate and he went back into the palace to talk more with Jesus. The more they talked the more Pilate wanted to release him. But when he confronted the Jews with his renewed intentions to release Jesus, they accused Pilate of not being loyal to Caesar. He brought Jesus to the Pavement called *Gabbatha* in Hebrew, and decided to crucify him (John 19:4-16).

"Stations of the Cross"

At this point in the narrative tradition has entered to establish fourteen stops or stations between Pilate's palace and Golgotha. These stations mark events reported in the Gospels or invented by tradition. Each Friday at three o'clock in the afternoon the Franciscans retrace the steps of the tradition.

Station One marks the site where Jesus was condemned. The building today is a Muslim school called El-Omariye. Entrance is gained by a flight of steps. Tradition holds that this was the site of the Praetorium, where Pilate's judgment hall was located and Jesus was sentenced. The original staircase, known as the Scala Santa, is supposed to have been taken to Rome by Helena. Today it is displayed in the church near St. Giovanni in Laterano.

Station Two marks the site where Jesus received the cross. The station is located on the road outside Station One opposite the Chapel of the Condemnation. Under the arch Pilate said, "Behold the man." Nearby is a Greek Orthodox monastery which claims to be the site of the prison of Barabbas.

Station Three marks the spot where Jesus fell the first time. It is around the corner, positioned to the left of the second station, where there is a small museum and a store. This station does not mark a biblical event but a probable tradition.

Station Four marks the site where Jesus met his mother. The area is marked by an Armenian Catholic church built in 1881. Tradition says that Mary exchanged a glance with Jesus and that, when Jesus fell, she pushed through the crowd to comfort him.

Station Five marks the place where Simon the Cyrenian took the cross from Jesus (Luke 23:26). This station was constructed by the Franciscans in 1895.

Station Six marks the place where Veronica wiped the face of Jesus.

Tradition states that she was one of the weeping women who followed Jesus. Tradition further states that Veronica was the lady who had an issue of blood for twelve years before Jesus healed her. The cloth, which allegedly contains the blood and sweat from Jesus' face and the imprint of his features, is in St. Peter's in Rome.

Station Seven marks the place where Jesus fell the second time. Across from the station is a column where some say the Romans fastened the death sentence. It is called the Gate of Judgment. The Franciscans bought the site of Station Seven in 1875.

Station Eight recalls where Jesus spoke to the daughters of Jerusalem (Luke 23:28). It is marked by a stone with a Latin cross and the Greek word *nikē* (victory).

Station Nine marks the place where Jesus allegedly fell a third time. The station, located up a flight of twenty-eight steps, is marked by the shaft of a column enclosed in a pillar of the door of a Coptic church.

Station Ten marks the place where Jesus was stripped of his clothes. Stations Ten through Thirteen are at the traditional site of Calvary.

Station Eleven marks the site where Jesus was nailed to the cross. It is located in the right nave of the Church of the Holy Sepulcher, the section which belongs to the Franciscans. The site is marked by a silver-covered altar made in Florence in 1558 and by a mosaic made in 1938.

Station Twelve marks the place where Jesus died on the cross. A disc marks the spot where the cross was fixed. On a platform two feet high stands a Greek altar.

Station Thirteen recalls the taking down of the body of Jesus from the cross. Over the altar is a wood statue from the sixteenth century.

Station Fourteen is the tomb in the Church of the Holy Sepulcher.

The Church of the Holy Sepulcher

Six religious communities have certain rights in the Church of the Holy Sepulcher today. These rights are protected by the "Status Quo," an arrangement dating from 1757 which states that there will be no change or innovation either in possession or in the exercise of ritual. The six groups are the Franciscans, Greek Orthodox, Armenian Orthodox, Syrian, Coptic, and Abyssinian. The Copts have two rooms, and a chapel at the rear of the sepulcher itself, but are restricted to certain days. The Syrians and Abyssinians are even more limited in their rights. These rights include the use of lamps, decorations, pictures, and candles, as well as the rights to clean and make repairs. These rights are worked out in detail since the right to repair a wall or to hang a picture implies possession of that wall or picture.

There is a paved court in front of the Church of the Holy Sepulcher. It measures some fifty-four by eighty feet, and lies over an ancient cistern. A number of chapels mark each side. The court was the scene of bloodshed on a number of occasions when various religious communities came to blows over the rights of the sanctuary. The last such occasion was in November, 1901, when fifteen Franciscans were wounded by Greek monks.

The door on the right has been closed since the time of the Crusades, while the key and the right to open the other door are in the hands of two Muslim families. Entrance is free, the fee being paid by the community using the basilica. Once inside, the Muslim doorkeepers rest on the left. Some say they are there to keep the rival Christian groups at peace with one another.

Directly in front of the door (on the inside) is a polished red stone measuring about four by eight feet. It is called the "Stone of Anointing"; it marks the place where Joseph and Nicodemus prepared the body of Jesus for burial. On the right is Calvary, which is some seventeen feet above the floor of the building and measures thirty by thirty-seven feet. The top is divided into two chapels; the one on the right belongs to the Latins. About one-third of the platform rests on the rock below, the remainder rests on structure. A silver disc with an opening in the center marks the spot where the cross was fixed. On each side of the altar is a black marble disc marking the hole where the cross of one of the thieves stood. On the right of the altar is the place where the rock was split by the earthquake. The crack runs through the entire rock and can be seen below in the Chapel of Adam.

Under the dome is the *Anastasis* or the site of the sepulcher itself. The upper narrow gallery belongs to the Greeks; the lower, wider gallery is divided between the Latins and the Armenians. In the center is the sepulcher—twenty-seven feet long, nineteen feet wide and high, covered with marble and adorned with sixteen pillars.

Scattered throughout the building are numerous other sites marking biblical and postbiblical events. Included are the spots where the women watched the crucifixion, the place from which the Jewish officials mocked Jesus, the place where the soldiers divided his clothes, the place where Jesus appeared to Mary, and the column of the flagellation. It should be mentioned again that the many claims made are, of course, to be regarded as traditions rather than as proven facts.

Man at His Worst, God at His Best

Harold Hazelip

Crosses are in style today. They may be found on women or men. They come in bronze, silver, and gold, or as costume jewelry set with stones.

Beautiful crosses are worn like astrological signs and amulets. The cross has become a kind of decoration for church towers, walls, and tombstones.

But the cross in ancient times was no pretty decoration. It was the symbol of disgrace, the "electric chair" or the "gas chamber" of that time. It was the place reserved for traitors, misfits, and criminals.

In the second century A.D. the Christian writer Justin carried on a debate with Trypho, a Jewish rabbi, over the claims of Christianity. Trypho argued that the Old Testament contained the proof that Jesus could not be the Messiah. After all, Deuteronomy 21:23 said clearly, "For a hanged man is accursed by God." Who would believe in a crucified Messiah, Trypho wondered.

The apostle Paul wrote, "For Jews demand signs and Greeks seek wisdom, but we preach Christ crucified, a stumbling block to Jews and folly to Gentiles, but to those who are called, both Jews and Greeks, Christ the power of God and the wisdom of God" (I Cor. 1:22–24). The Gospels tell the story of the crucifixion very simply. People in the Roman world knew the details. Some elaboration from history is almost necessary for us if we are to understand what Jesus went through for us and for all mankind.

Details of the Crucifixion

Following the verdict of condemnation by the Roman governor, Jesus was scourged, an event the Gospels summarize with one word (Matt. 27:26). The scourge was a whip made of leather thongs, studded with sharpened pellets of lead, iron, or bone. The victim was stripped and tied in a bent position to a pillar, or stretched on a frame; his back was literally ripped to pieces.

Then the soldiers had their fun with Jesus. They plaited a crown of thorns for his head, put a reed in his right hand for a scepter, arrayed him in a purple robe, and saluted him: "Hail, King of the Jews!" (Mark 15:16–20). Rather than acting from hatred, they probably were only playing games with a man they considered to be a "pretender."

Then the procession toward Calvary began. The Greek word for the place was *kranion,* which we have in English as "cranium." The Latin term in *calva,* which means a "bare head or skull," and accounts for the word *Calvary* (Luke 23:33, KJV). For the procession. the "criminal" was placed in the center of a square of four Roman soldiers. A board was carried before him, probably whitened with gypsum, with the charge against him painted in black letters. The inscription for Jesus read, "This is the King of the Jews" (Luke 23:38).

The victim was expected to carry the cross, or a part of it. The upright beam may have already stood from previous crucifixions, but the crossbeam had to be carried. Jesus may have been weakened by the flogging; Simon of

Cyrene, a passerby, was forced to help Jesus carry the cross (Luke 23:26). A multitude of people followed, including some women who "bewailed and lamented him." Jesus turned to them and said, "Daughters of Jerusalem, do not weep for me..." (Luke 23:27, 28).

They Reach Golgotha

When they reached the place of crucifixion, the cross would be laid flat, and the victim laid on top. Jesus was offered medicated wine (a narcotic) to drink. This would dull the pain; Jesus tasted and refused it (Matt. 27:34).

Halfway up the upright beam, there was usually a ledge of wood which projected as a saddle on which the body could rest. Otherwise, the nails would tear through the hands from having to bear the victim's full weight. The nails were driven, his body was suspended. Instead of the usual curses from the victim, Jesus said, "Father, forgive them; for they know not what they do" (Luke 23:34).

Before the victim was nailed to the cross, he was stripped except for a loincloth, and his clothing fell to the soldiers as incidental income. There were probably six articles of clothing: a belt, sandals, girdle, turban, and tunic—all of about equal value—and a robe, which was used as a cloak by day and a blanket at night. Jesus' robe had no seams and the soldiers cast lots for it.

The robe was the only thing of value he possessed. Robes were ordinarily made at home, usually a mother's gift to her son as he left home. Soldiers gambling for the robe may have caused his thoughts to turn toward Mary, who stood near the cross. Jesus saw John, and said to his mother, "Woman, behold, your son!" Then he said to John, "Behold, your mother!" John understood, and took Mary to his own home (John 19:25-27).

The cross was apparently near a highway. People going to and from the city would taunt him: "You who would destroy the temple and build it in three days, save yourself! If you are the Son of God, come down from the cross" (Matt. 27:40). The priests, the rulers, the soldiers all joined in the ridicule.

Two robbers were crucified with him, one on either side, increasing the shame of his death. They were not petty criminals or burglars; they were brigands—reckless adventurers. At first, both of them joined the mockery. Luke tells us that one of them changed his mind and said, "Jesus, remember me when you come into your kingly power" (Luke 23:42).

The End Comes Quickly

Jesus was crucified at nine in the morning, and at noon darkness came over all the land for three hours. About three in the afternoon he cried with a loud voice, "My God, my God, why hast thou forsaken me?" (Matt. 27:46). The drama was drawing to an end.

He was thirsty. When they held a sponge full of vinegar to his mouth, Jesus said, "It is finished" (John 19:30). Then he prayed the brief prayer he may have been taught by his mother to pray at night, from Psalm 31:5: "Father, into thy hands I commit my spirit!" (Luke 23:46). Then he bowed his head and died.

At that moment, "the curtain of the temple was torn in two, from top to bottom; and the earth shook, and the rocks were split; the tombs also were opened, and many bodies of the saints who had fallen asleep were raised" (Matt. 27:51, 52). The centurion who was in charge of the crucifixion said, "Truly this was the Son of God!" (Matt. 27:54).

Only one merciful note seems to mark the entire crucifixion. Usually crucifixion was a lingering death. One might last for days. But Jesus died quickly. The next day was the Sabbath; the bodies must be down from the crosses. When the soldiers came to hasten the end, they found Jesus already dead. "One of the soldiers pierced his side with a spear, and at once there came out blood and water" (John 19:34).

The Meaning of the Cross

This is the story of the cross. Reflecting on the meaning of the cross is like trying to take in the grandeur of a great mountain peak: it cannot be done from one angle alone. We must come to it from different directions. The New Testament uses many images to convey to us its meaning. Sometimes the cross is described as the breaking down of hostility or the renewal of a friendship; Paul talked of God's reconciling us to himself (Eph. 2:16). Sometimes the image is drawn from the courtroom. We are the accused; we know our guilt. But to our surprise the judge acquits us when we have no defense at all. The word is "justification." At other times the image is of slaves who are about to be auctioned but for whom someone pays the price and says, "You're free." The word is "redemption."

All of these words suggest that the cross—horrible as it was—made all the difference in our lives. When people have thought of Jesus going to the cross in his love for sinners, they have said, "God must be like that." God was, in Christ, reconciling the world to himself, not counting our sins against us (II Cor. 5:19). The cross is most of all the proof of God's love.

Your response and mine to the cross? We are to be crucified with him (Gal. 2:20). When we have died with him to sin through our repentance, and have been buried with him in baptism for the forgiveness of our sins, he takes up his dwelling place in us.

The Garden Tomb

32   Christ's Tomb

Jesus was led from the palace, the place of the pavement, to be crucified. On the way his captors made Simon of Cyrene carry his cross. A great crowd followed Jesus on his death path, including a large number of crying women. Jesus told them not to cry for him, but for themselves. Two other men were also to be crucified.

They arrived at Golgotha, an Armaic word meaning "the skull." The word appears only three times in the Bible (Matt. 27:33; Mark 15:22; John 19:17). Golgotha was located near Jerusalem. Hebrews 13:12 indicates that Jesus suffered outside the city walls. However, the site was not far outside the walls, but "near the city" (John 19:20). Matthew's statement, "And those who passed by…" (Matt. 27:39), may indicate that Golgotha was by a well-traveled road. It was visible from some distance, as indicated by the expression, "women looking on from afar" (Mark 15:40; cf. Luke 23:49). This has led some to think it was a hill, but nowhere does the Bible indicate that the crucifixion took place on a hill. Further, only in John 19:41 is there indication that the tomb was near the site of death and that it was in a garden. All of these suggestions do not enable us to locate the site of the crucifixion and burial with absolute certainty.

Upon his arrival at Golgotha, wherever it was, the officers gave Jesus a drink of wine mixed with gall, but he refused it. Jesus was crucified with two thieves, and while dying uttered seven meaningful sayings, among which are: "My God, my God, why have you forsaken me?" "Father, into your hands I commend my spirit," and "It is finished." When he died the earth quaked, tombs were opened, and darkness came upon the earth at midday. The Roman centurion in charge of the crucifixion said, "Truly this was the Son of God." Having found Jesus dead within a relatively short time, the Roman soldiers pierced his side (Matt. 27:32–56; Mark 15:21–41; Luke 23:26–49; John 19:17–37).

The Holy Sepulcher

From early times Christians have regarded the site of the Church of the Holy Sepulcher as the place of Christ's death, burial, and resurrection. Tradition states that the site of Calvary was taken by the Romans, where they erected a statue of Jupiter-Serapis, while over the tomb they constructed an altar to Venus. In A.D. 326 Constantine exposed the tomb and began to build a basilica. The tomb was covered before the end of that century by a rotunda thirty-seven feet high and forty feet in diameter. The church was destroyed in 614 A.D. by the Persians but immediately it was rebuilt. A separate church was built over the site of Calvary; it was not until the tenth century that the two sites were brought into one building as they are today. The current Church of the Holy Sepulcher was constructed by the Crusaders.

The Garden Tomb

There are many today who believe that the Garden Tomb, rather than the Church of the Holy Sepulcher, is the true site of Christ's burial. This controversy is not new. Some sixteen theories concerning the site of the death and burial of Jesus were promoted between 1840 and 1876, of which twelve argued in favor of the Holy Sepulcher and the other four against it. In 1840, Otto Thenius first suggested that the hillock outside the Damascus Gate, with ancient cisterns dug into its side, was the authentic Calvary.

In 1882 General Charles (Chinese) Gordon, while sitting on the roof of a house in Jerusalem, noted that the hill behind the present-day Arab bus station looked just like a skull. Two small dark caves formed the eyes, a ridge made the nose, and a lower opening in the ragged cliff suggested the mouth. It gave the clear impression of a skull. In 1867, a Greek doing construction work at the foot of the hill had found a rock-hewn tomb there. The tomb was cut from solid rock and was assigned by some to Roman times, but by others to the Byzantine period.

No tradition earlier than the nineteenth century regards the site of Gordon's Calvary or the Garden Tomb as authentic. The site of the Garden Tomb is 650 feet north of the present Damascus Gate, a part of the modern wall of Jerusalem. The tomb is cut into solid rock and is fourteen feet wide, ten feet deep, and seven-and-one-half feet high. The controversy as to whether the Church of the Holy Sepulcher or the Garden Tomb is the site of Christ's death and burial continues to rage. It is noteworthy that both sites are merely the suggestions of tradition.

Archaeologists and historians of first-century A.D. Jerusalem speak of three walls of the city. The current walls were built in fairly recent times and are thought to follow the walls built by Hadrian in the second century. Therefore, the question is not where the walls fall today, but where they stood in the first century. The authenticity of the Holy Sepulcher site depends in part upon where the second wall of the city rested. If it curved to the west, the Holy Sepulcher would have been inside the city and thus would be removed as a possible site of the death of Jesus. However, if it curved to the east then the church remains a possible site. At present it is impossible to establish the course of the second wall and to determine with certainty whether the Church of the Holy Sepulcher was in or outside of Herod's city of Jerusalem at the time when Jesus was crucified.

As a postscript to the above uncertainties, let us remember that it is not exactly where, or even when, Christ was crucified, buried, and raised from the dead that matters, but the fact that it happened. Actually, it matters little whether the site of the Holy Sepulcher or the site of the Garden Tomb is the correct one. The point of supreme importance is that Jesus lived, died, and lives again. This is a part of the solid evidence that he is the divine Son of God and our Savior.

Good Morning!

Batsell Barrett Baxter

On Sunday in the spring of each year, designated by many as Easter Sunday, the entire Christian world centers its thoughts on the resurrection of the Lord. It is one of the few events in the life of Christ for which the exact time of the year can be determined. The resurrection of Christ came at Passover time. Passover always falls on the first Sabbath after the first full moon after the vernal equinox. We use the same factors to calculate the date of Christ's resurrection. March 21 designates the change from winter to spring. We wait for the first full moon, then for the first Sabbath or Saturday, and the day following is the anniversary of the first day of the week on which Christ was raised from the dead.

The Resurrection Was Central

The early Christians preached the resurrection as a central part of the gospel. All four Gospel writers tell of Christ's resurrection from the dead. Luke puts it in these words: "But on the first day of the week, at early dawn, they went to the tomb, taking the spices which they had prepared. And they found the stone rolled away from the tomb, but when they went in they did not find the body. While they were perplexed about this, behold, two men stood by them in dazzling apparel; and as they were frightened and bowed their faces to the ground, the men said to them, 'Why do you seek the living among the dead? Remember how he told you, while he was still in Galilee, that the Son of man must be delivered into the hands of sinful men, and be crucified, and on the third day rise.' And they remembered his words, and returning from the tomb they told all this to the eleven and to all the rest" (Luke 24:1-9).

Notice in this reading that the women had come to the tomb to anoint the dead body of Christ. They and the other disciples saw him die and saw him buried. At that point their hopes vanished and they gave up their expectations of his establishing a kingdom. When the women brought the news of the empty tomb to the apostles, Peter and John ran to the tomb to see for themselves. Peter entered first, then John. Later John wrote, "Then the other disciple, who reached the tomb first, also went in, and he saw and believed; for as yet they did not know the scripture, that he must rise from the dead" (John 20:8, 9).

The Apostles Proclaimed It

Once they were convinced, however, that Christ had risen from the dead the disciples began to declare it everywhere they went as a cornerstone of their Christian faith. In order to notice the degree to which they made the resurrection a central part of the faith let us look at several passages of Scripture. For example, in the selecting of an apostle to take the place of Judas, Peter said, "So one of the men who have accompanied us during all the time that the Lord Jesus went in and out among us, beginning from the baptism of John until the day when he was taken up from us—one of these men must become with us a witness to his resurrection" (Acts 1:21, 22).

A little later we read in Acts 4:33, "And with great power the apostles gave their testimony to the resurrection of the Lord Jesus...."

When Paul wrote to the Romans he described the act of baptism in terms of Christ's burial and resurrection: "Do you not know that all of us who have been baptized into Christ Jesus were baptized into his death? We were buried therefore with him by baptism into death, so that as Christ was raised from the dead by the glory of the Father, we too might walk in newness of life. For if we have been united with him in a death like his, we shall certainly be united with him in a resurrection like his" (Rom. 6:3-5).

Your Faith Is Vain, Unless...

These are just a few of the evidences that the apostles and other disciples preached the resurrection from the dead as a cardinal principle of Christianity. Nothing was more significant, as evidenced by their emphasis upon it, than the fact that Jesus had been raised. The crucial nature of this fact is seen in an important paragraph from Paul's first letter to the Corinthians: "Now if Christ is preached as raised from the dead, how can some of you say that there is no resurrection of the dead? But if there is no resurrection of the dead, then Christ has not been raised; if Christ has not been raised, then our preaching is in vain and your faith is in vain" (I Cor. 15:12-14). Our hope of life eternal depends upon Christ's resurrection.

From this dismal picture Paul then turned to the brilliant light of the resurrection: "But in fact Christ has been raised from the dead, the first fruits of those who have fallen asleep. For as by a man came death, by a man has come also the resurrection of the dead. For as in Adam all die, so also in Christ shall all be made alive. But each in his own order: Christ the first fruits, then at his coming those who belong to Christ" (I Cor. 15:20-23).

The Apostles Staked Their Lives

The resurrection of Christ is the crucial matter in Christian faith. The apostles staked their lives on it. They left homes and families, risked goods and reputation, and eventually suffered martyrdom because of their faith in Christ's resurrection. They were eyewitnesses of the resurrected Lord. They had seen him alive, they saw him die. In agony they watched him die on the cross and then watched as he was buried in the tomb. A period of despondency followed until on the first day of the week he began to appear to them alive again. Mary Magdalene saw him, then the other women. He appeared to ten apostles in an upper room; then one week later he appeared to the Eleven in the same place. He ate breakfast with seven by the Sea of Galilee. He walked with two disciples on the way to Emmaus. He appeared to Peter alone. He was seen by five hundred brethren at one time. There were other appearances and then finally he ascended from the presence of the Eleven on top of the Mount of Olives.

Saul of Tarsus was a brilliant young Jewish lawyer. He had studied at the feet of Gamaliel and was extremely zealous in his persecution of Christians. Then on the Damascus road the Lord appeared unto him and Saul came to believe that Christ was the Son of God. His whole life was changed. He became an apostle and ultimately died as a martyr for his faith. On the subject of resurrection we have quoted him more extensively than any other of the apostles. He, who knew all of the arguments which the high priest and the others gave for not believing in Jesus, came to be the foremost proclaimer of the risen Christ.

The resurrection of Christ is crucial. Because Christ was raised from the dead, we know that he is no mere man, but rather the divine Son of God. He is worthy of honor, respect, and worship. We must obey his commandments, if we expect to reach heaven.

We close with the words which Christ spoke to Martha on the occasion of her sorrow at the death of her brother Lazarus. Jesus said, "I am the resurrection and the life; he who believes in me, though he die, yet shall he live, and whoever lives and believes in me shall never die. Do you believe this?" At that point Martha said to Jesus, "Yes, Lord; I believe that you are the Christ, the Son of God, he who is coming into the world" (John 11:25–27).

Ask of yourself the same question Jesus asked of Martha. Do you believe in Christ as the divine Son of God? If you do, have you ever confessed him before your fellow men, as he has asked you to do? Have you repented of your sins deeply and genuinely, and then submitted to the beautiful symbolical act of baptism, which suggests Christ's death and resurrection? This is the way that you come into the family of God. This is the way that you express your faith in your resurrected Lord.

Emmaus Today

33 Emmaus

The story of the two disciples walking from Jerusalem to Emmaus ("warm well" or "warm springs") on the very day of the resurrection occurs only in Luke, consuming most of the twenty-fourth chapter. The two disciples were walking toward the village and discussing the events of the past days when another drew near to them. The third party was Jesus, but "their eyes were kept from recognizing him" (Luke 24:16).

The stranger asked, "What is this conversation which you are holding with each other as you walk?" (v. 17). At this point the two men stopped walking and looked at Jesus with sad faces. One of the men, Cleopas, asked if he were the only visitor in Jerusalem who had not heard about the happenings. The stranger inquired further and they told him that Jesus of Nazareth had been a prophet known for his deeds and words before both God and the people. They indicated that their religious authorities arrested him, tried him, and arranged with the Romans to have him crucified.

The two disciples were disappointed because they had expected Jesus to be a redeemer in Israel, but it had been three days since his death and there was apparently no hope remaining. They also told the stranger that some of the women who had been part of their group were now claiming that they had seen a vision of angels who said Jesus was alive. Some of the men had gone to the tomb and it was certainly empty.

It was the stranger's turn to talk. He began by calling the two disciples foolish men, slow of heart to believe what the prophets had written. He asked, "Was it not necessary that the Christ should suffer these things and enter into his glory?" Then, "beginning with Moses and all the prophets, he interpreted to them in all the scriptures the things concerning himself" (Luke 24:26, 27).

As they approached Emmaus, the stranger prepared to bid them farewell as he was apparently going further. They urged him to spend the night since it was near the evening. He agreed. At table the stranger took the bread and blessed it and broke it. When he gave it to them, their eyes were opened. The stranger, whom they now knew to be Jesus, vanished out of their sight.

They asked each other, "Did not our hearts burn within us while he talked to us on the road, while he opened to us the scriptures?" They did not delay but left the table and returned to Jerusalem in time to find the eleven apostles still gathered along with others. The apostles told the two men, "The Lord has risen indeed, and has appeared to Simon!" (Luke 24:34).

Then Cleopas and his friend told the apostles of the events on the road and around the table while Jesus was breaking bread. As they were sharing these experiences, Jesus appeared, frightening them. Jesus told them to look at him and handle him. He even ate with them to convince them that he had indeed risen in the flesh. Luke continues with Jesus' giving a form of the Great Commission (Luke 24:44–49).

According to Luke 24:13, Emmaus was sixty stadia from Jerusalem, or about seven miles (the Roman stadium is about 600 feet). This reading is found in an early third-century papyrus and in Codex Vaticanus, as well as other manuscripts. Most English translations record a distance of about seven miles. However, Codex Sinaiticus and the Palestinian Syriac record 160 stadia, which is about twenty miles.

The text indicates that Jesus met the two disciples during their walk. They recognized him as a "visitor to Jerusalem," a phrase which suggests that he joined them not far from Jerusalem. They made the trip to Emmaus during the day and then walked back that night. Alfred Plummer concludes that it is absurd to suppose these two walked forty miles in one day and arrived in time to find the disciples still gathered together and conversing. On the other side, Edward Robinson, F. M. Abel, and J. W. Crowfoot, early explorers of the land of Palestine and acquainted with the habits of the people, find no difficulty in a forty-mile walk on one day.

Some seven sites have been proposed for Emmaus, with two being leading candidates. El-Qubeibeh is seven miles west of Jerusalem. Ancient ruins of the Greek, Byzantine, and Crusader periods mark the countryside around el-Qubeibeh. Located between el-Qubeibeh and Jerusalem is Nebi Samwil, called "Mount Joy" by the Crusaders because they caught their first glimpse of Jerusalem from this hill. Nebi Samwil is the traditional site of the tomb of the prophet Samuel.

The traditional site of Emmaus is 'Amwas (Nicopolis), twenty miles west of Jerusalem. Eusebius identifies 'Amwas as the biblical Emmaus in his *Onomasticon,* and comments that Emmaus is now "Nicopolis, a famous city of Palestine." Jerome followed Eusebius; the Crusaders also accepted this site.

The town of 'Amwas is located on the main Jaffa-Jerusalem road. Two arguments against this being the correct site are its distance from Jerusalem, which suggests that the disciples walked forty miles on the day Jesus rose from the dead, and the fact that Josephus indicates the place was a governmental center while the place visited by Jesus seems to have been more of a village.

Excavations were conducted at 'Amwas as early as 1875. Five buildings were uncovered. The latest is a twelfth-century church (Crusader period). Under this building was a larger church whose floor was twenty-eight inches below the floor of the Crusader church. This larger basilica (150 by 170 feet) is placed in the third century.

Is Your Bible Open?

Harold Hazelip

For hundreds of years scholars had attempted in vain to unlock the secret of ancient Egyptian hieroglyphics—literally "sacred carvings." The characters looked strange and unfathomable. Then in 1799 an officer in Napoleon's expedition discovered a stone slab near the mouth of the Nile River which became known as the Rosetta Stone.

On the Rosetta Stone was an inscription in three languages. One of these languages was Egyptian hieroglyphics, another was Greek. An English physicist named Thomas Young compared the Egyptian hieroglyphics to the other languages and was able to identify the name of Ptolemy. Eventually the young French scholar Champollion was able to decipher the hieroglyphic system of writing. This might never have been possible without the Rosetta Stone.

Missing the Bible's Point

Many people think of the Bible as needing something like a Rosetta Stone. The Bible is a collection of writings spanning many centuries. It contains poetry, history, and prophetic oracles. There are verses that are simple, and others that seem impossible to understand. There are references to ancient history and peoples about which we are ignorant.

The Bible has often been misunderstood or misapplied. The Nazis led a movement to discard the Old Testament from the collection of Scripture. They scoffed at it as a "Jew book" consisting of the "stories of herdsmen." Even today the Bible is being used by some in South Africa to support the politics of apartheid. They argue that since "God created . . . every living creature . . . according to their kinds," people of different ethnic origins should be kept completely separate from one another (Gen. 1:21-25).

In Leo Tolstoy's *War and Peace,* Pierre Bezukhov had watched the destruction of his beloved Russia by the forces of Napoleon and was asking the meaning of these tragedies. One day a friend pointed him to Revelation 13:18, which describes the beast who carries the mysterious number 666. Pierre began to study and concluded that the awful beast was none other than Napoleon. He gave the letters in Napoleon's name numerical equivalents and found that they would total 666. After further reflection, Pierre decided that he himself was the one prophesied in the Book of Revelation to destroy the beast.

On the Emmaus Road

People have so often missed the point the Bible is making. In the last chapter of the Gospel of Luke, two men were walking dejectedly from Jerusalem to Emmaus. They were talking of the things that had happened over the Passover weekend. Jesus joined them but they did not recognize him. He asked about their conversation. They explained sadly how Jesus of Nazareth, "a prophet mighty in deed and word before God and all the people," had been crucified. "But we had hoped that he was the one to redeem Israel. Yes, and besides all this, it is now the third day since this happened." Then they told of women who had visited his tomb and found it empty. The women had even seen a vision of angels who said that Jesus was alive.

Jesus interrupted, "O foolish men, and slow of heart to believe all that the prophets have spoken! Was it not necessary that the Christ should suffer these things and enter into his glory?" And Luke adds, "And beginning with Moses and all the prophets, he interpreted to them in all the scriptures the things concerning himself" (Luke 24:13-27).

The two men invited Jesus to stay the night with them. As they sat for the evening meal, he gave thanks for the food. Their eyes were opened and they recognized him, but he vanished. They said to each other, "Did not our hearts burn within us while he talked to us on the road, while he opened to us the scriptures?" (Luke 24:32). They returned to Jerusalem and told the apostles what had happened.

These disciples, as pious as they were, had missed the point of Scripture. Their problem was not in knowing too few facts of Scripture; they had not heard the message of Scripture. They had approached Scripture with preconceived notions. In their understanding there was no room for a suffering Messiah. Instead of overthrowing the physical power of Rome, Jesus had died on a horrible cross. How could he be their savior?

Our Approach to Scripture

It would be a mistake for us to look self-righteously at the blindness of these disciples. Someone has commented, "Whenever you read the Bible and it makes you feel self-righteous, you've misunderstood it." In their blindness we should see something of ourselves. We too can become blind to the real meaning of Scripture.

How can we penetrate the Scriptures today—understand them for ourselves? Perhaps you have followed the usual procedure of beginning at the first of the Bible and reading it through. In an effort to hear the Bible more clearly, why not try a different procedure? Try reading it backward once. Begin with the closing section of Scripture—the Epistles—Romans through Revelation. A picture emerges in these letters of a scattered, struggling community in the Roman Empire who believe they have found in Jesus Christ the true revelation of God. They have committed themselves to him, body and soul, in life and death. They never talk of him as a martyred saint. They write of new life, new hope, new power which has come into the world. They locate this power in the person of Jesus Christ—his death, his burial, and resurrection. They are not embarrassed that he was crucified, or that such a death is a stumbling block to some and foolishness to others. Whoever reads their testimony today must be moved by their sincerity, their conviction as they speak of Jesus as the Revealer of God and the Savior of man.

Then move backward to the Acts of the Apostles. You will discover the beginnings of the church, the way people from various backgrounds became

Christians. You will see the determined march of the gospel from Jerusalem to Rome.

Moving further back to the beginning of the New Testament, you will discover four Gospels. Here are the sources for our knowledge of the life and teachings of Jesus Christ. Don't edit them—read them! See and hear a disturbing Savior who issued a loving call to discipleship. Note his promises and his rebukes. The Gospels are good news, but they are set against the background of God's judgment on our sin.

In the Gospels you will meet a man so simple that children loved and understood him, yet so demanding that his disciples found it impossible to follow him perfectly. He loved the loneliness of the hills and the lakes, but gave himself freely to the crowds. He was gentle and patient, yet threatening and rebuking. You see in him what God is like. Executed by the Romans, he still has an enormous impact on the human race today.

Now perhaps you are ready to read the Old Testament. There you will find the history of God's people told largely through the story of great events: the creation, the call of Abraham, the exodus, the preaching of the prophets. Throughout the Old Testament Scriptures you will find the hopes and the promises of a coming Messiah, which Jesus fulfilled.

The Key to the Bible

What those disciples discovered as Jesus talked with them at Emmaus was that the Scriptures are not merely a loose collection of unconnected books. There is a central story to the book, and the center of the story is Christ.

You may sit before a page covered with lines and figures which appear senseless at first. But all at once there flashes through your mind the formula by which you can solve the mathematical problems on the page. Now everything falls into its place until at the end you have the solution to the problem before you.

The Bible may appear to be an insoluble puzzle. But once you find the key in Jesus Christ, the pieces of the Bible begin to fall into place and make perfect sense. Christ is the Rosetta Stone of the Bible.

It is up to you to hear him, to do his will. He commanded his disciples to go into all the world and tell his story to every creature. And then he promised, "He who believes and is baptized will be saved; but he who does not believe will be condemned" (Mark 16:16).

The Mount of Olives as Seen from the Northeast Corner of the Old City

34　Mount of Olives

The mountain directly east of the city of Jerusalem is known as the Mount of Olives, suggesting the abundance of olive trees upon its slopes in ancient times. The mountain is called "Mount of the Ointment" in the Talmud. It was a Sabbath-day's journey from the city, meaning three thousand feet or five stadia.

The Mount of Olives is actually a ridge which runs along the east side of the city of Jerusalem parallel to the ravine known as the Kidron Valley. There are three separate peaks on the ridge; these are known today as Mount Scopus, the Mount of Olives, and the Mount of Offense. The entire ridge is about two-and-one-half miles long. The northernmost peak, at an altitude of 2,963 feet above sea level, is the highest. Its name, Scopus, comes from a word which indicates seeing, or overlooking, in this case, the city of Jerusalem. We also get our modern terms *microscope* and *telescope* from this word. The famous Hebrew University has been erected on top of this mountain.

The middle peak rises about 100 feet higher than Jerusalem at approximately 2,700 feet above sea level. Looking to the east, one has a magnificent view of the Jordan Valley and the Dead Sea (on a clear day) some fourteen miles away and some 4,000 feet down in the Great Rift. Beyond are the mountains of Moab, while to the southeast is the area known as the wilderness of Judea, the site of the temptations of Jesus. Looking west from the mountain, one has a beautiful panoramic view of the city of Jerusalem, with the temple mount and its Muslim holy buildings in the foreground and the Old and the New City behind. In addition to olive trees, there are abundant stands of pines near the top of the mountain. The wind blows quite hard in this area, bending the trees in a permanent southeastern direction. The Mount of Olives has a special meaning for us, because it was our home during our stay in Jerusalem. The Intercontinental Hotel, erected on the southern brow of the Mount of Olives, provides a magnificent view of Jerusalem, just across the Kidron Valley to the west.

The southernmost peak, which some do not even consider part of the same ridge, is called the Mount of Offense, the Mount of Corruption, the Mount of Evil Counsel, or Mount Scandal, because Solomon is thought to have built pagan altars here for his foreign wives (I Kings 11:7, 8).

From the biblical narrative it appears that Bethany was on the east side of the Mount of Olives, with Bethphage located nearby, possibly a bit nearer to the top of the mountain. The Garden of Gethsemane was on the lower slope of the mountain toward the west.

Biblical Events

A number of events during Christ's ministry occurred on or near the Mount of Olives. Apparently Jesus spent the final week of his life before the crucifixion teaching in Jerusalem during the daytime, but retiring to the Mount of Olives each evening. His triumphal entry crossed the mountain as he came from Bethany to Jerusalem at the beginning of the week. On his way into the city on one of the mornings he saw a fig tree and because of its barrenness caused it to wither away. According to Luke, it was from the Mount of Olives that Jesus looked down upon the city of Jerusalem and wept over it because of its sinful rebellion against God (Luke 19:41, 42). After having preached in the temple area, Jesus returned to the Mount of Olives and sat down with his disciples to answer their questions concerning the destruction of the temple and the end of the world (Matt. 24-25; Mark 13).

The Mount of Olives was also the site of the ascension of Jesus. Jesus had predicted his ascension, talking about "his departure" (Luke 9:31), and the fact that "the days drew near for him to be received up" (Luke 9:51). John indicated that he would be glorified (John 7:39; 12:16, 23). Mark indicated that Jesus "was taken up into heaven, and sat down at the right hand of God" (Mark 16:19).

According to Luke, Jesus taught his disciples about the fulfillment of Old Testament prophecy and about their role in proclaiming his death and resurrection. Then he led them as far as Bethany, where he lifted up his hands and blessed them. While Jesus was blessing his disciples he was carried away into heaven. The disciples returned to Jerusalem and were constantly in the temple (Luke 24:44-53). Acts also tells about the final conversation with the disciples and about the ascension, including the testimony of two angels that he would return in like manner (Acts 1:6-12).

Divergent Claims

There are three sites claimed for the ascension, two Jericho roads, three paths of the triumphal entry, and four Gardens of Gethsemane. These divergent claims are, to say the least, distracting. In spite of the fact that no one can know with absolutely certainty the specific spots where the events in the life of Jesus occurred, many buildings have been built claiming identification with this or that event. When Constantine, the first "Christian" emperor, built churches in Palestine, he built at three sites: the places of the birth, resurrection, and ascension of Jesus. The church which he started at the ascension site in A.D. 325 was destroyed in 614 by the Persians. The church was in part restored, according to the testimony of Arculf in 670, but it was pulled down again by al-Hakim in 1010. The Crusaders rebuilt on the ruins and other rebuildings have taken place in later centuries.

At a slightly different site Arculf saw a structure which had a series of concentric circles with doors leading into the innermost circle. The inner room was without a roof and in the center were, it was claimed, the last footprints of the Lord before he ascended. This structure was rebuilt by the Crusaders as an octogon and Saladin converted it into a mosque, adding a roof. The most impressive building today is the Russian Orthodox Monastery belltower on the crest of the mountain. Built sometime in the nineteenth century, the tower has six stories and 214 steps.

On the slope of the Mount of Olives, facing the temple area, is the largest and oldest Jewish cemetery in the world. Dating back to biblical times, it is a choice burial site because many expect the resurrection to take place first on the Mount of Olives. Tradition holds that those buried here will be raised first. Reference to Zechariah 14:1-11 is made. For those of us who are not likely to be buried there, it is comforting to remember that when Jesus returns, the righteous of all the earth will be caught up to meet him in the clouds to be with him forever (I Thess. 4:16-18).

"Why Do You Stand Looking into Heaven?"

Batsell Barrett Baxter

When he had concluded his description of the life of Jesus, including his birth, his active ministry, his crucifixion, and resurrection, the inspired writer Luke brought his Gospel to a close with these impressive words, "Then he led them out as far as Bethany, and lifting up his hands he blessed them. While he blessed them, he parted from them, and was carried up into heaven. And they returned to Jerusalem with great joy, and were continually in the temple blessing God" (Luke 24:50-53).

Sometime later Luke followed his history of the life of Christ with his history of the beginning of the church, which we know as the Book of Acts. As was indicated a moment ago, he closed his first history with the telling of Christ's ascension. In the opening chapter of Acts, he tells again of Christ's ascension, "And when he had said this, as they were looking on, he was lifted up, and a cloud took him out of their sight. And while they were gazing into heaven as he went, behold, two men stood by them in white robes, and said, 'Men of Galilee, why do you stand looking into heaven? This Jesus, who was taken up from you into heaven, will come in the same way as you saw him go into heaven'" (Acts 1:9-11).

A Spirit Presence for a Sense Presence

Jesus had spent some thirty-three years on the earth, growing from infancy into manhood, living the perfect life as an example for those of us who would follow, teaching the profound truths of God's will for man, and giving his life on the cross as the means of redeeming us from our sins. Those who lived in that first century, especially his disciples, had the opportunity of eating with him, talking with him, and seeing him in all of the normal activities of life. What an experience it was for these few to have the privilege of such an intimate association with the divine Son of God. But, while here on the earth in the flesh, Jesus could associate with only a few, whereas the multiplied millions on earth needed a close and intimate association with him. It was because of the limitations of his physical life on earth that he said to his disciples toward the end of his earthly ministry, "Nevertheless I tell you the truth: it is to your advantage that I go away, for if I do not go away, the Counselor [or Holy Spirit] will not come to you; but if I go, I will send him to you. And when he comes, he will convince the world of sin and of righteousness and of judgment" (John 16:7, 8). Because Christ was for all men, not just a few, it was necessary for him to substitute a spirit presence for the sense presence of his earthly ministry. That is what he did when he ascended from the Mount of Olives that day long ago.

After Abraham Lincoln's death, someone said, "Now he belongs to the ages." In an infinitely more important way, Jesus, who had been limited by time and place during his earthly sojourn, after his ascension belonged to all men everywhere. Christ is no longer locked in ancient history, but is present in the here and now, available as a constant spiritual companion to every person on earth. The first great value of the ascension is that it makes every person on earth a contemporary of Christ. A spiritual fellowship with Jesus Christ is just as real a possibility for you and for me today as it was for those who walked beside him in ancient Israel. This would not be true if he had not ascended from the earth.

Lord of the Universe

There is a second important meaning to the ascension. When Jesus exchanged his physical presence among men for a spiritual presence available on a far wider scale to all mankind, he became Lord of the universe. Shortly after Jesus' death, resurrection, and ascension, Peter preached his great sermon on Pentecost, on the day when the church had its beginning. Toward the close of his sermon he said, "This Jesus God raised up, and of that we all are witnesses. Being therefore exalted at the right hand of God, and having received from the Father the promise of the Holy Spirit, he has poured out this which you see and hear.... Let all the house of Israel therefore know assuredly that God has made him both Lord and Christ, this Jesus whom you crucified" (Acts 2:32–36).

The apostle Paul, in one sense a latecomer among the apostles, since he did not live with Jesus, is best suited of all the apostles to emphasize that we live by faith, not by sight (II Cor. 5:7). Paul and the other early Christians were saying, in effect, "Jesus has now been taken from us, but he is present nonetheless. He is present with us, just as God is present with us. He is in heaven, reigning over us as Lord and Savior."

Our Pioneer and Forerunner

The ascension of Jesus has a heart-warming message for us here in this life. We live in a precarious world. The failure of a nuclear plant leaves fear and uncertainty behind. A tragic famine leaves thousands starving. A deadly disease takes a loved one away. Life is full of uncertainties and dangers. Without the encouraging word of the ascension, we would be left to doubt. But the New Testament affirms "that in everything God works for good with those who love him" (Rom. 8:28). The chapter goes on, "If God is for us, who is against us? He who did not spare his own Son but gave him up for us all, will he not also give us all things with him?... It is God who justifies; who is to condemn?... Who shall separate us from the love of Christ?... No, in all these things we are more than conquerors through him who loved us" (Rom. 8:31-37).

When we face the difficulties of life and are uncertain about the future, when we wonder whether life is worth its cost, we find great assurance in passages like this one from the Book of Hebrews: "Therefore, since we are surrounded by so great a cloud of witnesses, let us also lay aside every weight, and sin which clings so closely, and let us run with perseverance the race that is set before us, looking to Jesus the pioneer and perfecter of our faith, who for the joy that was set before him endured the cross, despising the shame, and is seated at the right hand of the throne of God" (Heb. 12:1, 2). Jesus is our "pioneer" and our "forerunner" who "opened the way."

Our Hope for Eternity

The ascension also has another meaning that is extremely important to all of us. None of us likes to think of his own life coming to an end in death, with nothing significant beyond. If death were the final end, then life would be in the deepest sense meaningless, going nowhere. We thank God that this is not true, however. Paul wrote to the Corinthians, "If for this life only we have hoped in Christ, we are of all men most to be pitied. But in fact Christ has been raised from the dead, the first fruits of those who have fallen asleep. For as by a man came death, by a man has come also the resurrection of the dead. For as in Adam all die, so also in Christ shall all be made alive. But each in his own order: Christ the first fruits, then at his coming those who belong to Christ" (I Cor. 15:19-23).

Just as Christ was raised from the dead, never to die again, so will we be. As Christ was taken up into heaven, so will we be. Paul wrote to the Thessalonians, "For the Lord himself will descend from heaven with a cry of command, with the archangel's call, and with the sound of the trumpet of God. And the dead in Christ will rise first; then we who are alive, who are left, shall be caught up together with them in the clouds to meet the Lord in the air; and so we shall always be with the Lord" (I Thess. 4:16, 17).

Christ Supreme in our Lives

Finally, it should be obvious that, if the ascension has any meaning in our lives, it must mean not simply that Christ reigns supreme in the universe, but also that we strive to open our hearts and minds to him so that he may reign supreme in our lives. What value is there in remembering his ascension unless we exalt him to the supreme place in our hearts and minds, that he may, indeed, be Lord of our lives?

May each of us believe in him as the divine Son of God, make known that faith before those who are about us, courageously turning away from the sins of the world, and then be buried with Christ in baptism for the forgiveness of our sins. This is the simple way in which he calls men to come to him and salvation.

The Valley of Hinnom

35 The Valley of Hinnom

In Hebrew the valley of the son of Hinnom is Gei Ben-Hinnom, which was eventually contracted into the name *Gehinnom*. Gehinnom or Gehenna became a common expression for hell. Today the valley is known as Wadi er-Rababi.

Tradition records a number of possible sources for the name of the Hinnom Valley. For example, the valley was at times the site of child sacrifice, giving birth to the idea that the valley was named after the children who groaned (Heb., *noham*) or the spectators who groaned (Heb., *nohaminn*) on the spot. The biblical phrase, valley of the son of Hinnom, suggests that it was probably named after a man named Hinnom. Some have thought that Hinnom was the original Jebusite owner.

Hinnom in the Old Testament

When King Solomon "did what was evil in the sight of the Lord, and did not wholly follow the Lord, as David his father had done, [he] built a high place for Chemosh the abomination of Moab, and for Molech the abomination of the Ammonites, on the mountain east of Jerusalem" (I Kings 11:6, 7). Solomon built these places of worship on the southern brow of the city overlooking the Hinnom Valley's easternmost section.

Ahaz, who began his rule in 735 B.C., "burned his son as an offering, according to the abominable practices of the nations whom the Lord drove out before the people of Israel" (II Kings 16:3). An alternate reading is that he "made his son pass through the fire," suggesting the ritual practices in the Hinnom Valley at the altar to Molech. The parallel text says, "He burned incense in the valley of the son of Hinnom, and burned his sons as an offering" (II Chron. 28:3).

Manasseh, Ahaz's grandson, was a wicked king who ruled fifty-five years in Jerusalem, beginning when he was twelve years old. "He burned his sons as an offering in the valley of the son of Hinnom...and did much evil in the sight of the Lord, provoking him to anger" (II Chron. 33:6).

In one of his great sermons against Judah, Jeremiah recounts in a lengthy statement some of the evil done: "And they have built the high place of Topheth, which is in the valley of the son of Hinnom, to burn their sons and their daughters in the fire; which I did not command, nor did it come into my mind. Therefore, behold, the days are coming, says the Lord, when it will no more be called Topheth, or the valley of the son of Hinnom, but the valley of Slaughter: for they will bury in Topheth, because there is no room elsewhere. And the dead bodies of this people will be food for the birds of the air, and for the beasts of the earth; and none will frighten them away" (Jer. 7:31–33).

Child Sacrifice

The fiendish custom of infant sacrifice to the fire gods seems to have been kept up at Topheth at the southeast end of the valley of Hinnom. The name *Topheth,* according to rabbinic tradition, is derived from the root *Toph* or "drum"—drums were used in the valley to drown out the cries of the children who were made to pass through the fire.

When Josiah's high priest, Hilkiah, found the book of the law in the temple, reform began. Josiah, who died in 608 B.C., cleaned up the valley of Hinnom. He defiled Topheth, which was in the valley of the son of Hinnom, so that no one would burn his son or daughter as an offering to Molech (II Kings 23:10). He broke down the altars and images of the false gods and burned the bones of their priests (II Kings 23:10-14; II Chron. 34:4, 5). After Josiah defiled the altars to Molech, the valley appears to have become a cesspool into which the sewage of the city was conducted.

One Jewish source describes the child sacrifice in detail. The image of Molech is depicted as a figure surrounded by seven fences. His body was hollow, serving as a place to kindle a fire. His face was shaped like a calf, his hands were outstretched, ready to receive offerings. Those who brought a fowl to sacrifice were permitted to pass only the first fence. The individual who offered a goat entered through the second. The one bringing a sheep passed through the third fence. A calf allowed a man to enter through the fourth fence, a cow through the fifth, and an ox through the sixth. The one who brought his son as an offering was permitted to go through all seven fences and to approach Molech. The source indicates that the man would kiss his son and lay him in the arms of Molech, which were red-hot from the fire burning inside the idol. Spectators would bring drums and beat them vigorously so that the cries of the child would not grieve the father.

Jesus on Gehenna

Jesus used the word *Gehenna* several times to refer to the state of the lost: Matthew 5:22, 29,30; 10:28; 18:9, 23:15, 33; Mark 9:43, 45, 47; Luke 12:5.

Today the Hinnom Valley is identified as a steep, precipitous ravine that begins near the Joppa Gate and stretches around the west and south of the city until it joins the Kidron Valley. However, this is not the only valley suggested as the biblical Hinnom. Both the Kidron on the east and the Tyropoeon in the center have also been identified with Hinnom.

God's Wrath
Harold Hazelip

The French atheist writer Jean-Paul Sartre wrote a play called *No Exit*. Three characters sit in a room and carry on ceaseless conversation. They never sleep. Not even for a moment do they escape the penetrating gaze of each other. At times their conversation is hostile, at other times only boring. The awful thing about their plight is that there is "no exit" from the room where they are. So they carry on this conversation for eternity.

This is Sartre's version of hell. Of course, he does not think of hell in the distant future. For Sartre, it is right now. So he concludes the play with the statement, "Hell is other people." At least the idea of hell—of endless suffering—is meaningful even to this atheist writer.

Perhaps you remember Dante's *Inferno*. He describes a tour into the realm of the dead. Here we find incredible speculation about the "geography" of hell. Dante divides it into many levels. And, with his vivid imagination, he is able to consign the sinners to their respective places.

What Is Hell Like?

Dante's work, and many others, may have had more impact on us than we recognize. When you mention "hell" today, the imagination goes to work as to what it will be like, who will be there, and a host of other questions. If we follow Dante or Sartre, our imagination may lead us to some absurd pictures of hell. We need to hear once more what the Bible says.

The Bible has three principal descriptions of hell. First, it is a place of punishment—often described as "the lake of fire" (Matt. 18:8, 9; Rev. 20:11–15). Jesus described it as a place where people weep and gnash their teeth in pain (Matt. 25:30). Second, Jesus referred to hell as destruction: "And do not fear those who kill the body but cannot kill the soul; rather fear him who can destroy both soul and body in hell" (Matt. 10:28). The punishment is eternal; the hopes of the suffering ones are destroyed. Third, the Bible refers to hell in terms of isolation and banishment: the worthless servant will be cast "into the outer darkness" (Matt. 25:30). And the Lord will say, "I never knew you" (Matt. 7:21–23). There is a fact which recurs in each of these descriptions: The Bible regularly teaches that evil will be punished. The Bible speaks as consistently of the punishment of the evil as it speaks of the reward of the righteous.

God's Love and Hell

A question often asked today is, Isn't eternal condemnation inconsistent with a God of love and with a Savior who sacrificed himself for the lost? So many people are sure that the idea of an eternal hell is incredible. They think that God in love will deliver all men. This is not, however, what Scripture teaches. C. S. Lewis claimed in his last book that he had met no people who fully disbelieved in hell and also had a living, life-giving belief in heaven.

Instead of rejecting the teaching of the Bible regarding hell, let's try to understand this teaching. We do not understand the Bible's teaching concerning God's wrath unless we recognize it as the other side of the coin of God's goodness. Paul wrote, "Note then the kindness and the severity of God" (Rom. 11:22). God's goodness is seen in the fact that he once offered his covenant of grace to poor, miserable slaves in Egypt. In the New Testament he offers a place of celebration at his banquet—Jesus called it a marriage feast (Matt. 22:1-14). Jesus' parable of the ten virgins emphasizes the celebration (Matt. 25:1-13). He invited with the words, "Everything is ready; come to the marriage feast" (Matt. 22:4). And some gratefully accepted the invitation.

But there were also those who chose to be left out. They were invited to the feast but were too busy with other things. Five of the ten virgins did not take it seriously enough to be prepared. One of those men invited to the wedding feast came in, but without his wedding garment. He did not appreciate God's gift to him.

The point of these parables is that God's wrath is only upon those who choose it. God is not capricious in his judgment. We ourselves choose our destiny.

In the Old Testament, the great prophets—Amos, Hosea, Isaiah, and others—reminded God's people that they had broken their covenant. Because they had broken faith, God would send on them a "day of the Lord" which would engulf them in destruction. This reminder was intended to point them to God's final offer of salvation. There was always the chance that their repentance would alter their fate.

In the New Testament, Jesus reminds us that God is giving us our final opportunity to repent. His parable of the sheep and the goats tells us with certainty that there will be a balancing of the accounts. His parable of the ten virgins reminds us that some were irrevocably shut out from the celebration. The New Testament closes with the Book of Revelation, which tells us that those works of evil which now seem to triumph will ultimately be destroyed. God is good. His goodness demands that he finally balance the accounts. He is now giving us the time to repent.

We Choose!

Hell is something people choose. We may wish that death could end it all. If life becomes too painful, one can always commit suicide for an early escape. But Christianity insists that there is no such escape. Each one of us will live forever.

Every individual man will one day be claimed by either God or Satan. God now claims all on the grounds that he made them. Satan hopes to claim them all by conquest. Man will certainly learn that he can make no claim in and of himself. One of C. S. Lewis's characters, the demon Screwtape, says "They will find out in the end, never fear, to whom their time, their souls, their bodies really belong—certainly not to them whatever happens."

In Lewis's book, *The Pilgrim's Regress,* a character named John asks his

Guide if there really is a "black hole," meaning hell. When the Guide says yes, John wonders if God is really kind and good. The Guide replies that nowadays God is often accused of cruelty. To the contrary, God should be accused of taking risks. He has taken the risk of making men free. When man commits sin, God saves him from it if he can. But God does not save people against their will. If God forces us, we are no longer free.

Then Lewis asks, "What more can you ask God to do? To cancel man's sins and offer miraculous help? He has done that on Calvary. To forgive them? Some will not accept forgiveness. To finally leave alone those who refuse him? Alas, this is what he does. And once a man separates himself from God, what can he do but wither and die?

We Can't Evade Responsibility

We try to avoid our responsibility by being full of questions. How many will be saved? Many or few? Why did he die for all if only few are saved? Jesus' response was, "Strive to enter by the narrow door" (Luke 13:24).

Or we ask, When will the end of the world come (Matt. 24:3)? Jesus did not answer this question with a date, but with a command: "Watch therefore, for you do not know on what day your Lord is coming" (Matt. 24:42).

This brooding over how many will be saved, or over the position of the hands of the clock of the world, is brooding over something that is not our business. Speculation about such questions only leads us away from the real question: Am I ready for the coming of the Lord?

God's intention, the Bible insists, is not doom but deliverance. But your decision is serious. Heaven is something you can miss. Hell is a real possibility.

Think seriously about God's invitation to life. Faith in him is still a possibility for you. And repentance from your sins. In baptism, Christ's saving blood can be applied to your soul's needs and you can have the hope of eternal life.

Royal Tombs

36   David's Tomb

The City of David was the name given to the fortified city of Jebus after David captured it. The Jebusites had successfully withstood the conquest of the land under Joshua (Josh. 15:63). When David was elected king by all the tribes of Israel, it became necessary to capture Jebus in order to unite the kingdom and to have the use of the vital highway running through that city.

The conquest of the city (1003 B.C.) is described in II Samuel 5:6–9 and I Chronicles 11:4–7 as a daring deed engineered by David and led by Joab, who thereafter became David's commander-in-chief. David transferred his capital from Hebron to Jerusalem and undertook the building of several

259

major projects: the "House of Cedars" (II Sam. 5:11; I Chron. 14:1), the "House of the Mighty Men" (Neh. 3:16), and the structure known as "David's Tower" (Song of Songs 4:4). David's city was located on the southeasternmost hill of Jerusalem, Mount Ophel, one section of what would later become a much enlarged Jerusalem.

The traditional site of David's tomb is located outside David's city, across the Tyropoeon Valley, on the western hill which has been called Mount Zion since the time of Josephus. This site was inside the city walls which Herod built, but was well outside the original city of David.

The Search

The search for the tomb of David has gone on for a long period of time. Miscellaneous traditions have located the tomb in Bethlehem, or near Gethsemane, or on the southwest hill of Jerusalem (Zion). Beginning with Josephus in the first century A.D., the western hill acquired a connection with King David. By the tenth century local Arab and Jewish tradition located the tomb of David on present-day Mount Zion and the tradition was accepted by Christians during the first Crusade. The Bethlehem tradition was based on the idea that the "City of David" was Bethlehem and not Jerusalem. From the fourth to the seventh century, travelers were directed to Bethlehem to see David's tomb. Both Jerome and Arculf mention it. In 1850, de Saulcy persuaded many that the "Tombs of the Kings," north of the Old City, included the location of David's burial spot.

The facts concerning David's tomb are meager, but it can be known with certainty that David's death and burial took place in Jerusalem (I Kings 2:10). Also, in his sermon on Pentecost, Peter mentions that David's tomb "is with us to this day" (Acts 2:29), indicating that the tomb was within sight of the place where he was standing.

In spite of abundant archaeological work there is a general lack of evidence for anything connected with David's original city of Jerusalem. There are two reasons for this lack of evidence. First, much of the early city was built on terraces which were frequently in need of repair. During the repair work a great deal of the city slid down the hill to destruction. Second, where David's city occupied the summit of the hill, archaeologists have found that the rock has been extensively quarried. Herod the Great in the first century B.C. and Hadrian in the second century A.D. used this area as a source of stone for the buildings they were constructing north and west of Ophel.

Tombs on Ophel

Among the structures destroyed by quarrying on the southeast ridge of Mount Ophel are two tunnellike cuttings out of the rock which Raymond

Weill in 1913–1914 identified as royal tombs. The long one (fifty-four feet long, eight feet wide, and five to thirteen feet high) is thought by some to be David's tomb, the other is thought to be that of Solomon. There is no definitive archaeological evidence, however, for assigning these tombs to David and Solomon, though their size and form suggest a wealthy burial.

Weill's proposed tomb of David may well be the true site. The two long tunnels, which were at one time filled with twentieth century rubbish, are carved out of a natural rock, even as David's tomb must have been. Much of the tomb has been cut away and one can only speculate about what the original entrance may have looked like. The Kidron lies off to the left of the present entrance (viewed from the inside) and the Hinnom just ahead. Today, the ancient City of David is an uncommercialized area that is being developed into an Israeli national park.

In any case, it was in this area that David's men took the city of Jebus to make it the City of David, Jerusalem. It was here that so many of the events of David's life took place: it was to this area that he moved the ark; here he sinned with Bathsheba and plotted Uriah's death to cover his sin; here he allowed his old friend Jonathan's crippled son, Mephibosheth, to sit at the royal table; here he felt the revenge and treachery of Absalom; and in his last days it was on these very hills that he witnessed Adonijah, his son, trying to take over the kingdom from Solomon. It was here that David died. All that is known for sure about his burial site is that it is nearby.

David's Son and His Kingdom

Batsell Barrett Baxter

In recent months there have been reports in the news that a major American publisher intends to publish a "condensed" version of the Bible. We have seen condensed versions of the major works of fiction for a long time. Children may pick up a simplified copy of Dickens' *Tale of Two Cities*. Busy people can find *Gone with the Wind* condensed into a few hundred pages. But the Bible? How would you condense it? And what would you choose to leave out?

There is a sense in which it would be impossible to condense the Bible, for any such work would reflect the disposition of the "condenser." What parts of sacred Scripture could one leave out? On the other hand, thoughtful Bible students have long recognized that there is a theme running through the Bible, a thread which runs through its narrative, poetry, and prophetic sections. Indeed, for thousands of years God's people have been "telling the story." And "telling the story" means proclaiming the theme which runs throughout the sixty-six books which make up the Bible.

The Central Theme

Have you ever stopped to think what that theme or thread might be? Some of the greatest literary and musical works known to us have tried to find that thread. George Frederick Handel's greatest composition was *the Messiah*. He explained that his purpose was to tell in that great work the one great story of redemption. And so his oratorio begins with the Old Testament. There we hear about the hopes of the people of God in the Old Testament—hopes for redemption, for a Messiah, for liberation. Then we hear the voice of fulfillment. From Genesis to Revelation, there is a story, a thread running through God's Word. It is the story of redemption.

The story comes to its climax in the life and ultimately in the death and resurrection of Jesus. On the day of Jesus' crucifixion there were undoubtedly many people, including the disciples, who concluded that they had hoped in vain. We find them going back to their old occupations (John 21). Jesus was not the Redeemer of Israel, they reluctantly concluded. It is little wonder that the men on the road to Emmaus were in despair. "We had hoped...," they said. Apparently they had placed their hopes in the wrong person. It is little wonder that the disciples, behind their closed doors, had given up their hope also. Jesus could not be the answer to their hopes. They had long felt that the Old Testament breathed an air of expectation. But now their expectation had come to a bitter end.

Christ's Resurrection

Have you ever noticed what led these disciples to hope again? It was the resurrection. The resurrection changed all of their old ideas about what the Old Testament was really saying. Indeed, it was to despairing men on the road to Emmaus that Jesus opened the Scriptures and said: "O foolish men, and slow of heart to believe all that the prophets have spoken! Was it not necessary that the Christ should suffer these things and enter into his glory?" The text goes on, "And beginning with Moses and all the prophets, he interpreted to them in all the scriptures the things concerning himself" (Luke 24:25–27).

Likewise to the disciples behind closed doors, he said, "These are my words which I spoke to you, while I was still with you, that everything written about me in the law of Moses and the prophets and the psalms must be fulfilled.' Then he opened their minds to understand the scriptures, and said to them, 'Thus it is written that the Christ should suffer and on the third day rise from the dead' " (Luke 24:44–46). After the resurrection, the disciples recognized a new way of reading the Old Testament. It was the story of Jesus. All of their hopes from childhood found their fulfillment in Jesus.

Establishment of the Church

God's plan comes to completion with the establishment of his church, or kingdom in Jerusalem on the day of Pentecost. Christ's life had been lived. His teaching had been done. He had died on the cross, had been buried, and had been raised from the grave, the first fruits of them that are asleep. Jesus had told his disciples to remain in Jerusalem until they were "clothed with power from on high" (Luke 24:49).

It was on Pentecost Sunday that the Holy Spirit fell upon the apostles. Here is the way the Scriptures describe the scene, "When the day of Pentecost had come, they were altogether in one place. And suddenly a sound came from heaven like the rush of a mighty wind, and it filled all the house where they were sitting. And there appeared to them tongues as of fire, distributed and resting on each one of them. And they were all filled with the Holy Spirit and began to speak in other tongues, as the Spirit gave them utterance" (Acts 2:1–4).

Gathered in Jerusalem on that day were devout Jews from many different geographic regions. Miraculously, as the apostles spoke, each person heard clearly in his own native tongue. It was the apostle Peter who preached the primary sermon on that important beginning day of the church. He began his sermon, "Men of Judea and all who dwell in Jerusalem, let this be known to you, and give ear to my words." At that point he anchored his sermon in Old Testament prophecy, comparing the events of Pentecost with a prophecy from Joel.

The death of Jesus was no accident. It was a part of the eternal plan of God, as indicated further in Peter's sermon: "Men of Israel, hear these words: Jesus of Nazareth, a man attested to you by God with mighty works and wonders and signs which God did through him in your midst, as you yourselves know—this Jesus, delivered up according to the definite plan and foreknowledge of God, you crucified and killed by the hands of lawless men. But God raised him up, having loosed the pangs of death, because it was not possible for him to be held by it" (Acts 2:22–24).

Peter next quoted David, Israel's greatest king, who had foretold the coming of the Messiah. Peter then continued, "Brethren, I may say to you confidently of the patriarch David that he both died and was buried, and his tomb is with us to this day. Being therefore a prophet, and knowing that God had sworn with an oath to him that he would set one of his descendants upon his throne, he foresaw and spoke of the resurrection of the Christ, that he was not abandoned to Hades, nor did his flesh see corruption. This Jesus God raised up, and of that we all are witnesses. Being therefore exalted at the right hand of God, and having received from the Father the promise of the Holy Spirit, he has poured out this which you see and hear." Then Peter brought his sermon to its climax, "Let all the house of Israel therefore know assuredly that God has made him both Lord and Christ, this Jesus whom you crucified" (Acts 2:29-36).

And what kind of kingdom has the descendant of David who would sit upon his throne in Jerusalem established? It is a spiritual kingdom—Christ is the king and his followers are the faithful and loyal subjects.

Becoming a Christian

This kingdom began on Pentecost, when some three thousand people at the end of Peter's sermon responded by asking, "Brethren, what shall we do?" Peter responded, "Repent, and be baptized every one of you in the name of Jesus Christ for the forgiveness of your sins; and you shall receive the gift of the Holy Spirit" (Acts 2:37, 38). These three thousand responded to Peter's directions and were baptized into Christ. Multitudes more were added in the days and weeks and months which followed. The beginning was the same in every case: the gospel of Christ was preached, people heard it and believed in him as the divine Son of God, they repented of their sins, and climaxed their obedience to the Lord by being baptized in water for the remission of their sins. At that point God added them to his kingdom, or family, or church.

The Lord's kingdom was really a new way of life, based upon the teachings of Christ. It was a way of life which Jesus had exemplified as he lived on the earth, letting love dominate his every act. It transformed a little band of disciples into a great spiritual kingdom with a new center for their lives, with new purposes for living, with a new joy in their hearts, and with a new eternal destiny ahead of them. Christ's kingdom continues to be the hope of the world!

The Wailing Wall

37 The Wailing Wall

The Wailing Wall, also known as the Western Wall, is a section of the wall which surrounded the Herodian temple and formed the support of the high platform of the temple complex. The height of the wall is some seventy feet with some sixteen more courses of stone under the current ground level. The wall is exposed for some 165 feet, only a small part of the total 1,560-foot Western Wall.

The Jews write down their wishes and prayers on small bits of paper, fold them carefully, and insert them into crevices between the stones of the

Wailing Wall. They believe the messages will be read by God. The practice is several centuries old.

When David had finished his house and had defeated his enemies, he said to Nathan the prophet, "See now, I dwell in a house of cedar, but the ark of God dwells in a tent" (II Sam. 7:2). Nathan told him to build a temple, but that night God told Nathan that David's son would be the one to build the house for God. God said, "You [David] have shed much blood and have waged great wars; you shall not build a house to my name" (I Chron. 22:8). Nathan relayed God's message. and David yielded (II Sam. 7). David collected materials for the future temple, including one hundred thousand talents of gold and one million talents of silver. David provided bronze, iron, wood, jewels, and stones. He also had craftsmen trained to carry out the work (I Chron. 22, 28, and 29).

Solomon's Temple

Solomon was given instructions for the building of the temple and charged to carry out what David had planned for. David charged the leaders to help Solomon. He also spelled out arrangements for the temple services, for the duties of the priests, the music, the gatekeepers, the treasuries, officers, and judges (I Chron. 22-27).

Construction began in April/May 966 B.C. and was completed in October/November 959 B.C. The laborers were Israelite men but Hiram and the Phoenicians furnished both the lumber and the skilled craftsmen (I Kings 5). The logs were floated from Tyre to Joppa and then brought over land to Jerusalem (II Chron. 2:16).

The basic plan for the temple approximately doubled the dimensions of the tabernacle, but retained the general layout of courtyard, porch, and double chamber. The building was ninety feet long, thirty feet wide, and forty-five feet high (I Kings 6:2). When the temple was built, the stone was prepared at the quarry so that no hammers or axes broke the silence of the site. The Holy of Holies was a cube lined with paneling, separated from the Holy Place by a partition of cedar paneling, with double doors of olive wood (I Kings 6:16, 20, 31, 32).

Solomon dedicated the temple by bringing the ark into the Holy of Holies, making a speech, praying a long prayer, blessing the people, and offering up sacrifice on the new altar (I Kings 8). The dedication apparently took eight days.

When the prayer had been completed and Solomon's sacrifices consumed, the glory of the Lord filled the temple (II Chron. 7:1). The temple became the dwelling place of God and typified the way of salvation by which man can come into the presence of God (Heb. 8:1-15; 9:23, 24).

As the result of widespread apostasy characterized by the building of high places, in Rehoboam's fifth year Shishak was permitted to attack and take the treasures of the temple as a measure of divine judgment (II Chron. 12:2-9). Asa put the votive gifts of his father in the temple; and later when Baasha, king of Israel, made war on Judah, Asa used the silver and gold from the temple to buy an alliance with Ben-hadad of Damascus (I Kings 15:15-24).

When Athaliah usurped the throne of Judah from Joash, the young boy was hidden in the temple until he was old enough to rule (II Chron. 22:10—23:15). During the reign of Athaliah, the temple fell into disrepair, largely as a result of priestly carelessness. This continued until Joash decided to restore the temple. Since no money was available for repairs, either from the temple treasury or the king's budget, a box was set up for free-will offerings. As money was collected, the workmen were hired and repairs were made (II Chron. 24:4-14).

The idolatry practiced by Athaliah was so influential that the people persuaded Joash to leave God when Jehoiada the priest died. Zechariah rebuked Joash and was stoned to death in the temple court. Shortly afterward an attack by Syria dealt Jerusalem a damaging blow and Joash sent the temple treasures to Hazael, king of Syria, as tribute (II Chron. 24:15-24; cf. II Kings 12:17, 18).

Nebuchadnezzar carried Jehoiakim and the vessels of the temple into Babylonian captivity (II Chron. 36:7). Additional vessels were taken out of the temple to Babylon during the reign of the succeeding king Jehoiachin. When Zedekiah rebelled against Nebuchadnezzar, the city fell and the temple with it. The vessels of precious metal were removed and the temple was burned. It seems that the ark, cherubim, and other wooden objects, now stripped of their gold, perished in the flames.

In the fourteenth year after the destruction of Jerusalem (572 B.C.), Ezekiel was taken back to Jerusalem in a vision. An angel measured the temple as he watched. The return of the Lord to the temple is pictured, and instructions about the altar are given (Ezek. 40-43).

The Second Temple

Cyrus ordered the temple of Jerusalem rebuilt (II Chron. 36:22, 23). Soon after the return of the Jews, the altar was rebuilt and sacrifices were resumed (Ezra 3:1-7). In the second year after their return, they began to rebuild the structure. The completed foundation caused some to rejoice, but elderly people who had seen the temple of Solomon wept over the inferiority of the new one (Ezra 3:8-13). Opposition forced construction to halt but the prophets Haggai and Zechariah promoted the project and work began again

(Ezra 5:1, 2). The temple was finally dedicated and the feast days were celebrated (Ezra 6:16–22).

Nothing in the Bible indicates that God's presence ever filled this second temple. It lasted until about 20 B.C. (a hundred years longer than Solomon's temple), when Herod remodeled it.

Herod's Temple

The New Testament has over one hundred references to the temple. Parts of the temple specifically mentioned in the New Testament include the pinnacle (Matt. 4:5), its noble stones (Luke 21:5), Solomon's portico (John 10:23; Acts 3:11; 5:12) and the Beautiful Gate (Acts 3:2, 10).

Shortly after his birth, Jesus was brought to the temple to be presented to the Lord. This involved a sacrifice of either two turtledoves or a pair of young pigeons by his parents (Luke 2:22–24). During this activity, a righteous man named Simeon sang praises to God while holding the baby in his arms (Luke 2:25–35). A prophetess named Anna who lived in the temple also came to adore Jesus (Luke 2:36–38).

The next recorded visit of Jesus to the temple was at age twelve when he stayed behind after the Passover and sat among the teachers, listening to them and asking them questions (Luke 2:41–52). During his temptation by Satan he was brought to the pinnacle of the temple and urged to jump off in order to test God (Matt. 4:5–7). John's Gospel records several trips Jesus made to Jerusalem during his ministry. On the first trip, he cleansed the temple of the merchants selling animals and exchanging money.

Near the end of his life, Jesus' triumphal entry into Jerusalem climaxed when he went "into the temple; and when he had looked round at everything, as it was already late, he went out to Bethany with the twelve" (Mark 11:11). The next day he again cleansed the temple of those exchanging money and selling birds and animals. Hearing Jesus was in the temple, the lame and blind went to him and were healed (Matt. 21:14). "And he was teaching daily in the temple" (Luke 19:47).

Jesus engaged in controversy with the Pharisees in the temple area, and spoke warnings and woes to them (Matt. 22–23). He sat down next to the treasury, observed the worshipers giving their money, and made a comment about a widow and her mites (Mark 12:41–44). Once, as they were leaving the temple, some of his disciples mentioned the buildings. He replied, "Truly, I say to you, there will not be left here one stone upon another, that will not be thrown down" (Matt. 24:2). As Jesus left the temple for the last time (the Gospels do not mention his going back), he predicted its destruction.

After Jesus' ascension, the disciples frequented the temple daily (Luke

24:53; Acts 2:46). Peter and John were on their way to pray in the temple when they met the lame man at the Beautiful Gate and healed him (Acts 3:1-10). Peter then addressed the people from Solomon's portico (Acts 3:11-26). After Peter and John were arrested and set free, and the disciples began sharing their possessions with others, Luke records, "Now many signs and wonders were done among the people by the hands of the apostles. And they were all together in Solomon's portico. None of the rest dared join them, but the people held them in high honor" (Acts 5:12, 13).

Shortly afterward, the apostles were arrested. Upon their release by an angel, they entered the temple at daybreak and taught (Acts 5:19-21). They were brought before the council but were released on the advice of Gamaliel. "And every day in the temple and at home they did not cease teaching and preaching Jesus as the Christ" (Acts 5:42).

When Paul took four men to the temple in connection with a vow they had made, the Jews were stirred up against him and seized him. Paul was dragged out of the temple, the gates were shut behind, and the mob would have killed him had not the Roman officials come to the rescue. He spoke to the crowd; when they refused to listen any longer, he was taken back to the barracks, where it became known that he was a Roman citizen (Acts 21:17—22:29).

Some call Herod's temple the "second temple," following the tradition that Herod merely remodeled the structure Zerubbabel had erected. Others insist on calling Herod's temple the "third temple," suggesting that he completely reworked the area. Construction of Herod's temple began about 20 B.C., with the basic structure taking about one-and-one-half years to complete, although subsidiary work was still being carried on nearly fifty years later (John 2:20).

According to Josephus, Titus attacked Jerusalem in August of A.D. 70. After the fall of most of the city, the temple area remained the last Jewish stronghold. In the attack on the sanctuary itself, the structure was accidentally set on fire, against the wish of Titus. The last of the temple complex, along with about six thousand people who sought refuge there, perished.

Eusebius (fourth century A.D.) mentioned that it was sad to see the temple area in destruction. He commented that the destruction had already lasted more than four times as long as the seventy years of ruin during the Babylonian captivity. The platform seems to have remained in ruins until the arrival of the Muslims in the mid-seventh century.

Dome of the Rock

Today the Dome of the Rock and the al-Aksa Mosque dominate the platform. The Dome of the Rock was erected in the mid-seventh century by

Abd al-Malik. It is basically an octagonal structure, supporting a drum and dome. On each of the eight walls are five windows, while another twelve windows grace the drum. It is the oldest existing monument of Muslim architecture. Many repairs have been made to the building, the most recent being in the 1950s.

Each of the eight sides measures sixty-three feet, and the mosque has a total diameter of 180 feet. The total height, not counting the crescent, is 108 feet. Four gates permit entrance to the structure.

Inside is the rock, some fifty-eight feet long, fifty-one feet across, and four to six-and-a-half feet high. Traditions place the offering of Isaac on Moriah, the threshing floor of Ornan, and the altar or Holy of Holies of the three Jewish temples on this rock. A Muslim legend claims that Mohammed ascended into the heavens astride his horse from this rock.

Jewish people assemble at the Western Wall to pray and lament, especially on the eve of the Sabbath and of festivals. The wall has symbolized Jerusalem for many generations, calling to their minds the ideal of Jewish independence and Jewish consciousness.

"No Other Name"

Harold Hazelip

One no longer needs to travel to a foreign city to witness a wide variety of religious choices. The competition is great. A professor of religion in a major Eastern university recently commented that within a twenty-block radius in his home city, forty or fifty Oriental religious movements thrive. There is an unprecedented interest among Americans in Eastern religions.

Nineteenth-century writers such as Ralph Waldo Emerson and Walt Whitman read the "sacred writings" of some of the Eastern religions. But this earlier interest was confined mostly to intellectuals and centered on doctrinal ideas in Oriental philosophy. Today rather large numbers of people who are not intellectuals are involved; they are more interested in the religious and devotional practices of the Eastern religions.

By one estimate, three million Americans espouse the teachings of three thousand religious and nonreligious cults. They range from people who worship the devil in dark basements in New York and San Francisco to people who follow one of several new messiahs claiming to be God's messengers.

An estimated forty million Americans dabble in astrology. There are said to be more than twelve thousand professional astrologers, as well as tens of thousands of part-time astrologers. It is claimed that meditation techniques, mixed with religious ideas, reduce stress and tension, improve health, increase self-confidence and productivity, heighten intelligence and creativity, and reduce the need for drugs—all for an investment of forty minutes a day.

The Question of Truth

In the midst of all of these claims, we must ask about truth. In our tolerant times the various approaches to salvation stand rather peacefully together. The average person may decide that many religions contain at least a kernel of truth, so it is of secondary importance as to which religion we claim as our own.

Soon after Christianity began, the apostles were being interrogated by a court in Jerusalem. A lame man had been healed and the city was filled with excitement. The question was, "By what power or by what name did you do this?" The apostle Peter explained, "...by the name of Jesus Christ of Nazareth, whom you crucified, whom God raised from the dead...this man is standing before you well.... And there is salvation in no one else, for there is no other name under heaven given among men by which we must be saved" (Acts 4:8-12).

Most believers in Christ have taken this claim for granted: "There is salvation in no one else." Jesus himself said, "I am the way, and the truth, and the life; no one comes to the Father, but by me" (John 14:6). We may be perplexed by such an exclusive claim to truth. But if Jesus had claimed less, we would probably not be interested in the claim at all.

Challenges to Christ's Claim

Besides the cults which deny this claim, Donald Miller in his *Finality of Jesus Christ in Today's World* has listed a half dozen current challenges to the belief in the finality of Christ. First, non-Christian religions have become aggressive. Religions from the East have begun to build impressive buildings in the West, particularly in the United States. These religions are experiencing a revival of interest and are bidding for universal acceptance.

Second, communism qualifies as a quasi-religion and controls over a billion people. Third, there is a resurgence of nationalism with some of the new nations claiming ultimate loyalty from their people. Fourth, secularism prospers today. Someone has remarked, "How many people get along without God, and never seem to miss him!"

A fifth challenge to the claims of Christ is "neo-paganism." Miller cites D. H. Lawrence's novels which, he says, "seek to resuscitate the spirit of the ancient fertility cults." There are recent books which revive the most vulgar and primitive forms of paganism—a deifying of sex and its worship as the seat of the vital life force of man.

And there is religious syncretism. Arnold Toynbee insisted that we should look for a "common essence in the great world religions." He argued that Christianity should give up its claim to unique and final truth.

Democracy has helped to produce a religious pluralism. Many forms of belief and unbelief exist side by side with the same rights and privileges. We may forget that the right to hold a view does not mean that the view is right. The Christian should be courteous toward those whose beliefs differ from his. But this is not the same as saying that differences are unimportant or that it really does not matter what one believes as long as he is sincere in believing it.

The early Christians believed that Jesus is for everyone. They proclaimed this wherever they went. They believed that the world had too many religions. They went out to make the simple announcement—as you find so often in their sermons in the Book of Acts—that the God everybody has been searching for in all of these religions has shown up in the world unexpectedly! He's here! So the search is off.

The Book of Acts records that these messengers went by the temples of the Greek gods and pointed to all the sculptures of those gods, as Paul did in Athens (Acts 17:16–34). And they said, "The God you worship but do not know has revealed himself to us. It happened this way. There was a carpenter in Nazareth who went about doing good. He was crucified but God raised him from the dead. There are hundreds of people alive who are witnesses. It can be checked!" That was the good news of the gospel.

Christ Is Unique

Our twentieth-century problems are not all that different. We still long to know about God. We see ourselves and we ask about the meaning of our existence. We wonder about the power which determines the outcome of history. As someone has put it, "The religions of man are the deep and frightening questions; Jesus Christ is God's saving answer."

What is so special about the gospel? The truth that God became man in Jesus Christ! The other religions represent man seeking God; the gospel shows God seeking man. In the great religions of the East, believers resemble drops of water which flow into the ocean and are dissolved in it. In the nothingness of nirvana the individual finds his fulfillment by ceasing to exist as an individual.

But God's message of love draws us into fellowship with him. He calls us by name. We are his. Here, in his service, we truly become ourselves. We find our real identity as sons and daughters redeemed at great cost and welcomed home. Our names are written in the book of life for all eternity. We are not erased in eternity, we do not disappear; we enter into eternal fellowship with God.

How is this great goal of life attained? The various religions provide men with laws, instructions, and "travel information" from Confucius, Buddha, and others. Once Peter asked Jesus, "Lord, to whom shall we go?" Then he answered his own question: "You have the words of eternal life; and we have believed, and have come to know, that you are the Holy One of God" (John 6:68, 69).

The early church was utterly uncompromising in her claim for the finality of Christ. If she had been willing to join the other religions as one big happy family, she would have escaped persecution. Those other religions escaped the troubles which Christianity faced because of its uncompromising nature. But the shrines of Artemis and Isis and Mithras and the Caesars are now covered with the dust of many centuries. Christianity lives.

So you believe the claims of Christ. Are you following him? The way to begin is so simple. You simply go through a likeness of what he went through to redeem us. He died, was buried, and was raised for our salvation. We die to sin in repentance, are buried with him in baptism, and are raised to a new relationship with him and a new life before men (Col. 2:12; 3:5).

The Pool of Siloam

38   The Pool of Siloam

The Siloam Pool lies in the lower section of the ancient area of Jerusalem known as Ophel. Ophel is the southeastern hill which lies south of Mount Moriah (the temple mount), west of the Kidron Valley, and east of the Tyropoeon Valley. Jerusalem was first settled on Ophel, an area of about eleven acres, because water was readily available and also perhaps because the steep walls to the east and west made the height easy to defend.

The word *Siloam* means "sending" or "sender." The Arabic spelling is *Silwan*. This is the name of the modern Arab village in the Kidron Valley surrounding the Pool of Siloam and the Gihon Spring. It appears that the

275

name of the old pool, which was built before Hezekiah and called "Sent," was transferred to the new pool, which was built by Hezekiah.

The Jebusite Shaft

When David was thirty-seven, he was anointed king over all Israel. At that point, he moved his capital from Hebron to Jerusalem. However, Jerusalem was in the hands of the Jebusites, who first had to be conquered. David told his leading military men, "Whoever would smite the Jebusites, let him get up the water shaft to attack the lame and the blind, who are hated by David's soul" (II Sam. 5:8); furthermore he offered the position of commander of his army to the man who accomplished the task (I Chron. 11:6). The Jebusites had constructed a horizontal tunnel from the Gihon Spring to the west. After digging ninety feet under the city, they hit a natural cave. From the cave they dug a vertical shaft forty-five feet long. From the top of the shaft, they fashioned a sloping curving tunnel some 135 feet long which ended in a staircase which led to the city's summit. During a siege, water could be gained by going down the stairs and sloping tunnel to the vertical shaft, which would act like a well.

Apparently it was this shaft to which David referred and which Joab climbed, gaining access to the city. Kathleen Kenyon wrote, "There is every reason to suppose that this watershaft is the method by which the Jebusites had access to the spring in time of war, and that it was the means whereby the capture of the town by David was achieved."

Hezekiah's Tunnel

At a later time, when Hezekiah was king of Israel, the Assyrian king Sennacherib invaded Palestine and ultimately besieged Jerusalem. In antici-pation of his approach Hezekiah made elaborate preparations. "He planned with his officers and his mighty men to stop the water of the springs that were outside the city; and they helped him. A great many people were gathered, and they stopped all the springs and the brook that flowed through the land, saying, 'Why should the kings of Assyria come and find much water?' " (II Chron. 32:3, 4). Then, he had a tunnel dug to channel the water inside the city to what became known as the Pool of Siloam.

As S-shaped underground tunnel was discovered in 1867 by Charles War-ren; it wound through the rock underneath Mount Ophel some 1,749 feet to the Pool of Siloam. The Gihon and Siloam Pool are only about 900 feet apart but the tunnel winds to make up the extra distance. The tunneling was done by starting at both ends and, by a remarkable feat of engineering, finally meeting in the middle. Hezekiah's engineers planned so expertly that when workmen, beginning at opposite ends of the tunnel, met, they were off only about twelve inches in elevation.

When Sennacherib laid siege to Jerusalem he and his men were unable to use the water which Hezekiah had brought within the city. Ultimately God miraculously destroyed 185,000 Assyrian soldiers and the remainder of the force was withdrawn (II Kings 19:35, 36). In summarizing Hezekiah's reign, II Kings 20:20 says, "The rest of the deeds of Hezekiah, and all his might, and how he made the pool and the conduit and brought water into the city, are they not written in the Book of the Chronicles of the Kings of Judah?"

It is possible for visitors to Jerusalem today to walk through Hezekiah's tunnel. For us, it proved to be one of the most rewarding experiences of our trip. The passageway is two to three feet wide and five to six feet high and there is a constant stream of water passing through it. Normally the water is only a foot or so deep, so wading is easy, but occasionally the Gihon Spring gushes forth in an abundance of water and the tunnel may be filled nearly to the top. The spring gushes forth intermittently from a natural cave one or two times a day, though in the rainy season, it may issue forth four or five times a day. The water is cool and clear and fills the Siloam Pool at the southern end of the tunnel with beautiful, clear water. Eighteen stone steps descend to the present Pool of Siloam, which is fifty by fifteen feet. Stumps of ancient columns can still be seen in the water.

The Man Born Blind

While in Jerusalem for the feast of the Tabernacles (John 7:2) Jesus and his disciples passed a man who was born blind. The disciples used him as the basis for a question, "Rabbi, who sinned, this man or his parents, that he was born blind?" (John 9:2). Jesus replied that sin had not brought about his blindness—the man was born blind so that the power of God could be demonstrated. Jesus made some clay by spitting on the ground and spread it on the man's eyes. He told the man to go and wash in the Pool of Siloam. The man went, washed, and returned, seeing.

At another time those who were talking with Jesus told him of several Galileans who, while sacrificing, were attacked and killed by Pilate's soldiers. Jesus asked, "Do you think that these Galileans were worse sinners than all the other Galileans, because they suffered thus?" He responded that there was no connection between their suffering and sin and that all needed to repent. He then used the illustration of the eighteen people who were killed when the Tower of Siloam fell (Luke 13:1-4).

In a city where traditions reign and false claims are constantly being made, the visitor finds it refreshing to locate something that by its very nature has to be authentic. The tunnel of Hezekiah is a good example. Such a tunnel through solid rock beneath the city could not be moved nor its course changed. The pool at the end of the tunnel may differ in size or in appearance, but it must be at the same location as the pool known in Jesus' day. It was here, at this exact location, that a man washed the clay from his eyes and could see. Walking in this tunnel and wading in the Pool of Siloam provided a memorable experience.

Has Suffering Any Meaning?

Batsell Barrett Baxter

One of the most puzzling of all problems is the problem of human suffering. Why must humanity suffer? Why must there be heartache and disappointment? Why must there be disease and death? Even more specifically, why must the innocent suffer?

This question must have been in the minds of the poor, diseased, lame, broken pieces of humanity who waited patiently around the Pool of Siloam in ancient Israel. It is the question that fills the mind as one waits in the emergency room of a large modern hospital for word about a friend or relative who has been struck down in an accident. It looms large again when we visit a home for the aged or a ward in a hospital and see those who are reaching the very end of life, limited in their ability to see, or walk, or speak, or even to think. It is especially distressing if they are not only old and infirm, but also poor, forgotten, and unwanted. There are other kinds of suffering, too, as those who make regular pilgrimages to the cemetery to place flowers on the grave of a lost companion would tell us. Heartache, loneliness, disappointment, and even despair are all about us, if only we have eyes with which to see. Suffering everywhere! One wonders why.

A Result of Man's Sin

Many answers to the problem of human suffering have been given and many of those answers are very wrong. One of the answers often given seems plausible because it has in it a large element of truth, but it is not the whole answer. There are many evidences of suffering as a result of man's sin. The man who drinks heavily, after a while, pays the price in his own body and in the tangled strands of his own life. The liar, the cheat, the hypocrite also inevitably suffer. But, to say that this is the explanation of all suffering is to speak too quickly. Think of the innocents who suffer. Job in the Old Testament is an example. He was one of the best men on earth, yet he suffered grievously.

On one occasion Jesus faced this same question, as indicated in the Gospel of John, "As he passed by, he saw a man blind from his birth. And his disciples asked him, 'Rabbi, who sinned, this man or his parents, that he was born blind?' Jesus answered, 'It was not that this man sinned, or his parents, but that the works of God might be made manifest in him'" (John 9:1-3). When the innocent suffer, it is not because of their own sins. We must look for other reasons.

There is another explanation of suffering: God cannot do anything about it. The argument is that if God were infinitely powerful and if he loved man with an infinite love, he would not let man suffer. But it is hardly convincing to say that he who created the universe is powerless to remove suffering. In view of all that God does for us, neither is it convincing to say that he does not love man and does not want man to be free of suffering. There must be other elements in the situation, and there certainly are.

The Nature of the Universe

For example, the very nature of the universe helps to explain suffering. Think for a moment of what we call the laws of nature. As we look at the whole universe it is a system of order. Scientific experiments made in one part of the world can be verified through the same experiments in another. There is uniformity throughout the natural laws of our universe. There must be, or our world would not work. This uniformity, this system of order, has much to do with man's suffering in the world. For example, take the subject of fire. The same law accounts for both the fire with which we cook our meals and heat our homes and the fire which will burn our houses and destroy our lives. The only way in which a world can possibly work is for the laws to be constant. When man uses God's laws of nature as he ought to use them, he prospers and is happy. When he misuses those laws, he suffers.

When God made man a creature of freedom he opened the door to suffering. It could be no other way. When God made the universe he made it possible for man to use his freedom to find the good, but this inevitably included also the possibility of evil and suffering. Why does man suffer? It is sometimes because he, or his ancestors, or his neighbors, have misused their freedom. In some way he or those about him have violated some of God's laws and have thus destroyed that which God created perfect and whole.

Is Suffering Always Evil?

When the subject of human suffering is mentioned, man generally assumes that all suffering is evil. Is this really true? Look at it this way: Man's primary purpose in existence is to honor and glorify God, and to become as godlike as it is humanly possible to become. Now this being so, everything that takes man away from God is evil, and everything that brings him toward God is good.

When we have accepted this standard we can see the events of our world in a different light. It is quite possible that the riches, the honors, the pleasures of this world are actually hindrances rather than helps. It is quite conceivable that illness, loss of money, or even loss of friends might ultimately serve some good purpose. We do not say that when we become sick, or when we suffer, we are to rejoice, but we do believe that if we accept these things in the proper manner, they can be a blessing.

Much of the pain that we suffer is remedial in character. There is a passage in the letter to the Hebrews in which God tells us that he allows us to suffer because of his love for us: "For the Lord disciplines him whom he loves, and chastises every son whom he receives" (Heb. 12:6).

Suffering also has the power to beautify and ennoble the character and the spirit of the sufferer.

God Helps Us in Time of Trial

There is a final point to be made. Our God does not stand off at a distance and ignore our sufferings. He helps us bear them and gives us the strength to triumph through them.

What a tragedy it would be to miss the joys of heaven and the freedom from suffering that God makes possible for all of us! Yet, he will not force us to be saved. He has offered salvation through his Son Jesus Christ and allows us to make the decision whether we want to follow him to eternal life in heaven or reject him and spend eternity in endless suffering. If you are not now a Christian, believe in Christ, repent of all your past sins, make known your faith in Jesus as Lord, and be buried with him in baptism for the remission of your sins. Then, redeemed, justified, saved, spend your life happier than you have ever been, as you look forward to the wonderful world that God has prepared for us.

Jaffa (Joppa) Today

39 Joppa

Located on the Plain of Sharon on a promontory jutting out into the Mediterranean Sea, Joppa was one of the oldest and most important harbors in the ancient Near East. The harbor, formed by reefs in a semicircle about 350 feet offshore, allowed ships to enter from the north, while the sandy beaches nearby welcomed smaller boats.

Located about forty miles west of Jerusalem, Joppa stands at the center of the country's coastal strip. Tel Aviv, connected to the northern part of Joppa, was founded in 1909, and together they boast a population of nearly half a million people. The average January temperature falls between 47°

and 57°, while the reading in August is likely to be between 72° and 89°. Joppa receives about twenty-one inches of rain each year. It rises about 125 feet above the sea and is the only natural harbor between Egypt and Haifa. Two good springs supply the city with water and land around Joppa is very fertile. Joppa has been occupied for nearly 3,500 years. After a Hyksos fortress was built there in the eighteenth century B.C., the site saw Egyptians, Canaanites, Jews, Greeks, Romans, Moslems, Crusaders, Arabs, and Zionists settle its hillside.

The city of Joppa is also known as Yafo, Japho, and Jaffa. The spelling *Joppa* is used in the New Testament and reflects Greek influence. Several explanations are offered for the origin of this city's name. According to a Semitic legend the site was named after Japheth, son of Noah, who supposedly established the town after the flood. Perhaps it is more likely that the city is named after the Hebrew word *yafeh,* which means "beautiful." The earliest mention of Joppa in the Bible comes in Joshua 19:46, a description of the borders of the inheritance of the tribe of Dan. Since the city was so well fortified, it is doubtful whether the army of Joshua ever subdued it. Some suggest that Joppa was not part of Israel until David took the coastal area.

A Port for Temple Supplies

On two different occasions Joppa was used as a port to receive materials necessary to the construction of the temple in Jerusalem some forty miles away. Hiram, the king of Tyre, in correspondence with King Solomon was promised wheat, barley, oil, and wine. In turn he replied, "We will cut whatever timber you need from Lebanon, and bring it to you in rafts by sea to Joppa, so that you may take it up to Jerusalem" (II Chron. 2:16). Later, Zerubbabel and others who returned from exile gave the Sidonians and Tyrians food, drink, and oil so that they would "bring cedar trees from Lebanon to the sea, to Joppa" (Ezra 3:7).

Modern Joppa still has a street named Tarshish, recalling the destination of an earlier traveler leaving from the city's harbor. A part of the story of Jonah reads, "He went down to Joppa and found a ship going to Tarshish; so he paid the fare, and went on board, to go with them to Tarshish, away from the presence of the Lord" (Jon. 1:3).

Dorcas and Peter

Dorcas (Tabitha in Aramaic) was a Christian who lived in the city of Joppa in the first century. She was known for her good works and love; and when a sickness took her, she was laid in an upper room in one of the houses of the city, while the apostle Peter was sent for. Peter, lodging in the nearby town of Lydda (the present-day Lod, near the airport), came at the request of her many friends and raised her from the dead (Acts 9:36–42). After this event Peter remained in Joppa in the home of Simon the tanner, until he had a vision on the housetop and was directed by God to go to Caesarea to preach to Cornelius.

Visitors to Joppa today will be shown the "house of Simon the tanner," but the structure actually dates back only to 1730. A first-century house has been uncovered, however, in the same general area. A courtyard and the walls of an adjoining room are preserved to a height of about six feet. Since the general area of Joppa is relatively small, we may legitimately conclude that the owner of this house must have been a neighbor of Simon. Evidence indicates that this house and those about it were destroyed in A.D. 66 when revolt against Rome broke out. Through the centuries many famous people have visited Joppa. In March of 1799 Napoleon captured the city. James T. Barclay, the first missionary supported by the Churches of Christ in America, arrived in Joppa in 1851 and then went on to Jerusalem to live and work for several years.

While the modern buildings are not the buildings known to Peter and the early Christians, the hill on which ancient Joppa was built is the same and the sea with its reefs forming a natural harbor is the same. As one visits this scene and rereads the stories of the Bible there is a special feeling of nearness to those who lived and served the Lord there so long ago.

"Full of Good Works"
Batsell Barrett Baxter

Today as we are standing near the historic old city of Joppa, I think of a woman who lived here two thousand years ago. I don't know how widely she was known in the old city; perhaps we know more about her than did many of her neighbors. We remember her not because she was rich or famous, but because she was the kind of person you would immediately identify as a Christian.

We remember her because of the story told about her in the Book of Acts. We know nothing about her family or friends or children, if there were any. All we know about her is Luke's story: she died and left many mourners whose lives she had touched. Peter raised this woman from the dead. But what is most striking about her are the few details about her life that have been recorded.

Here's the story as it appears in the final paragraph of Acts 9, "Now there was at Joppa a disciple named Tabitha, which means Dorcas.'' Tabitha in Armaic and Dorcas in Greek mean gazelle, a lovely and graceful creature of the deer family. Continuing our reading, "She was full of good works and acts of charity.'' When she died, her friends called for Peter, who came from nearby Lydda. When he arrived, ''they took him to the upper room. All the widows stood beside him weeping, and showing coats and garments which Dorcas made while she was with them.'' Peter raised her from the dead. As a result many believed in the Lord. That's all there is. We would like to know more about this good woman, but that's enough. Actually, the only thing that we know about her character is that "she was full of good works and acts of charity.'' She had made garments for others, and so had touched their lives. it is as if the writer Luke had said, ''Now, there was a model Christian.''

"Good works" in the Life of a Christian

We recognize that there must be something paradoxical about describing Dorcas as a model Christian on account of her good works, for we are repeatedly told by Paul that ''no human being will be justified in [God's] sight by works of the law'' (Rom. 3:20). There were always those people who thought of their good works as earning credit before God. People like the righteous Pharisee whose prayer, in the eighteenth chapter of Luke, is nothing more than bragging to God about his generosity and his fasting. The Scriptures are very plain, however, that good works do not save us. It is only Christ who saves! Salvation is a gift from God, never earned by our works, though, of course, we must respond in obedient faith to the commands of God in order to receive the free gift of salvation.

But, let's come back to Dorcas. It wasn't that Dorcas and others like her had tried to earn credit before God. They had been so moved by the love of God that it was natural for them to turn their love toward others. Apparently Dorcas had become so accustomed to her works of charity that it never occurred to her that she was doing something special. Her good works were as natural to her as her own accent. She knew that in Jesus Christ ''we are his workmanship, created in Christ Jesus for good works'' (Eph. 2:10). Perhaps she also knew, in the words of Paul, that ''God is at work in you, both to will and to work for his good pleasure'' (Phil. 2:13).

Who Is a Christian?

There is a great deal of confusion in the minds of many people about what it means to be a Christian. What does a Christian look like? Some think in negative terms, of the Christian's avoidance of certain vices. Others think in positive terms about Christians as being self-sacrificing in their concern for others. Nearly everyone assumes that a Christian is a person who practices the golden rule, obeys the Ten Commandments, and lives by the Sermon on the Mount. Some people regard going to church as important, others do not. Some put little emphasis on "becoming a Christian" just so long as a person lives a decent, honest, and generous life. What do the Scriptures say?

If we read the New Testament Scriptures carefully, we learn that a Christian is one who has believed in Christ as the divine Son of God and has accepted him as Lord and Savior. This foundation of faith and commitment must also include a confession of Jesus before our fellow men, a repentance from our past sins, and being baptized for the forgiveness of our sins (Rom. 10:9, 10; Luke 13:3; Acts 2:38). After our initial response to the Lord's call through obedient faith, God adds us to his church (Acts 2:47). But that is only the beginning, as the story of Dorcas clearly shows.

It is significant to remember that according to the most complete description of the judgment scene which we have in the Scriptures, Matthew 25:31–46, when we stand before God in that great final day, he will evaluate our lives in terms of how concerned we were about the hungry, the thirsty, the naked, the sick, strangers, and those in prison. It is important to "become a Christian" and it is also important to live a generous, helpful kind of life afterward.

The Mind of Christ

The picture we find in the New Testament of the early Christians indicates that the mind of Christ had become so much a part of their thinking that their natural, spontaneous impulses were to live clean, pure lives, and to share their time, energy, and resources with everyone who was in need.

As we read about the lives of the early Christians, it is very obvious that the life of faith was also a life of good works. We read of Christians who stirred one another up to good works (Heb. 10:24). They visited one another in prison (Heb. 13:3), and they practiced hospitality by taking in strangers (Heb. 13:2). They were reminded that "pure religion" involved taking care of widows and orphans (James 1:27). Indeed, it was considered a mockery of the faith to say to one who was hungry and needy, "Be warmed and filled," for empty phrases like this do not take care of the needs of the body (James 2:16). Undoubtedly, as I Peter 2:12 suggests, it was the good work of the Christians which most impressed the unbelievers of ancient times.

We remember that Jesus taught that his disciples must be salt and light (Matt. 5:13, 14). We all know that salt preserves and saves, while light illuminates. The real point, however, is that *we* are to be salt and light. Paul wrote to Titus, "Remind them to be submissive to rulers and authorities, to be obedient, to be ready for any honest work" (Titus 3:1). He wrote to the Galatians, "Bear one another's burdens, and so fulfil the law of Christ. . . . And let us not grow weary in well-doing . . . let us do good to all men, and especially to those who are of the household of faith" (Gal. 6:2, 9, 10). In the final book of the Bible, Revelation, John quotes the voice from heaven as saying, " 'Write this: Blessed are the dead who die in the Lord henceforth.' 'Blessed indeed,' says the Spirit 'that they may rest from their labors, for their deeds follow them!' " (Rev. 14:13).

A Touched Life Touches Others

What does a Christian really look like? Does some particular behavior distinguish Christians from others? A Christian looks like Dorcas, who quietly touched the lives of others because her life had been touched. A Christian looks like those early disciples who took care of orphans, widows, strangers. He looks like the Samaritan who placed himself in danger in order to help another. He looks like those people to whom Jesus said, "I was hungry and you fed me, thirsty and you gave me drink." A Christian may not dress in any distinguishable way, nor speak a special language that distinguishes him. Instead, a life of good works is the mark of a Christian— especially when those good works become as natural as his own accent.

Caesarean Coastline

40   Caesarea

Coastal Caesarea is to be distinguished from Caesarea Philippi. The city of Caesarea on the Mediterranean Sea is uninhabited today. It is located midway between Haifa and Tel Aviv, in the midst of the very fertile Plain of Sharon. This area is known today for its citrus fruit. The Mount Carmel range is about eight miles to the north.

Herod's City

According to Josephus, Herod the Great observed that "there was a city by the seaside that was much decayed, [but] was capable of improvements."

287

This city was Strato's Tower. Herod "rebuilt it with white stone, and adorned it with several most spendid palaces" (25-13 B.C.). Herod had noted that there was no good haven for ships from Dora to Joppa and that the sailors were "obliged to lie in the stormy sea." Herod "overcame nature and built a haven larger than Piraeus [the port of Athens]." Josephus notes that "abutting the harbor were houses, also of white stone, and upon it converge the streets of the town, laid at equal distances apart."

Herod renamed the city Caesarea after Augustus Caesar (emperor of Rome from 27 B.C. to A.D. 14, who had given Herod the title of king). Caesar's temple, "remarkable for its beauty and grand proportions," stood facing the harbor. Josephus notes that the buildings in the city were "all constructed in a style worthy of the name which the city bore." Herod also "appointed games every fifth year and called them in like manner 'Caesar's Games.' "

The harbor is considered one of Herod's most remarkable building works. Three hundred yards south of the harbor stand the remains of a Roman theater. Excavated from 1959 to 1964, the theater was built by Herod. Concerning the theater one writer commented, "The rulers of those times were neither the most humane nor the most refined people in history but they knew how to build. And they knew where. The theater is a monument to their taste and skill."

Caesarea also boasted a Roman hippodrome. This race course, built inside the Herodian city, measures 1,056 feet by 264 feet. A square granite pillar, thirty-five feet long, lies in the center of the complex, which was able to seat twenty thousand spectators. Near the pillar are three conical blocks which were polished to shine like mirrors. These reflected the sun into the horses' eyes during the race—resulting in frightened horses and a more exciting race.

Biblical History

After the conversion of the Ethiopian in Acts 8, Philip passed on to Azotus and other towns until he came to Caesarea (Acts 8:40). He apparently settled here. On Paul's return from his third missionary journey, he stayed in Philip's home. Philip, who was known as an evangelist, was the father of four unmarried daughters who were known for their prophesying (Acts 21:8, 9).

A Roman army officer named Cornelius was stationed at Caesarea. Through a vision Cornelius, himself a Gentile, was told to send to Joppa, some thirty miles to the south, to ask the apostle Peter to come to Caesarea (Acts 10:1-8). Peter and the messengers of Cornelius, along with some Christians from Joppa, arrived in Caesarea to find a crowd in Cornelius' house. After some teaching and discussion, Cornelius and some of his associates became Christians (Acts 10:23-48). Peter remained in Caesarea for a number of days (Acts 10:48). He later went to Jerusalem, where he told the apostles of the events in Caesarea (Acts 11:11–17).

Toward the end of Paul's second missionary journey, he left Ephesus and sailed to Caesarea. On that occasion he visited the church and went on to Antioch (Acts 18:22). After completing his third missionary tour, he was arrested in Jerusalem. The officials decided to transfer Paul to the prison in Caesarea. He was moved there at night by an armed escort. Paul rode a horse on the fifty-mile trip from Jerusalem in the hills to Caesarea on the plain. Paul was delivered to Felix, who placed him in Herod's praetorium under guard (Acts 23:23–35).

During his imprisonment in Caesarea, Paul made several appearances before civil authorities. The first appearance occurred five days after Paul's arrival. The Jewish high priest, Ananias, along with some elders and their spokesman Tertullus, came to plead their case against Paul before Felix.

Paul was kept in custody but was allowed some freedom and visits from friends. He was arraigned before Felix and his wife Drusilla (a Jewess) to speak about the Christian faith. After some discussion, he was sent away. Felix later talked with Paul several times, hoping Paul would offer him money for pardon. The matter ended two years later when Felix was replaced and left Paul in prison (Acts 24).

Porcius Festus was the next governor and he heard Paul soon after his arrival. The Jews came from Jerusalem to present their case. As an attempt to please the Jews, Festus asked Paul if he would stand trial in Jerusalem. Paul appealed to Caesar (Acts 25:1–12).

Paul also told his story before Festus and King Agrippa, along with Agrippa's wife Bernice. Following this speech it was decided that Paul would be sent to Rome (Acts 25:23—26:32).

The remains of Herod's city are scattered throughout the area today. Much of the building material used by Herod was reused by the Byzantines and the Crusaders. It is interesting to note that until the excavations at Caesarea were conducted, nothing was known of the Roman procurator Pontius Pilate except the material in the Gospels and Josephus. In the excavation of the theater a stone was found which bears this inscription (as restored): *Tiberieum/Pontius Pilatus/Praefectus Iudaeae*—"Tiberius [the Roman emperor of the period] /Pontius Pilate/Prefect of Judea."

New Eyes for Old

Harold Hazelip

The most famous conversion story in all history is the conversion of Saul of Tarsus. Indeed his conversion is an outstanding argument for the truthfulness of Christianity. No one was held in greater esteem by the rulers of his nation. No one was more deeply prejudiced against Christianity. His conversion occurred on his trip to Damascus to persecute Christians.

To become a Christian, he had to turn his back on impeccable credentials. He rehearses these in Philippians 3: "If any other man thinks he has reason for confidence in the flesh, I have more: circumcised on the eighth day, of the people of Israel, of the tribe of Benjamin, a Hebrew born of Hebrews; as to the law a Pharisee, as to zeal a persecutor of the church, as to righteousness under the law blameless. But whatever gain I had, I counted as loss for the sake of Christ. Indeed I count everything as loss because of the surpassing worth of knowing Christ Jesus my Lord. For his sake I have suffered the loss of all things, and count them as refuse, in order that I may gain Christ and be found in him" (Phil. 3:4–9).

Before Saul's Conversion

What caused such a change in Saul, who became Paul the apostle? There were no social ties with Christians to influence him. His change in religious convictions meant the loss of his friends and becoming an object of persecution and hatred by his own people. No unbeliever has ever had so great an opportunity or such important reasons to disprove the claims of Jesus Christ as Saul had—if they could be disproved.

The Acts of the Apostles gives three accounts of Saul's conversion (chs. 9, 22, 26). If we combine them, and note additional details in his letters, the resulting picture is of a man who began with a very mistaken estimate of Jesus and the movement which grew out of his life, death, and resurrection.

Paul later wrote, "I formerly blasphemed and persecuted and insulted him; but I received mercy because I had acted ignorantly in unbelief. . . . I am the foremost of sinners" (I Tim. 1:13, 15). Luke's account describes Saul as one who consented to the murder of Stephen (Acts 8:1; 22:20). He led a house-to-house persecution of Christians, resulting in their being imprisoned (Acts 8:3). Saul is described as "breathing threats and murder against the disciples of the Lord" (Acts 9:1). In a speech before King Agrippa, Paul said, "I not only shut up many of the saints in prison, by authority from the chief priests, but when they were put to death I cast my vote against them. And I punished them often in all the synagogues and tried to make them blaspheme; and in raging fury against them, I persecuted them even to foreign cities" (Acts 26:10, 11).

One of those foreign cities was Damascus in Syria, 150 miles away from Jerusalem. The journey on foot took about a week. Saul obtained authority to bind Christians in Damascus and bring them to Jerusalem for trial. But he never completed his mission.

What happened? How could God reach this man? When the Ethiopian treasurer was converted to Christ, an angel had sent Philip, an evangelist, to teach him. When Cornelius, the Roman soldier, was converted, an angel was sent to tell him how to find a preacher of Christ. When Lydia, the Philippian jailor, and other Europeans heard the gospel, Paul and his helpers had been directed toward them by a vision Paul saw in the night (Acts 16:9).

But could God send a preacher to Saul? These were the very people he wanted to imprison or kill. Instead, the Lord himself appeared to Saul in a dazzling light at midday on the road to Damascus.

Unless a traveler was in a great hurry, he usually rested during the midday heat. But Saul was on an angry mission. When the dazzling light overwhelmed him, he heard a voice ask, "Saul, Saul, why do you persecute me?" (Acts 26:14). Saul responded, "Who are you, Lord?" He must have wondered. Something about Stephen lingered in his mind. How could a bad man die like that—with a prayer on his lips for his murderers? Was this Stephen's voice? Or the voice of another who had been killed? The answer he received was stunning: "I am Jesus whom you are persecuting" (Acts 26:15). Saul had thought that every man who believed that Jesus was alive ought to die. Now there was no escape from this truth. He had been wrong. When he realized his guilt, he asked, "What shall I do, Lord?" (Acts 22:10).

Mistakes Paul Did Not Make

We may learn an important lesson from what Paul did not do in his effort to cope with guilt. He did not blame someone else for his wrongdoing. Sometimes we blame our environment, our heredity, the structures of society. I would resent it if someone else looked at my action and said, "Don't blame him—he's not responsible. He was born that way." The essence of human personality is that we are responsible beings. We are not puppets. Other factors affect our lives, but we are responsible for our decisions. Adam blamed Eve and Eve blamed the serpent. Adolph Eichmann shrugged, "I was not responsible for the final solution to the Jewish problem. I was just a bureaucrat doing what I was told." Paul did not deny responsibility for his actions.

Other people deny the reality of moral standards. Guilt is a hangover from a primitive era. Like the ancient Stoic who denied the reality of pleasure and pain, we may refuse to face our guilt. But denying the existence of right and wrong is too high a price to pay to get rid of our conscience pangs. Paul did not attempt this escape mechanism.

Nor did Paul attempt to repay God for the evil he had done. A husband wrongs his wife and then heaps gifts upon her in an effort to compensate for what he has done. But how can you restore destroyed lives? Paul did not attempt to atone for his own wrongdoing.

Accepting God's Forgiveness

Instead, Paul allowed himself to be forgiven by God. When the Lord confronted him on the Damascus road and rebuked him for his wrongdoing, there followed words of hope: "Rise, and go into Damascus, and there you will be told all that is appointed for you to do" (Acts 22:10). Saul waited three days and nights. He could not see. He neither ate nor drank. Then Ananias came—one of those people he meant to imprison or kill. Instead of heaping condemnation upon him, Ananias said, "Brother Saul, receive your sight" (Acts 22:13). This was the warm greeting of a fellow Israelite. He assured Saul that he had a future in the very enterprise he had tried to destroy—the church of Jesus Christ: "The God of our fathers appointed you to know his will, to see the Just One and to hear a voice from his mouth; for you will be a witness for him to all men of what you have seen and heard. And now why do you wait? Rise and be baptized, and wash away your sins, calling on his name" (Acts 22:14-16).

Paul could not repay God for the wrongs he had done. But he could be forgiven by going through a likeness of what his Lord had gone through to redeem him. He could die to his old way of life, be buried in baptism, and be raised to a new life of service. And so Paul became a Christian. He even became an apostle in the very church he had tried to annihilate!

The wrongs you have done will not go away. But by the mercy of God, they can be forgiven and your life can be changed. You will no longer have to say, "How bad I am! How could I ever have done such a thing?" Instead, you will be able to say, "How good God is! Imagine—after all that I have done wrong—he did not give up on me!" The fact that you are still breathing means that God has not given up on you. God patiently keeps on—he wants you to live, he has hope for you. There is release from guilt. Instead of looking at Christ and the world through narrow, selfish eyes, you can begin to look at the world through the eyes of Jesus Christ!

When I Can Find a Moment

Harold Hazelip

Christopher Morley has a character in one of his novels talk about the importance of time. He thinks all time is wasted if it does not give some awareness of beauty and wonder. He is especially impressed by the large city and wonders how much time is wasted there. He says, "Well, here are some 6,000,000 people. To simplify the problem . . . let us assume that 2,350,000 of those people have spent a day that could be called, on the whole, happy: a day in which they feel satisfaction. . . . Very well, that leaves 3,650,000 people whose day has been unfruitful: spent in uncongenial work or in sorrow, suffering, and talking nonsense. This city, then, in one day has wasted ten thousand years, or one hundred centuries. One hundred centuries squandered in a day!" This thought makes the character feel quite ill, and he tears up the scrap of paper on which he has been figuring.

Time: we seem to have either too little or too much. How can I possibly do everything that must be done before five o'clock? Or before next week? We never seem to catch up. For others, time drags along like a tortoise, and there is nothing to fill it. There are no objectives to be reached, no deadlines to be met.

Paul Before Felix

The apostle Paul was arraigned before a governor named Felix. Paul made his defense and Felix delayed his decision on the case. Some days later, Felix brought along his wife Drusilla and they listened to what Paul had to say about his faith in Christ. But when Paul discussed purity of life, the mastery of passions, and the coming judgment, Felix became terrified, and interrupted him: "You may go for the present . . . when I can find a moment, I will send for you" (Acts 24:25, Moffatt). Two years later another governor succeeded Felix and he left Paul in custody.

Felix put one of the more persistent fallacies of the human mind into words here: that a person can ever *find* time. We seem to think that we will accidentally stumble into a great block of time that will be available for a hard or disagreeable task which we want to escape for the moment. We are able to lose time, but we never seem to find it. We have to make time for what we want to do.

Life is like going into a department store with a limited amount of money. If you buy this, you can't buy that. Unless life is planned carefully, it may turn into a shopping spree which spends all of its money at the first counter. It may happen to be only cheap, gaudy jewelry, but if it catches the eye, that settles the matter.

Felix promised to hear Paul again when he could find a moment. Antonius Felix was governor of Judea from A.D. 52 to 59. He had been a household slave of Antonia, mother of Claudius Caesar, the reigning Roman emperor. He became a favorite of Claudius, and this led to his advancement from the status of a slave to that of governor. Tacitus, the Roman historian, says that "he exercised the power of a king with the mind of a slave." This brief description agrees with the text of the Book of Acts. Felix held Paul, knowing he was innocent, hoping to be bribed for his release.

Felix was married successively to three princesses. Drusilla, who accompanied him to hear Paul, was the youngest daughter of Herod Agrippa I, who beheaded the apostle James and imprisoned Peter for a time. Drusilla had been married to Azizus, king of Emesa, an insignificant little kingdom. Felix used a sorcerer to win her from her husband.

Nonconversions in Acts

The Acts of the Apostles records many conversions. There were the three thousand on Pentecost who were cut to the heart by Peter's sermon. The Ethiopian nobleman was reading the prophet Isaiah when Philip began preaching Christ to him. The devout Roman soldier, Cornelius; Lydia, who closed her business to worship God on the sabbath; Saul, who was conscientious even while persecuting Christians—all of these became Christians.

But the apostles also met cases of nonconversion, including King Agrippa and Governor Felix. Felix was only one example of many in the Bible which remind us that time is not at our disposal. Because God is in control of time, we dare not dismiss the urgency of his invitation. The prophet Isaiah said, "Seek the Lord while he may be found, call upon him while he is near" (Isa. 55:6). There is a note of urgency in his appeal.

The Note of Crisis

Mark indicates the urgency of God's appeal very clearly when he first tells us about Jesus' preaching. There came a special moment for Jesus' arrival on the stage of public notice. It was "after John was arrested." Then we are told, "Jesus came into Galilee, preaching the gospel of God, and saying, 'The time is fulfilled and the kingdom of God is at hand; repent, and believe in the gospel'" (Mark 1:14, 15). The time is fulfilled: there is an urgency in the hour. God has come at this particular moment with his invitation. And he summons us to repent because the hour has arrived. It is the time for decision.

The parables of Jesus ring with a note of crisis. We are called on to decide about God and his kingdom. Jesus' story of the banquet has people making excuses—very good excuses: "I have married a wife . . . I have bought some land . . ." (Luke 14:15-24). Those who rejected the invitation were not evil. Their tragedy was that they were going on with life as if it were "business as usual." Perhaps they thought they had an infinite amount of time to accept such an invitation.

Jesus' story of the rich fool (Luke 12:16-21) presents one who thought his whole life could proceed as he wanted. He was going to spend his life tearing down barns and building bigger ones. God called him a fool; his whole existence was self-centered.

Do you recall the cry of the rich man in torment? "Go warn my five brothers." The answer came back: "They have Moses and the prophets." That is, they have their opportunity at this very moment (Luke 16:19-31).

Jesus once condemned his own generation for being very astute in judging the signs of the weather, but unable to recognize the "signs of the times" (Matt. 16:3). Do we go on buying and selling, marrying and giving in marriage, without recognizing the real priorities in life?

Making the Time

The words *now* and *today* ring through the New Testament. "Behold, now is the acceptable time; behold, now is the day of salvation" (II Cor. 6:2). "Today, when you hear his voice, do not harden your hearts" (Heb. 4:7).

Do you recall the old television series, "Run for Your Life"? The central character had been told that he had only a limited time to live. This put his values in place and gave a special urgency to his plans. He became more determined to do the things which were especially important to him. Time was precious.

This is what is at stake when Jesus says, "The time is fulfilled and the kingdom of God is at hand, repent, and believe in the gospel" (Mark 1:15). The coming of God's kingdom presents an opportunity that we dare not spurn.

We live under the illusion that there will always be a better time for putting our lives in order, for finding the real priorities of life. But missed opportunities can so easily be gone forever. Today is the only time you and I have. Let's learn from Felix's failure. We will not find the moment; we will have to make the time to obey God. Jesus called for belief, and repentance. He also called for a new birth which is consummated in baptism, marking the end of the old life and the beginning of the new. "Behold, now is the day of salvation."